Readings at the Edge of Literature

Readings at the Edge of Literature   Myra Jehlen

The University of Chicago Press   Chicago and London

Myra Jehlen is the Board of Governors Professor of Literature at Rutgers University. She is the author of *American Incarnation: The Individual, the Nation, and the Continent* and is the coeditor of *The English Literatures of America, 1500–1800.*

The University of Chicago Press, Chicago 60637
The University of Chicago Press, Ltd., London
© 2002 by The University of Chicago
All rights reserved. Published 2002
Printed in the United States of America
11 10 09 08 07 06 05 04 03 02   5 4 3 2 1

ISBN (cloth): 0-226-39600-2
ISBN (paper): 0-226-39601-0

Library of Congress Cataloging-in-Publication Data

Jehlen, Myra.
    Readings at the edge of literature / Myra Jehlen.
      p.   cm.
    ISBN 0-226-39600-2 (cloth : alk. paper)—ISBN 0-226-39601-0 (pbk. : alk. paper)
    1. American literature—History and criticism.   I. Title.
PS121 .J44 2002
810.9—dc21

                                                        2002018008

Contents

Acknowledgments

The essays collected here, having been written over many years, represent not just an episode but a whole history of friendship and collegiality. Reflecting on this history, I see that I was accompanied, on the road to the edge of literature, by a great many people of excellent conversation: Sacvan Bercovitch, Lauren Berlant, Richard Brodhead, Paola Colaiacomo, Rosa-Marie Colombo, Mario Corona, Genèvieve Fabre, Barbara Gelpi, Maurice Gonnaud, Giles Gunn, David Halperin, Evelyn Keller, Christopher Kutz, Amy Lang, Frank Lentricchia, George Levine, Helene Moglen, Franco Moretti, Donald Pease, Richard Poirier, Barry Qualls, Arnold Rampersad, Jessica Riskin, Forrest Robinson, Michael Rogin, Cecilia Tichi, Patricia Meyer Spacks, Michael Warner, and Marilyn Young. I take this book as an occasion, made festive thereby, to thank them for their intelligence and wit, their writings, and their contributions to mine.

Introduction

This introduction comes in two parts because the essays it presents come together in two ways, the first historical, the second formal. The title, however, *Readings at the Edge of Literature,* applies generally. All the essays read for what I am calling the "edge" of literature, a point on the horizon of every sentence and story, where the writing meets up with an apparently definitive unknown and is unable to say anything more. Jorge Luis Borges wrote about this point in "The Approach to Al-Mu'tasim" in which the narrator describes a novel about a student who discovers the existence of a supremely wise teacher and sets out to find him by retracing the rays of his wisdom to their source. The student finally arrives at a house where, from behind a door with a curtain, "emanates a great radiance." When he asks to see Al-Mu'-tasim, a voice bids him enter. "The student draws back the curtain and steps forward. The novel ends."

It has arrived at what I take to be an epistemological impasse. The novel in Borges's story does not seem to have the means to imagine what the wise man might tell the student; at any rate, the quest for knowledge stops short. This ending may be taken by some readers as illustrating the thesis that a literary representation is a self-contained invention, not a method of discovery. This thesis, however, rests on definitions of invention and discovery that in my view exaggerate their opposition. Invention is less autonomous, I think, and discovery more mediated than current accounts have them. They are moreover intertwined. Inventions proceed in the hope of discovery, and Borges's story unfolds line by line in necessary relation to a possibility that the student can describe to us what lies behind the curtain. Without this possibility, the tale goes nowhere, in fact it never starts. The student is seeking for ultimate truths and, while the plot forecasts that he will not attain them, his ambition to know is motive and motor for everything that happens in it. The ending does not abrogate his ambition, quite the contrary. The student has established the existence of a supreme wisdom and even located it, and the novel ends with the legitimation of his quest.

It ends also with the insistence that the knowledge he has been seeking, however generic, is not abstract. It may be out of reach, but it is knowledge of this world. On this point, Borges is categorical. For the novel to have worked, the narrator explains, it was essential that "the extraordinary and unseen Al'Mu-tasim should give us the impression of a real character, not that of a jumble of insipid superlatives." The novel's author was "under an obligation of seeing to it that the [prophet] be no mere convention or phantom." Indeed, the "incredible voice of Al'Mu-tasim" which "urges the student to come in" is "a man's voice." The threshold of wisdom is a real doorstep situated "at the rear" of a "gallery" and concealed by a "cheap and copiously beaded mat curtain."

While he calls for a flesh and blood prophet, Borges's narrator is perfectly aware that the novel is totally fantastic. But it is not thereby any less connected to the real. By insisting on the reality of both the conditions of the search for Al'Mu-tasim and of the sage himself, Borges indicates, I think, that the knowledge sought, by both the student and the novel in which he is the hero, is a *literary* knowledge. However fantastic the author's imaginary world, he is saying, it is made out of real materials and it proffers a material kind of understanding. The goal of the quest, Al'Mu-tasim's wisdom, is itself of the same stuff as cheap beaded curtains behind which you can hear men's voices. The line connecting them eventually becomes the dotted line of the threshold and then disappears from sight. "The novel ends." It has reached the edge of literary knowledge, or, rather, one of its edges, since the narrator describes it and then continues writing his story. The student's search for the great Al'Mu-tasim, step by step, edge after edge, has enacted the peculiar, indwelling epistemology of literature.

I

It is no accident that I made my way to the subject of the relation of literature and knowledge through reading American literature. American literature seems to be especially engaged with that relation, whose moral and psychological

implications this literature develops to wonderfully surprising, though sometimes tragic ends. The essays in the collection mostly treat American texts of
the eighteenth and nineteenth centuries, and within these texts, issues of
political and social culture. I have taken up this culture through its fictions, in
other words through its mythmaking self-representations. The American
mythology is not more forceful than many others but it is peculiar in proposing that the nation's ways and values encompass the universal potential. The
knowledge its writers pursue to the edge of literature is the meaning and
value of a cosmic America, a goal that intensifies the dilemma of the Borge-
sian threshold. American writers write their way not only to the edge of a local knowledge, but often to the edge of America, which they then seem to
conceive as the edge of the world. They can be brilliantly perceptive about life
in America but have little or no sense of life beyond America. Unforgiving in
descriptions of slavery or of the bigotries of small-town society, they yet retain their conviction that America is ultimately good the way we might say
life is good: not meaning that it is by any means always pleasant but that it is
not to be quarreled with globally. At the edges of their writings, however,
looms catastrophic disenchantment, should the exploration of America prove
its claims too false.

There is a pattern in much of the classic American literature of an initial
radical challenge to ambient ways that is abandoned in disarray at the conclusion. This is what happens, for instance, in Mark Twain's *Puddn'head Wilson* and *Huckleberry Finn*. Two essays in this volume ("The Ties that Bind:
Race and Sex in *Puddn'head Wilson*" and "Banned in Concord: *Adventures of
Huckleberry Finn* and Classic American Literature") trace the process whereby
Twain started out to criticize aspects of his society and ended with an apologia. *Puddn'head Wilson* begins as a slashing satire of the idiocy of America's
way with race and concludes having demonstrated that even an invisible portion of black blood can make a man a murderer. *Huckleberry Finn* notoriously
ends by restoring an order it has bitterly denounced. But this restoration does
not involve reconciliation: the initial rejection of Hannibal's ways stands, it
just stands side by side with acceptance.

In fact, as I reread the essays I have collected here, it occurred to me that
they describe a congenitally paradoxical literature. American writers seem
bent not on resolving paradoxes but the opposite, developing them to their
utmost tension to produce accounts of the circumstances of American society that are as critically penetrating as they can be without puncturing its basic myths. Paradox is likely to feel not just congenial but realistic when one is
confronted by the dilemma of finding a critical distance to stand from a phe-

nomenon that seems to embrace all of reality, or all that is relevant in reality. When you are wholly in it, how do you see America whole? One way is Emerson's: standing in snow puddles on Boston Common and feeling uplifted into infinite space, he does not imagine he is about to levitate and does not want to. He stands solidly planted and becomes a transparent eyeball, an absurdity which would be blind anyway, in order to foil the common sense (useless in his paradoxical situation) that says you see what is before you, the ground when you look down and the sky when you look up. He wants to see the ground (the material and the quotidian) of the sky, and the sky (the spiritual and universal) of the ground. This is a recurrent feat of the American imagination: Thoreau looks into a stream to see the night sky, Melville's Ishmael grapples for the metaphysical truth of whale blubber. They were Romantics but need not have been; before the Romantic Renaissance, Franklin traced out the same figure in transforming the first American individualist into EveryAmerican.

Paradox is not an American creation but Americans may do it better, perhaps obviating the need for irony. Indeed, if irony is a refusal to overlook contradiction, a paradox might be described as a suspended irony. Suspensions are fragile states, however, and the American imagination is haunted by a vision of paradoxical affiliations coming apart: self-reliance becoming incommensurate with responsibility to others; declarations of the equality of all peoples with the pursuit of empire; or writing from nature and your individual soul with representations of the common ethos. "J. Hector St. John Crèvecoeur: A Monarcho-anarchist in Revolutionary America" explains Crèvecoeur's incongruous loyalism as an early example of the breakdown of the American paradox. He saw too clearly the irony in Jefferson's celebration of yeomen. "The Family Militant: Domesticity versus Slavery in *Uncle Tom's Cabin*" takes Stowe's work to be explosing the paradox of slavery in the nation of the free in order to salvage another paradox, the mutual dependence of individualism and the family, the American and America.

On the other hand, for all this unease and fragility, the existential doom awaiting the best of American writing is also the contrary effect of success. The making of America or, to be precise, the making of its dominant culture, involved working out a particularly effective way to deal with the threat to civic unity posed by the modern opposition of self and society. On the Atlantic's western shore, the threat was allayed by the resolution of the self-society duality into a trinity with America itself. The title of my book, *American Incarnation: The Individual, the Nation and the Continent,* sums up the suggestion that the United States developed a form of social cohesion based on the identification of each American as a self-sufficient fusion of himself, the United States and America. Believing that three can be one is proof of faith, however, while writing is the exercise of doubt. The classic American literature reads as if written in traction.

The essays appear neither in the order they were written nor of the writings they treat but in an order intended to expose the cultural and historical problem I have just sketched. An essay on Benjamin Franklin ("'Imitate Jesus and Socrates': The Making of a Good American") is about creating an American polity, the next about Crèvecoeur's fear of it. There follows an essay on the ways the classic American novel has engaged with Crèvecoeur's fears ("The Novel and the Middle Class in America"). The problems presented in all three explore the global reach of the idea of America. The next three (on *Uncle Tom's Cabin* and on the two Twain novels) explore the extreme difficulty for American writers of treating race and class, two issues that, by exposing unbridgeable faults in the terrain of the national mythology, have inspired a literature of transcendent resolutions or of despairing incoherence. The essay that follows, on the problem of method in feminist criticism ("Archimedes and the Paradox of Feminist Criticism"), opens a discussion of strategies of reading for political edges; that is, for the way both the expectations and the possibilities texts project are delimited by ideas about organization and power. This is the subject as well of the next four essays: "Why Did the European Cross the Ocean? A Seventeenth-Century Riddle," "History before the Fact: The Underdetermined John Smith," "History beside the Fact: What We Learn from *A True and Exact History of Barbadoes*," and "An Empire of One's Own: Virginia Woolf's *A Voyage Out*." These also have in common their historical subject, early American colonizations or the prehistory of New World mythology. On the other hand, form is the direct object of the last essay about the way architecture not only represents issues in the social role and philosophical nature of art but also develops these issues in unforeseeable ways. "Guggenheim in Bilbao" thereby expresses the underlying priciple of all the essays, that writing moves toward knowledge by an unfolding of forms.

II

In short, if literature has an epistemological errand, form runs that errand. The premise of this collection overall is that form is the essence of literature. Not form as opposed to content since content, in literature, is an avatar, a materialization of form; form therefore as an embodiment of ideas, attitudes, and emotions, as the way they realize themselves and acquire the language equivalent of mass and extension. Comic plots and end-stopped couplets have in common the technique of taking up this or that problem found in the world and, in giving it their shape, imparting to it an inherent logic that expresses the writer's understanding of how the problem really functions, or might function or ought to. The author does not know in advance where this logic will lead or what it may reveal about the real-life problem it has organized anew. That will emerge gradually as the formal process unfolds.

This process of the formal unfolding of knowledge is particularly fraught in American writing in that, as I have already suggested, the paradoxical relation of American writers to their native matter redoubles the paradox of all writing. Writing to the edge of literature is a more dramatic undertaking when the edge of the story is the edge of the world. Everything is at stake. It is difficult to imagine how life or the world can go on after the endings of classic American novels, except to abrogate or repeat what has already happened. Hester Prynne returns and will forever be a guardian of the moral order; Ahab is dead for having questioned the cosmic order and Ishmael draws the obvious lesson; Huck Finn heads out to the territory as if he were stepping off the planet; not even Isabel Archer has a future. It seems impossible for these novels to incorporate what emerges from the process of their writing. They react instead by going back to the values and ideas they had questioned in the beginning, though, as I said earlier, not to reconcile, just to stop fighting. *Puddn'head Wilson*'s racist conclusion, after it has become apparent that the problem of race in America cannot be solved without radical upheaval, is a dramatic instance of this pattern. Its dynamic is formal (emerging from the unfolding of its plot) and, in retracing it, I can illustrate the formal method that ties this collection together.

Puddn'head Wilson takes place before the Civil War and tells a tale of switched babies, black for white, white for black. The perpetrator of the switch is the mother of the black child and the nurse of the white. Observing the babies' marked resemblance, she determines to emancipate hers by the expedient of exchanging their little shirts, whereupon baby-slave is transformed into baby-master and vice versa. The obvious implication, when the switch works, is that slavery, and, more to the point since Twain was writing after its abolition, racially based social hierarchies, have no basis in nature.

As the plot unfolds, however, so does a different argument. The emancipated black baby grows into a petty thief on the way to turning assassin; while the enslaved white baby blossoms into a moral paragon. The sometime explanation that the black child is corrupted by his participation in the slave owners' culture does not account for the fact that he is much worse than his white peers. Nature not nurture is at issue: at the end, what the novel now considers the truth of his identity is revealed etched on his body, and the implication that he was always no-good because he was always black is irresistible. Cinderella was a born prince's consort; in *Puddn'head Wilson,* the role of Cinderella's tiny foot is played by a fingerprint taken when the black murderer was a fair-haired baby.

Twain would not be the first great writer to fall prey to the ill-begotten prejudices of his time, and the prejudices that accompanied the defeat of Reconstruction were certainly virulent enough to have poisoned any novel. Yet, the question remains why its author was evidently less affected by the racism of his surroundings when he conceived his story than when he finished it. The essay speculates as to whether, for all his antislavery sentiments, Twain was drawn up short by the concrete image his writing evoked, of the slave baby become a free man. A baby looks good in any color. But as the story goes on, the baby becomes a man and Twain apparently found the man dangerous to the point of justifying a complete turnaround: from having started out to define race such that black and white might change places, he ended up affirming the ineradicable inferiority of being black.

We say that writing has a momentum of its own, that things happen in the writing. Characters are invented and walk off on their own two feet to build themselves worlds their authors have not necessarily foreseen. In *Puddn'head Wilson,* the ambulatory logic of writing seems to have implied retreat. As Twain worked through the ramifications of his subversive scheme, he thought more conventionally, not less. This ideological devolution is launched when *Puddn'head Wilson,* through the logical evolution of its plot and of its characters, sets in formal motion a sequence of events that pass beyond the slave's emancipation; it installs him in the place of his former master. Twain ended up returning a slave to slavery because the development of the plot forced the issue of how the freed slaves were to be integrated. On this, he seems to have lacked the certainty he brought to the issue of slavery. He was therefore unable to press on to a conclusion that would be in line with the novel's initial project, to expose racism. Note that what baffled him now was a *better* grasp of the problem of race, namely, that it involved more than slavery and, for him, too much more.

A better grasp of America's defining problems through the work of literary form does not always entail a surrender and retreat. Sometimes, on the contrary, the new understanding is vitally enabling. The literary investigation embraces rather than flees the contradiction it uncovers, emphasizing that it has reached the edge of its understanding, instead of dropping a curtain and backing away. The Franklin essay turns on such a success in which literary form overcomes the limit of what can be said directly. The essay began as an effort to figure out why, every time I read the *Autobiography,* one sentence popped up before me like a fairy-tale gnome demanding the solution to a puzzle. The thirteenth and last of Franklin's practical virtues is Humility, which he defines this way: "Humility: Imitate Jesus and Socrates." So sharp an eye could not have missed the joke in urging a reader to compare himself to the most august figures in all history as a recipe for humility. If Franklin's final word of advice to ambitious young readers was literally ridiculous, he must have meant it to be. I suggest in the essay that the brilliance of Franklin's strategy lies exactly in making the reader laugh. The height of individual arrogance proffered as self-effacing modesty would be a paralyzing contradiction—unless it moved you to laughter.

Franklin takes to its extreme the paradox of modern selfhood requiring one to be a world unto oneself while granting everyone else the same global reach. He thereby gives evidence of, and imparts to the reader, a self-knowledge capable of reconciling infinite ambition, if not with traditional humility, then with something more reliable. The youth who even subconsciously recognizes the humor in Franklin's rule of humility will be armed against a dangerous egoism. In the self-knowledge implicit in getting the joke, he has a resource for controlling his own presumption. When the individual is the unit of social behavior, it is difficult to know where to ground morality. Here it is grounded in the ability to laugh at oneself. After making deep inroads into their Puritan abjection, Franklin badly needed to endow his young turks with a civilizing sense of humor. The *Autobiography* is an educational treatise teaching, along with self-sufficiency, a mitigating wit.

Wit, however, cannot be taught, it has to be experienced. The sense of a witty remark lies unparaphrasably in a specific conjunction of words designed to indicate at once the convergences and divergences of their meanings. Franklin often wanted to instruct his readers in a way of being that would enable them to take advantage of a self whose public face need not reveal its private thoughts. Rule number seven is another instance: "Sincerity. Use no hurtful Deceit." The ability to conceal your thoughts incurs an obligation to discriminate innocuous from harmful concealments. Sincerity has meaning only against a background of daily deceptions, as the point of humility lies in its relation to ambition.

But exactly what this relation is defies direct statement. Franklin does not mean "Humility: Remember you're just an ordinary human being," but just the opposite: that you had better practice humility precisely because you aspire to be extraordinary; besides, practicing humility is an excellent way to be better than anyone else. Only wit could articulate such a twisted idea. The witty definition of humility, moreover, conveys a moral knowledge that is not only more complex than the prosaic but also more radical because it penetrates to the level at which its terms reveal its contradictions. That basic level is essentially Al-Mu'tasim's doorstep: such supremely successful writing as Franklin's rule of Humility is still a trope on the formal limit of any writing. Franklin's wit takes what cannot be said and says it by revealing what makes it inexpressible. Al-Mu'tasim's wisdom is also inexpressible, or indescribable, but its glow, which we do see quite clearly shining behind the curtain, signals a knowledge that exceeds the possibilities of direct apprehension, or direct statement, and needs to be transformed in order to be accessible.

The necessary correlative of such knowledge is an external world to which the transforming language has access. The reading developed in the essay "History before the Fact: The Underdetermined John Smith," is a particularly clear instance of this dependence of the literary epistemological process on the accessibility of external worlds. This essay's subject is the problem of reading colonial chronicles, a set of documents that current historians are especially unlikely to trust as accounts of what really happened. Colonial historians, working out the past from texts whose views and values they mostly deplore, have found particularly persuasive the ideas that textual sources offer their own views of the world and nothing more. Unable to take archives at their word, these historians have found another way of dealing with the words, which is to treat them *as* words, stories whose connection to events and facts can never be ascertained. This means that while the stories are wholly unreliable, by the same token they are peculiarly telling about contemporary interests and attitudes. Taking a dim view of what their sources try to tell them, historians of colonization have become very adept at discerning subtexts, and, rather than reading the archives, they might be said to psychoanalyze them.

The paradigmatic text here is Michel de Certeau's interpretation of a painting that portrays the emerging European empire in the guise of an erect, armored Amerigo Vespucci contemplating a recumbent nude and female America. Reading the painting as an allegory of an imperial psyche that links "the erotic and the warlike," de Certeau offered an explanation consonant with his view that history writes its own story, archives are symptomatic rather than informative; that is, they inform about themselves.

Whatever it does to history, however, the idea that the written world is the only one we can ever know does away with literature by abolishing any distinction between literary and other writing. Literature starts from the assumption of an other, knowable reality in order to invent its own. Whether the invented world mimics the real one, interprets it, or turns its back on it entirely, is not important. In all these stances, writing produces something different from what already exists. Ironically, when historians deny having access to the real, they lose less than do literary critics. Historians still have their sources and they can still write about them, that being a close remaining option to writing about real events. Literary critics lose literature as such, and they also lose criticism which works by showing how—by what means and to what ends—the real has been transformed.

"History before the Fact" uses the method of literary criticism to read the literary component of a historical text—to show how the real has been transformed—and a historical fact drawn from outside the text is crucial to its reading. The text is an episode from John Smith's *Generall Historie of Virginia,* which tells the story of the honorary coronation of the Indian chief Powhatan. The scene features a very suspicious Powhatan being approached by a group of English envoys who, in order to make him look the part of a monarch, attempt to deck him out in a scarlet cloak while surrounding him with gifts. He accepts cloak and gifts but categorically refuses to kneel to be crowned. At length, worn out by "perswasions, examples, and instructions," the Englishmen resort to force: "by leaning hard on his shoulders, he a little stooped, and three having the crowne in their hands put it on his head, when by the warning of a Pistoll the Boats were prepared with such a volley of shot, that the King started up in a horrible feare. . . ." Regaining his composure, however, the Indian returns the kindness by offering the head of the legation "his old shoes and his mantell."

Smith's coronation scene is like de Certeau's Vespucci painting in picturing an encounter between the Old World and the New, except that Powhatan has more to say for himself. If the Indian does not emerge the winner in the exchange, he's not the loser either. The point of view from which the story is described is undividedly Smith's and Europe's, but the existence of a returning gaze is not ruled out. The narrator slyly equalizes the sides: everyone looks silly, the ceremony is a farce, and the Indian's apparent incomprehension may prove him sagaciously aware that the English are trying to flatter him into a damaging alliance. Though a true believer in the cause of the British empire, Smith here represents the conquest of America as a contest or an encounter, instead of the march of a natural destiny.

This is a perfectly reasonable reading, and as predictable. According to the theoretical account of colonization most widely followed today, colonial encounters generally feature the assumption by Europeans that they represent civilization, and those they encounter, a negative other. On this theory, the reading I have just proposed sketches a popular permutation of the basic dyad of European agent and other: an instance in which a European, John Smith, allows an other, Powhatan, more agency than his kind is usually accorded. There is no way to know what is going on outside the text, but the assumption that all human beings possess agency will imply that Powhatan's humanity seems to have forced itself subversively into Smith's narrative.

I do not say this interpretation is wrong, only incomplete. On a closer look, another factor is probably as important in shaping the encounter as the relation of European and other, namely Smith's own relation with his fellows. It could hardly be part of his role as a colonizer to make fun of his compatriots, still less to elevate Powhatan at their expense. So why does he make the Englishmen look even sillier than the Indian, while he himself stands apart signaling the reader with a wink and a nudge? When one recognizes that the little drama Smith has so vividly portrayed has three rather than two sides—the English, the Indians, and John Smith—it becomes apparent that he himself has two sides. In fact, he was in a personal quandary during this incident. Being in competition with the leader of the English delegation for the governorship of Virginia, Smith would not have been unhappy if the mission failed humiliatingly with his opponent bested by a savage. His pleasure in Powhatan's resistance, however, was complicated. Contrary to the implication of the first reading, organized by the dyad of Europe and the other, Smith, far from leaning toward a subversive empathy, advocated, in dealing with the Indians, more force and less flattery. If he favored straightforward treaties over spurious alliances, it was so as not to give men like Powhatan the illusion that they might treat as equals.

This second reading develops differently from the first by approaching the text through its form (style and tone). Smith's humor, like Franklin's, enables the writer to express a concurrence of mutually contradictory ideas and sentiments that otherwise threaten incoherence or, in this case, worse. Instead of revealing Smith to be duplicitous and possibly treacherous, the witty narration makes him the only one in the group a reader can trust. But here is the crux of the matter: while Smith appropriates the episode by an effect of form, for this effect to become apparent to us (for us to read it), we have to know something not directly told in his text, something which is literally its pretext. This requirement arises in all the essays, where formal readings presume a knowable world exactly because the knowledge within literary form is a knowledge of the world outside the text.

"Imitate Jesus and Socrates"   The Making of a Good
                                                                 American

This may be described as an occasional essay responding to
the occasion of a remarkable sentence in the *Autobiography* of
Benjamin Franklin.[1] The sentence offers a gloss for the last
virtue on a list of thirteen whose acquisition should make
Franklin perfect. To enlarge upon Humility, the final virtue,
he adds the injunction, "Imitate Jesus and Socrates." Either
Franklin's humor has for once failed him or such unaccus-
tomed loftiness from the creator of Poor Richard commands
serious attention.

• • •

Benjamin Franklin is best known perhaps neither as hu-
morist nor philosopher but as the calculating fellow Max
Weber saw embodying the crass spirit of capitalism and
whose apparent lack of interest in the darker mysteries of sex
and the psyche so depressed D. H. Lawrence. A man whose
idea of humility is imitating both the son of God and the
epitome of classical wisdom, however, must cherish a more
expansive sense of the personal self than Lawrence allowed.
For Franklin's concept of imitation is not that of Thomas à
Kempis. Franklin's American does not envisage submerging
his own in God's all-embracing Being but something like a
reverse Assumption—Ben Franklin as avatar of Christ and of
the greatest Greek of all. So the recommendation to humbly
imitate Jesus and Socrates, while characteristically pithy, is
also magnificently paradoxical. And while hitching the plain
to the superlative is an entirely familiar trope that need signal
nothing more than the paradox of democratic individualism,

paradox is not a word commonly associated with Benjamin Franklin. Yet I will suggest that his paradoxical thirteenth rule is a clue to another Franklin who more easily cohabits the same century as Rousseau and, far from ignoring the Hercynian Wood which was for Lawrence the image of the human heart, lumbers it assiduously.

This is not to claim that Franklin was a closet Romantic. But he was, I believe, as interested as the Romantics in the interior landscape, though he mapped it differently and was less awed by it. Foreshadowing Emerson, Franklin can be distinguished from contemporaries even as reflective as Thomas Jefferson through a more developed sense of the uses and abuses of the personal: hence indeed the very inspiration to write an autobiography, a form that originates in the perception of a dialectic of person and society, with the person defined antithetically through distance and difference.[2]

For an inherent capacity to stand alone is as essential to the architecture of the solid citizen of Franklin's *Autobiography* as it is to the excitable eccentric of Rousseau's *Confessions*. One may get a different impression at first when Franklin, addressing his memoirs to his son in the hope that he may cull from his father's life some useful hints for his own, begins by invoking filiopiety: "I have ever had a Pleasure in obtaining any little Anecdotes of my Ancestors," and so he hopes his son will be pleased to receive these anecdotes of his own ancestor. The opening move is toward rather than apart; Franklin's first gesture is, if not communal, at least familial. Going the opposite way, Rousseau's imperious opening sentence flies by all such nets: "I have resolved on an enterprise which has no precedent and which, once complete, will have no imitator." While Franklin writes for posterity, to reveal the means of his great success to descendants "as they may find some of them suitable to their own Situation, & therefore fit to be imitated," Rousseau records his *Confessions* because he is inimitable.[3] He modestly declines to judge whether "Nature did well or ill in breaking the mould in which she formed me" but has to admit that "I am made unlike any one I have ever met; I will even venture to say that I am like no one in the whole world."[4] A century before Freud, Rousseau locates sex at the core of individuality by confessing to a certain peculiar erotic preference heretofore concealed and now produced as the first evidence of his uniqueness. Franklin invokes some amorous peccadillos to prove himself just a typical young man—a little shrewder than most, harderworking, more ambitious, but *not* different.[5]

Rousseau claims that he is unique and Franklin that he is representative, but the difference between unique and representative is perhaps less than the dictionary claims. The American concept of representativeness—referring to

Franklin, Mitchell Breitweiser defines the representative man nicely as "a di-
gest of human nature itself, purified of time's local inflections"—is not really
the opposite of uniqueness.[6] When Franklin offers his exceptional career as
representative, he means that he believes everyone is potentially exceptional.
A certain kind of nursery school teacher reassures her jealous charges that
each one is special. This is either nonsense or demagoguery unless one conceives of a world without ordinariness, thus without norms or conventions.
An absence of norms and conventions, however, is just what characterizes the
dominant image of America as ahistorically transcendent and therefore sui
generis—unique. In that image, the individual American is unique as well in
deriving his identity not from his social context but from an individual distil-
lation of transcendent Americanness. Americans can each be unique and yet
all be identical, with one another and with America, and the most individual
American remains representative in his very autonomy. The American is
Everyman and Franklin is his supreme epigone.

The reason Rousseau declares himself unique in the *Confessions* is not the
reverse of this situation but its converse: eighteenth-century France and Europe were to their inhabitants profoundly historical situations constructed by
a pervasive immanence of norms and conventions from which, in order to
become his own man, the individual would have to separate himself, becoming exceptional (rather than representative). It is thus not a different but the
same logic of self-creation that inspired Franklin to present himself as representative and causes Rousseau to insist that he is unique, between them explicating the pun of the universal self, that each one comprises his own universe
while the universe of human possibilities is encompassed in each individual.
The *Autobiography* and the *Confessions* recount the birth of modern selfhood,
recapitulating in their phylogeny the ontogeny that transformed feudal con-
tinuities between individual and society into free-market dialectics. Two
adolescents upon leaving home and breaking traditional ties discover individual autonomy. That autonomy, however, having been purchased at the expense of any inherited access to food, shelter, or companions, immediately
brings up the problem of survival. How can self-possession generate posses-
sions?

At the ages of seventeen and sixteen, respectively, in 1723 and 1728, Franklin and Rousseau journeyed forth into the world, enacting not so much *Pilgrim's Progress* as *Paradise Lost* when, like a couple of Adams, they cast an
imperial eye on earth, leaving the heavenly heights for later.[7] A runaway en-
graver's apprentice, the penniless Rousseau broke his first youthful journey at
the house of his future patron and mistress whom he called Maman;[8] Franklin

put by all such atavisms, hired on as a journeyman-printer, and took a room in the house where he worked. But in the end they were both astute tradesmen working different markets. And in Franklin's market neither boyish charms nor confessions would have sold very well.

. . .

Instead of confession, therefore, Franklin professed, writing the *Autobiography* as a handbook for the investment and management of private selfhood in the rising market of a new nation. My emphasis here is not on "investment" and "management" but on "private" which, in the opening paragraphs of the narrative, is certainly Franklin's emphasis. He will recount "the Circumstances of *my* Life" (emphasis added), will trace *his* passage "from the Poverty & Obscurity in which I was born & bred to a State of Affluence & some Degree of Reputation in the World." Affluence and reputation add up to "a considerable share of Felicity" whose "conducing Means" he offers to share freely in the spirit in which he refuses ever to patent his mechanical inventions. Much like the latter, his strategies for advancement are individual creations that embody general laws of production less than one man's capacity to produce. By the time (some 275 words into the *Autobiography*) he acknowledges "the Inclination so natural in old Men, to be talking of themselves and their own past Actions," he has claimed "I," "me," and "my" twenty-eight times.

That number would not dismay him: "Most People dislike Vanity in others whatever Share they have of it themselves, but I give it fair Quarter wherever I meet with it being persuaded that it is often productive of Good to the Possessor & to others that are within his Sphere of Action." In fact he has come to think that "in many Cases it would not be quite absurd if a Man were to thank God for his Vanity among the other Comforts of Life."[9] Coming from one who a few pages later recalls with some emotion that Bunyan's collected works were the first of the books on which he spent all the hard-earned pennies of a straitened childhood, this encomium to the sin that names the town of sinners seems worth pondering. The more so that he endorses Vanity at the start of the *Autobiography,* whose declared purpose is to guide young Christian footsteps through the dangerous thoroughfares of the world.

That, however, is the explanation: Franklin means to direct his youthful readers *through* the world, not beyond it. They are to reach the Celestial City eventually, to be sure, but first they are bound for town where he will show them how to corner the Fair. This is not quite the apostasy it seems, for Bunyan himself harbored some ambivalence toward, if not the Fair's seductive display of goods and pleasures, then the vitality that has produced it. There may be wickedness but there is also exuberance in the cornucopia of "houses, lands, trades, places, honours, preferments, titles, countries, kingdoms, lusts, pleasures, and delights of all sorts, as whores, bawds, wives, husbands, children, masters, servants, lives, blood, bodies, souls, silver, gold, pearls, precious stones, and what not" that spills across Christian's path and also into the poem.[10] The trouble is that commerce mixes the potentially good pell-mell with the evil; selling and sold at Vanity's Fair, everyone and everything bears the taint of greed, and Bunyan can only think to pluck his Christian away fast. But as background for Franklin's turnabout, it is useful to see that before his predecessor fled Vanity, he himself revised its meaning. For in the image of the Fair, Bunyan has essentially reversed Ecclesiastes; the Preacher's argument about the world was that "all *is* vanity" (emphasis added); Bunyan's is that vanity *makes* all—produces all things.

The first effect of this revision is to render the opposition of heaven and earth even more stringent: by transforming vanity from merely a valuation of the world into the source of value in the world, the Puritan has rendered abnegation newly austere and acquisition more than ever profligate. Expressing a distaste not unlike Hobbes's for the new world of producing and self-producing individuals—Vanity is producing an expanded version of oneself, it is a capitalism of the self—Bunyan shudders and turns away. That he thus abandons a dilemma he cannot solve, the link between world-greediness and world-creation, is made plain by the allegory of Christian's helpless imprisonment. While on the site of Vanity and refusing to use its means of progress, he is entirely without power of self-propulsion and must await a deus ex machina to set him once more on his way. But if the seventeenth-century Bunyan espied the productive energy of the individualist self and was appalled by its selfishness, the eighteenth-century Franklin set about capturing this human lightning to empower a self-advancement that would be at the same time generally beneficial. It is important to an understanding of Franklin's concerns to see that his embrace of Vanity is *not* the opposite of Bunyan's rejection of it; that Franklin seeks only to transform Bunyan's idealism into an ideology—to recast general ideals into parameters of social and political relations.

The same order of revisionism is evident in another of Franklin's adaptations of Puritan thought which may illuminate this one. Through an interesting process, Franklin came to conclude that the purpose of God's Commandments lay not in God but in man; so that, "tho' certain actions might not be bad *because* they were forbidden by [revelation], or good *because* it commanded them, yet probably these actions might be forbidden *because* they were bad for us, or commanded *because* they were beneficial to us, in their own natures, all the circumstances of things considered."[11] Now, this may look like a reversal of orthodox Christianity but it is not, indeed it does not go nearly as far to secularize morality as did the outright separation of Christian and civic virtues that marked the Enlightenment elsewhere.

For Franklin does not divide Christianity from the secular order, he only shifts their positions. This method of secularizing actually ensures continuity with the same morality that governed the Puritan state and individual before. The discovery that revelation means first to serve man (rather than first to glorify God) ushers in a new secular era under the aegis of religion—under God. Social stability is thus retained and even reinforced. Through Franklin's glorious revolution the individual citizen is also reinforced, his earthly pursuits having appropriated divine prerogative at the same time as they are released from divine sanction. And a Vanity which seems blasphemous from the divine perspective (as Bunyan continues to see it even as he endows it with new secular capabilities), becomes from man's point of view a self-affirming energy. No longer a challenge to the deity but only to other men (indeed one way a benevolent God ensures beneficial competition among men), Vanity "is often productive of Good to the Possessor and to others that are within his Sphere of Action." For instance, it has produced the *Autobiography* whose good lies in turn in its production of productive young men, themselves made productive by Vanity.

Grown into a version of Rousseau's interiority-generating *amour-propre*, Franklin's Vanity is no longer the allegorical wraith it was for Bunyan. It has developed the corpulence of personal history, and when it expresses itself in the silver spoon and china bowl that Franklin's wife buys him to replace the wood and earthenware implements of his humbler days, Vanity is not only pride but pride in a job well done. Franklin's Vanity internalizes such doing well, indeed even doing good, and thereby converts the Vanity that was for Bunyan the agent of corruption into a trusty business partner. The same procedure operates in a converse way to complicate not a sin but a virtue, Sincerity, which it renders dualistic. Like Vanity, Sincerity would seem to be vitiated by such dualisms—a generally beneficial Vanity and a duplicitous Sincerity are on the surface contradictory. But Franklin's Sincerity becomes self-serving in the same degree as his Vanity becomes useful to others, so that both traits retain their original thrust but also acquire a dialectical capability that enables them to interact: to act in society.

Franklin's evolved Vanity provides a bridge between the opposing goals of the Puritan errand. By charting a route that enables the Pilgrim's Progress to

coincide with the Way to Wealth, Franklin translates the dichotomy that separates the Celestial City from the town of Vanity into a dialectic whose synthesis is a reformed Fair—an honestly conducted, socially beneficial, and personally profitable market. The road to this market passes through the country
of interiority, and it is to signal entrance into that country that the *Autobiography* begins with those twenty-eight invocations of the writer's own person
and, in case we have not been counting, sums them up pointedly as Vanity.

This conception of Vanity as ambition, which is only sometimes excessive, is what underlies the paradoxical arrogance of the precept that inspired
this essay, whereby one becomes humble by imitating Jesus and Socrates. Indeed in the context of redefining Vanity as the self's ambition to make something of itself, Vanity comes to inspire the pursuit of Humility, albeit a Humility that is also redefined. For while Franklin never says how we are to
imitate Jesus, he is quite specific about Socrates from whose method we
should copy the posture of "humble Enquirer." This means addressing others
"in Terms of modest Diffidence" and "never using when I advance any thing
that may possibly be disputed, the Words, *Certainly, undoubtedly,* or any others
that give the Air of Positiveness to an Opinion."[12] To be sure, Franklin admits,
an important part of this stance is mere pretense: Vanity inspires stronger
views than we are to express. But it is by no means all sham. Insofar as "the
chief Ends of Conversation are to *inform,* or to be *informed,* to *please* or to *persuade,*"

> I wish well meaning sensible Men would not lessen their Power of doing
> Good by a Positive assuming Manner that seldom fails to disgust, tends to cre-
> ate Opposition, and to defeat every one of those Purposes for which Speech
> was given us, to wit, giving or receiving Information, or Pleasure.[13]

All the definitions here and all the considerations are matters of exchange.
Humility has developed from a posture before God to a stance that permits a
man to trade goods with other men: that way, in giving one access to what
others have produced, Humility becomes no longer the opposite but the
complement of a Vanity that quickens one's own production.

• • •

An unprecedented individual autonomy has been reconciled with political
stability. This is very well, but there are difficulties. For reconciliation brings
its own hazards if only because it depends on contending dualisms: on paradoxes like the modest arrogance and arrogant modesty of thinking to imitate

Jesus and Socrates; and on possible contradictions in the individualist conception of selfhood between a much-expanded sufficiency and a commensurately greater vulnerability to sufficient others. The energy source of modern
man is dangerously unstable. Franklin needs not only to empower his ambitious readers but to warn them of the dangers and to devise protections. The
Autobiography expends about as much instruction warning as it does encour-
aging. For instance, the error that Franklin redresses by abandoning his con-
tentious style of debate is even more instructive than the correction.

In his sprightly youth, eager to be on his way, Franklin went too far.[14] At
the disputatious age of fifteen or sixteen, he happened to read a set of lectures
denouncing deism and at once espoused the opposite view, embracing deism
and concluding from its premise that a benevolent God would not have created man evil, that "vice and virtue were empty distinctions," and that individual conduct carried its own justification. It was then and in that spirit that
he discovered the Socratic method:[15]

> [I] became a real Doubter in many Points of our Religious Doctrine. I found
> this Method safest for my self & very embarrassing to those against whom I
> used it.
>
> I took a Delight in it, practis'd it continually & grew very artful & expert
> in drawing People even of superior Knowledge into Concessions the Conse-
> quences of which they did not foresee, entangling them in Difficulties out of
> which they could not extricate themselves, and so obtaining Victories that
> neither myself nor my Cause always deserved.[16]—

He continued to argue this way "some few Years" until events caused him
to reconsider whether systematically confuting established values and moral
laws was really to his advantage.

To wit, Franklin found that his freethinking friends "wrong'd me greatly
without the least Compunction": moral autonomy not only empowered him,
it also empowered others against him. A fast study, Franklin now "grew con-
vinc'd that *Truth, Sincerity* and *Integrity* in Dealings between Man & Man, were
of the utmost Importance to the Felicity of Life."[17] At this initial stage he was
not reclaiming the actual substance of Christian morality since truth, sincerity, and integrity are not rules of conduct but rules of the game. Although
later his list of virtues does include certain traditional rules of conduct, like
Chastity and perhaps Temperance, even these are redefined and, prodigiously,
the list itself emerges as a replacement for the Commandments.

In Franklin's secular theology the Ten Commandments yield to the thirteen Virtues, the last of which ("Imitate Jesus and Socrates") appears, in this context, at least profane if not blasphemous. Franklin has imitated not only Jesus but God and even that has not been enough to serve his large and complicated purpose—he has had to bring in a pagan Greek. This large purpose is the formulation of a moral ideology that can both regulate and enable the exercise of modern power, both that of the individual and that of the productive market. The complication comes from the newly complex nature of both, their separate and interactive dualisms which preclude any simple rules of conducts and require, precisely, contractual rules of the game. When Vanity becomes consonant with Humility in the pursuit of self-improvement (improvement now to encompass enrichment and advancement as well), morality in general has acquired a new complexity, a dualism that may be difficult to distinguish from duplicity.

Yet Franklin enshrines truth, sincerity, and integrity as a composite cardinal virtue that, since it is the originating virtue for any autobiography, in this context has primacy over all others. On the list of thirteen, truth/sincerity/integrity occupies the central place of number seven: "Sincerity. Use no hurtful Deceit. Think innocently and justly; and, if you speak; speak accordingly."[18] Once again, however, as with Vanity and Humility, the appended precept revises the orthodox definition in a way that seems at first to reverse it. The *O.E.D.* defines sincerity this way: "containing no element of dissimulation or deception; not feigned or pretended"; and *Webster's* concurs that sincerity is "marked by genuineness . . . free of dissimulation: not hypocritical: real, true, honest." For Lionel Trilling, who wrote a book examining the descent and meaning of sincerity in modern culture, it is an exact "congruence between avowal and actual feeling" or, more poetically, "the avoidance of being false to any man through being true to one's own self."[19] One probably false but telling etymological derivation has "sincere" being coined from the words *sine cera:* without wax, neither patched nor adulterated. In short, sincerity is an identification between appearance and reality. Any interpolation, any intervention or interpretation, certainly any private judgments about how hurtful this or that deception may be ought therefore to be fatal. Yet Franklin proposes such judgments as the heart of the matter: "Think innocently and justly," he urges, "and, if you speak; speak accordingly." Yet, technically, to be sincere a person should reflect as little as possible, be without policy, open and not silent, and speak not considerately but spontaneously.

Or as nearly spontaneously as possible, given that modern individuals have been rendered opaque to one another by a film of self-consciousness. Individualism makes us organically duplicitous by doubling our identity: when one's world is divided into private and public, one develops two selves. And sincerity, logically a contradiction in terms, emerged as a concept and ideal round about the sixteenth century to name and respond to a contradiction in the emerging concept and ideal of the self. Sincerity appears as a personal quality when personality, by definition and not deformity, becomes a mask. Acknowledging this contradiction, Trilling would have us settle for a partial sincerity; but perhaps because Franklin wrote two centuries earlier during a period of ideological transition when, generally, insurgent thinking disputes the roots of concepts, he addresses the issue more radically. His Sincerity is not partial but qualified ("use no hurtful Deceit"), and this qualification engages the fundamental issue of individualist relations. Franklin's Sincerity is a personal quality whose field is the community of others. It is an agreement among independent individuals not to exploit hurtfully their capacities to dissimulate, feign, and pretend.

The paradox of Franklin's prose demonstrates how sincerity can feign and pretend and yet be honest. Franklin explains in the *Autobiography* that he learned to write by imitation, copying out essays from the *Spectator* and even memorizing them so as to reproduce them as nearly as possible in their original idiom. This procedure finally yielded the clear, simple, forthright, unadorned writing that makes the *Autobiography* a founding text of the American Plain Style. Artless by the most careful design, its simplicity a complicated achievement, Franklin's prose is lucidly transparent—all the way down to its appearance, which is not at all genuine but entirely sincere. Its sincere message, the truth it both explicitly tells and embodies, is that truth is a sincere construction. Language is not identical with its message (Franklin's prose is functional precisely in not being directly expressive), and if we wish to speak effectively, to act efficaciously *and* ethically, we should rather widen the gap between words and their intended meanings than strive to close it. Each stage of the young Franklin's social and moral advancement entails a more definitive distinction—not an opposition but a separation—between speech and its effects, as between individual and community.

The Socratic stance he abandons had been by his own account *less* duplicitous than the truth, sincerity, and integrity he adopts instead, and which lead him, in all sincerity, to pretend to be less certain of his views than he really is. He never claims he actually became less certain nor does he advise real skepticism, only its forms. The real issue, which he defines more fully in the second part of the *Autobiography,* is rhetoric: "When another asserted something that I thought an Error, I deny'd my self the Pleasure of contradicting him abruptly, and of showing immediately some Absurdity in his Proposition; and in answering I began by observing that in certain Cases or Circumstances his Opinion would be right, but that in the present case there *appear'd* or *seem'd* to me some Difference, & c." Gradually he came never to assert a positive opinion of anything, and to "this Habit (after my Character of Integrity) I think it principally owing, that I had early so much Weight with my Fellow Citizens . . . and so much Influence in public Councils when I became a Member."[20]

So Franklin sets an example of integrity enhanced by hypocrisy, of sincerity morally superior to the reality it belies. This is an ethical system based on the assumption that appearance and reality are generically separate, a condition not at all to be regretted since the space that separates them is precisely the theater of morality. Indeed, were appearance and reality even potentially one, we could not act well or not as well as we are enabled to by the gap between private inclinations and the public behavior to which we pretend. As Vanity fuels productive activities that enrich society as well as ourselves, so a benevolent hypocrisy is needed to implement integrity: all this illustrating the general principle of the dualistic structures of both private character and public persona.

The *Autobiography* features a number of vignettes that show how this principle may be applied for fun and profit. One of these recalls an accident that late one afternoon broke up a completed printing form, requiring that Franklin work into the night to recompose it. The fortunate mending of this unlucky break, and its moral, came about when the conscientious printer was seen working late by an influential burgher who spread the news of his uncommon industry. Now, Franklin's industry was certainly more than ordinary, but it was not as uncommon as it appeared that night. The narrative makes no such distinction. On the contrary, it assigns the merit of the impressed observer's error to the truth as enlarging the truth itself: in the sentence following the gleeful account of how one Doctor Baird reported his amazement at seeing "him still at work when I go home from Club," Franklin adds parenthetically that he has mentioned his Industry, "tho' it seems talking in my own Praise, that those of my Posterity who shall read it, may know the Use of that Virtue, when they see its Effects in my Favour throughout this Relation," thus incorporating the exaggerated accounting into his own presumably more accurate one.[21]

There is much reality as well as appearance to justify Franklin's excellent reputation, and the good Doctor who reports seeing him at work earlier in the morning than others tells the real truth. But Franklin's point is not that appearance can (or should) substitute for reality; it is that reality needs appearance in order to achieve reality's own effects. "To show that I was not above my Business," goes another exemplum, "I sometimes brought home the Paper I purchas'd at the Stores, thro' the Streets on a Wheelbarrow." This could be a nice little emblem of bourgeois inauthenticity, but by Franklin's definition it is in no way insincere—no more than not expressing one's convictions forcefully or refraining from pointing out the flaws in an opponent's argument while planning how to expose them. This is not to say, although Franklin would not reject the proposition, that opportunism in the service of virtue is itself a virtue. Rather, the point of the wheelbarrow story is that virtue needs to be served by opportunism, or pretense, because without appearance the reality of virtue fails to realize itself: before appearing the real is not realized. When modern identity imagined itself freely self-created in an interior realm concealed by the ramparts of privacy, it created, as well a realm that was entirely exterior and free of any necessary connection to any individual. To be in the world (to be real for others) one has now to colonize it. Personal reality has to be personally created: once it is no longer inherited it ceases to be inherent.

What *is* now inherent is the power to create, which brings us back to the beginning of the discussion of Sincerity as a response to the dangers of the situation represented by Vanity: while Vanity is the force that drives the young man through the world, Sincerity keeps him in line; with the change of destination from the Celestial City to Vanity, it is what moralizes the Pilgrim's Progress. In other words, as Humility is to Vanity, so Sincerity is to Deceit: more or less slippery holds on the tail of the individualist tiger. Let go, and the gorgeous tiger may turn on you. A Humility that scorns ambition or a Sincerity that refuses to deceive are worse than useless.

• • •

To put this another way, for Franklin virtue is a political matter. The *Autobiography* is a rare document in American literature, a political treatise that does not deplore its subject as such. It is unabashedly a work of ideological persuasion. The most urban of the founders—not only a city-dweller but the creature of the city's economy and politics—Franklin takes streets and connected town houses, markets, and newspapers as natural features of the landscape. Closer in this respect to Hobbes and Locke than to Rousseau, Franklin, in his treatment of the political as an original state and his primary concern with civil life, is perhaps closest to an earlier thinker whose reputation casts him as Franklin's very opposite: Machiavelli. J. G. A. Pocock has found Machiavelli's republican themes most fully elaborated in the political debates of late eighteenth-century America where the problems of ensuring the survival and probity of a nonmonarchic government emerged with a special urgency un-mitigated by the remnants of earlier political traditions. Pocock does not mention Franklin, but he seems to me arguably the best expositor of the is-sues that characterize "the Machiavellian moment," meaning "a crisis in the relations between personality and society, virtue and corruption" arising from the recognition that because republican governments are radically historical (grounded not in claims of divine or otherwise transcendent order but in hu-man history) they are peculiarly prone to destabilization.[22] One source of in-stability is historical time, which has brought the republic about but threatens as well to bring it to an end. American ideology essentially neutralizes time by representing republican America—synonymous with the New World—as a transcendent universe that culminates history. But the other source of insta-bility Pocock identifies is civic corruption, and for that there is no permanent cure not worse than the disease.

Immunization is with a live vaccine. As without Vanity one would not seek improvements so energetically, so without the capacity to be corrupt, which is nothing else but free will, one would not be empowered to act cre-atively or morally. "The republican principle that virtue is active" means that republican virtue is also always divided.[23] Franklin, who is entirely commit-ted to an active morality (for whom there is really no other), insists that his readers understand the inevitable ambiguity that the power to act and activity itself generate. I have already noted several examples of this ambiguity in in-dividual conduct—exaggerations, lies, pretenses that are all said to enhance integrity—but the most fully developed instance in the *Autobiography* is di-rectly political in involving a group. Franklin's organization early in his career of the Junto, a club "for mutual Improvement" whose members provided one another with conversation and contacts, is one of the acts of which he de-clares himself most proud. More to the point, he holds it up as a prime exam-ple of civic behavior.

The Junto, however, was a secret society and after a time even a conspir-acy: a prime example, one would think, of republican corruption. When sev-eral of the Junto members wished to enroll their friends in this useful congre-gation, Franklin opposed expansion and suggested instead that each member establish "a subordinate Club, with the same Rules . . . and without inform-ing them of the Connexion with the Junto." The "Advantages" Franklin lists for this scheme detail the organic ambiguity of modern political ethics:

the Improvement of so many more young citizens by the Use of our Institu-tions; Our better Acquaintance with the general Sentiments of the Inhabi-

tants on any Occasion, as the Junto-Member might propose what Queries we
should desire, and was to report to Junto what pass'd in his separate Club; the
Promotion of our particular Interests in Business by more extensive Recom-
mendations; and the Increase of our Influence in public Affairs & our Power
of doing Good by spreading thro' the several Clubs, the Sentiments of the
Junto.[24]

These advantages were duly realized, Franklin reports, citing particularly how
the subordinate Clubs "answer[ed] in some considerable Degree our Views of
influencing the public Opinion on particular Occasions."

Franklin publishes the secret of the Junto in each of the three sections of
the *Autobiography,* both the fact of the Club and at almost equal length the fact
of its secrecy. Indeed, although concealment is recommended throughout the
narrative, this instance stands out. There is a crucial difference between individual and group concealment in that the former is unavoidable (since by definition a modern individual can never be fully known by others) while on the
contrary the latter is difficult to achieve and requires a positive act of deceit.
Private dissembling has a limited range both for good and evil—Franklin did
become more influential through his policy of never stating "a fix'd Opinion" despite never being without one. But even had that influence been for
the worse it was unlikely to significantly alter the course of events. Concerted
dissemblings are another matter, and the Junto did bring about important
changes in Philadelphia, creating institutions and inspiring long-term social
policies. And while one may be tempted to shrug off Franklin's own sharp
practices, he imbues them with more importance by associating them with
the covert operations of the Junto. One can only conclude that the *Autobiography* means to set an example if not of outright lying, then at least of personal
secretiveness and, in a good cause, of collusion. The good cause is basically the
same as Machiavelli's: the maintenance of a republican civil order conducted
with civic morality. The Junto (according to Franklin) plotted in the public
interest, for the social welfare, and even toward the expansion of democratic
rights. The contradiction in this is the same as that at the heart of private
morality, as benign and also as crucial. The Junto writes large the moral of the
whole *Autobiography.*

Given free will on the one hand and on the other the desired removal of
transcendent sanctions, how is civic morality to be preserved? How is the free
young man who is Franklin's Prince to be persuaded to act morally when he
has abundant power to do otherwise? The *Autobiography's* answer is Sincerity
and Humility. Not unlike Locke's notion of a society of competitive equals

nonetheless able to form communities of interest—the Junto is exactly such a community—Sincerity and Humility regulate our organic Duplicity and Vanity though a contractual ethic; they are ways of acting in common against the anomie of vain and self-seeking individualism. The separate members of a society are neither sincere nor humble; for this we thank God who makes us both able and prone to improve our initially exposed and lowly condition. To improve it both materially and spiritually: not being innately rich, we act so as to acquire; not being intrinsically sincere and humble, we can act sincerely and humbly. Franklin, like other Americans, has been read mostly in an American context, in which this notion of greater opportunities through the rectification of moral weakness offers a lay version of the doctrine of the Fortunate Fall. However, by promulgating Sincerity and Humility as not only personal but civic virtues (domesticating vice in the same way) he takes an additional step whose measure needs a transatlantic ruler.

I am proposing Franklin as an American Machiavelli with a New World perspective that enabled him to discern a possible resolution for the moral contradiction whose shocking exposure has earned Machiavelli centuries of infamy. When Franklin discovered that Revelation spoke for the benefit of man rather than the glory of God, he had the basic model for this possible resolution; the secularization he envisioned, bolder still as an affirmation of human prerogative than Machiavelli's separation of Christian and civic morality, is for the same reason no longer divisive. Christian values in Franklin's reversal of things become themselves socially instrumental. Instead of calling men out of history, they universalize history by investing it with their eternal validity. Thus far, however, the model is stable at the expense of being also static; the secular revolution has been prevented from destroying the old moral order (as freethinking threatened to do) but it seems to have also prevented from producing the New World it bravely announces. Having restored the laws of Revelation, Franklin could defend himself against the unscrupulous, but defense was not enough. He needed a concept of virtue that also enjoined action—republican virtue is *active*.

And so, in a passage early in the *Autobiography*, Franklin paradigmatically transforms Humility from a mode of acceptance into a way of acting. The passage follows directly the one cited earlier in this discussion in which he expresses his gratitude to the Lord for his Vanity:

> And now I speak of thanking God, I desire with all Humility to acknowledge, that I owe the mention'd Happiness of my past Life to his kind Providence, which led me to the Means I us'd & gave them Success.—My belief of This,

induces me to *hope,* tho' I must not *presume,* that the same Goodness will still be exercis'd towards me in continuing that Happiness, or in enabling me to bear a fatal Reverso, which I may experience as others have done, the Complexion of my future Fortune being known to him only: and in whose Power it is to bless to us even our Afflictions.[25]

At first glance this expresses an orthodox if perfunctory piety; the introductory phrase "[a]nd now I speak of thanking God" is a little offhand perhaps but the sentiment seems unexceptionable: Franklin recognizes his debt to God whose final determination of things he does not presume to know, let alone question.

A second reading reveals some possible heresies. The sentiment still seems proper, but one now notices that more than the tone is perfunctory; so are the invocations of Providence and Fortune, though ostensibly they are where true power resides. Like Machiavelli, Franklin wants to bring the relation of Virtue and Fortune (after the Middle Ages, increasingly meaning commerce) from the edges of the cosmic, where man meets God, into the center of civic life. (It is probably not by coincidence that Franklin's account of writing *Poor Richard's Almanack* offers as a single sample of its wares a proverb that weds Virtue and Fortune explicitly: "*It is hard for an empty Sack to stand upright.*")[26] In the narrative, the discussion of Virtue and Fortune follows immediately the seriocomic passage on Vanity and clearly sets out to balance it, indeed to overbalance it, since, as it has thus far been projected, the central drama of the book will lie in the acquisition of Fortune through Virtue. But the passage actually works to a different end, not succeeding in capturing the center of the stage for the Fortune-Virtue encounter and instead introducing a somewhat different drama in which Fortune is still a hero, or rather heroine, but Virtue, though it plays a key role, has become a supporting actor.

This new play features a new hero, Franklin himself. Franklin as a self: a hero not in the way that Christian is a hero of Bunyan's tale nor even the Prince of Machiavelli's, but much like Rousseau in his own story. Let me again seize an unusual opportunity for quantification and point out that Franklin's declaration of Humility uses the first-person pronoun thirteen times (out of some 120 words), more frequently still than in the Vanity passage. Humility, which here stands in for Virtue as such, having been broached as a force in itself ("I" and "Humility" appear on the first line grammatically as co-subjects of the sentence), disappears immediately never to reappear as an independent entity. Instead it becomes implicit in the person of Franklin, an aspect of his character; in Franklin's story of how he captured Fortune, Virtue is a means and neither a participant nor a victor in itself. The very submission with which the passage concludes turns Humility inside out; any reverses and defeats Franklin suffers in the battle with Fortune will be as much functions of his complex wholeness as his victories, a calculus that clearly moves toward Emerson's infinite self. The narrative sequence outlines the stages of the argument. First comes the Vanity passage in which Franklin owns and embraces his ego, even should it extend to egotism; then, with a backward glance at his claim on the first page of the book to have already conquered Fortune, he corrects himself with the stipulation that of course no one achieves such final mastery, not even he. But this bite of humble pie hardly causes him to lose any narrative weight. The next sentence abandons external or philosophical considerations altogether to launch into a biographical account tracing his lineage and the derivation of his name. One does not need a postmodern gloss on naming and its role in the constitution of subjects to get the point.

What, then, is the *Autobiography* saying about the relation of Fortune and Virtue and the way it organizes and moralizes the social lives of individuals? Specifically, does this transfer of authority from Virtue to Franklin doom or seriously undermine his Machiavellian mission to engender societal Virtue even at possible cost to individual advancement? The answer to both questions, I believe, is that Virtue remains as commanding, as imperative for Franklin as ever it was for Bunyan, Machiavelli, or for any moralists who defined morality as an end in itself in the image of a deity whose worship constitutes a final purpose, or in the name of an ideal, like the survival of the republic, whose fulfillment is its own sufficient reason. But although for Franklin morality is always instrumental—to personal advancement, to social betterment, to profit and production—it is not for that less essential. Humility, now a means and not an end, supporting actor rather than lead, is not thereby lesser. On the contrary, when "with all Humility" Franklin grants that Providence provides, Fortune disposes, and he only does the best he can, the last of these is nonetheless where the action is. As the condition for Franklin's activity, Humility emerges invigorated, activated: no longer a surrender of authority but a price paid for authority, or at most a duty paid to it like a tax which gives one the right of use. Interestingly, now that Fortune has become commerce, Virtue, represented here by Humility and Sincerity, has learned to trade. Humility negotiates with Vanity, Sincerity with an innate tendency to deceive. On the common ground of such trade, in a world whose parameters and meanings are defined by commerce, Fortune and Virtue are reconciled in a way that would have pleased Machiavelli, for the condition of their reconciliation is *vivere civile*, "active citizenship in a republic": "participation and action in a social structure" which permits the individual to guarantee order and morality by his own behavior.[27]

Such reconciliation emphatically does not mean synthesis nor any kind of mutually neutralizing fusion. Morality here flows from duplicity. Franklin's Virtues can constitute moral commerce as well as the morality of commerce precisely because they are not, like Bunyan's, singular characteristics nor, like those of Lawrence or Trilling, private singularities. Instead, Franklin conceives of Virtue as a dualistic node of individual identity, dualistic because identity is for him the complex product of realizing negotiations between private and public. The reconciliation of Fortune and Virtue therefore means their encompassment within a common site of interaction—often a marketplace.

At this market—a long way from Vanity Fair—personal ethics are essential; it will not function without them. The liberal social order Franklin envisioned depending significantly on the virtue of its individualist citizens—a government of laws *and* men—entails a degree of trust in the common political process that has not been characteristic of the American tradition.[28] In the famous passage from the *Notes on the State of Virginia* in which Jefferson renders yeomen the guardians of the national virtue, Pocock reads Jefferson's attempt to deal with the "Machiavellian moment." But even as Jefferson declares that it "is the manners and spirit of a people which preserve a republic in vigour," his faith in the popular virtue is highly qualified and, as Pocock notes, he seeks stronger bulwarks against corruption, in institutions themselves, specifically in the institution of agrarianism. The material incentives of fee-simple agriculture are to translate into spiritual values in order to guarantee America's integrity, while the "mobs of great cities add just so much to the support of pure government, as sores do to the strength of the human body."[29]

Those we commonly invoke to define the ideals of republican government, like Jefferson, not uncommonly hold this view: that cities are excrescences on the body of nature, diseases threatening to infect the whole nation, and that their relatively large populations constitute, beyond crowds, denatured "mobs." On the whole, Rousseau regrets civilization, especially as represented in the jejune urbanities of the Parisian beau monde. We tend to pass over such familiar diatribes, but the antiurban topos does have implications for the possibilities of the democratic process, cities being the original locales of democracy and in all ages its political centers. It seems worth noting that in contrast to Rousseau and Jefferson, Machiavelli and Franklin take the city to be the natural site for building the virtuous republic. Franklin especially stands out among his contemporaries by taking urban life entirely for granted. One implication of this premise has been seen in Franklin's projection of what might be called a morality of relations: that is, a moral system whose ground is the social and political dialectic, an idealistic ideology, an ethic of engagements whose sense does not translate very well into the idiom of the prevailing Jeffersonian view that morality begins at the city limits.

Franklin's American is a city builder: a paver of streets, an organizer of libraries and post offices, a money lender and currency printer, a newspaper and book publisher, in which occupations he also makes his fortune. Jesus and Socrates achieved an ideal apotheosis by sacrificing themselves for the common good. Franklin's pragmatism excludes even the possibility of self-sacrifice. The characters who suffer lasting harm in the *Autobiography* are incompetent or deluded, and socially irresponsible besides; for when one man profits in Philadelphia, everyone profits. There is a trick to it: to make the world safe for a fertile selfishness and duplicity, the good American agrees to be careful of the common good and reasonably honest. *Imitating* Jesus and Socrates is exactly the thing: real sincerity and humility would miss the point which is far less to *be* this way or that inside oneself than to *enact* a useful self in the world. Imitation is not less than being but its fulfillment. Standing on a peak discovering the Blue Ridge mountains, integrity may be sufficient; in the new world's shops and parlors, what is wanted is imitation.

The author of *Letters from an American Farmer* boasted that in
America "we have no princes, for whom we toil, starve and
bleed: we are the most perfect society now existing in the
world."[1] But he opposed the American Revolution and remained loyal to the English crown, though his French origin
alone should have made him its opponent. Before the war he
had declared that immigrants to America could never be expected to remain committed to European societies that condemned them to "involuntary idleness, servile dependence,
penury, and useless labour." His dignity as well as the fruits of
his labors secured here, the new American must inevitably
"love this country much better than that wherein he or his
forefathers were born" (50). It was only natural and right for
a man to owe his first loyalty to the land that he tilled. But
having thus argued, and in the process provided perhaps the
best known definition of "the American," J. Hector St. John
Crèvecoeur then found himself, overnight, pleading with
hostile neighbors to be allowed to return to France. His lands
expropriated and his family scattered, Crèvecoeur fled the
New World in September 1780. How did this come about,
and why?

His sincerity and loyalty to America were beyond question. The cited passages were written before the confiscation
of his farm, but he published them afterwards nonetheless, in
1781–82, when he was back in France and helping American prisoners escape across the Channel, to return home.
Thomas Jefferson praised the *Letters* enthusiastically, and recognizing their remarkable propaganda value, endorsed their

agrarian vision as altogether in accord with his own. In Europe Crèvecoeur was dubbed "The American Farmer." By the close of the war, the country he had left as an ignominious fugitive honored him on his return as French consul.[2] But this reinstatement should not be taken to mean that his loyalism had been a mere misunderstanding. Crèvecoeur's opposition to the Revolution was as serious and principled as his commitment to America. Making sense of this requires that we distinguish between two historical developments usually treated as one: the achievement of national independence on one hand, and the evolution of American democracy on the other.

These two developments have been linked through an interpretation of the Revolution that tends toward the teleological, in viewing it as fought essentially to achieve nationhood. This view was bolstered for a long time by the general agreement that "American society in the half century after 1775 was substantially what it had been in the quarter century before."[3] In the absence of significant social change in the new nation, it was reasonable to suppose that the Revolutionaries were politically motivated and sought independence from external control rather than any internal resolution or transformation. But recent studies have uncovered more social flux and conflict in colonial America than had been suspected, and rather less consensus about the overall national purpose. It is in this context of closer attention to the internal complexities and contradictions of early American society that I will be attempting to explain Crèvecoeur's political decision against the Revolution. In coming to this decision, however expressive it was of larger principles, Crèvecoeur responded specifically to his local experience in rural Pennsylvania.[4]

In the period before the Revolution, that society seemed to Crèvecoeur very nearly a paradise which, best of all, anyone could enter. For this is what he valued above all about America, the opportunity he saw it providing everyone to achieve abundant self-sufficiency, and the dignity of equal status among his neighbors and before the law. In America, he wrote, society "is not composed, as in Europe, of great lords who possess everything, and of a herd of people who have nothing." Here is "no invisible power giving to a few a very visible one" (46). Instead everyone had equally complete control of his life, and none had power over another's. The early *Letters* celebrate the resurrection of Europe's wretched, hopeless poor, to whom America promised:

If thou wilt work, I have bread for thee; if thou wilt be honest, sober and industrious, I have greater rewards to confer on thee—ease and independence,

... the immunities of a freeman. .... Go thou and work and till; thou shalt prosper, provided thou be just, grateful and industrious. (73)

One such happy story, the ascent of Andrew the Hebridean from emigrant to American, was a New World *Pilgrim's Progress,* depicting "the progressive steps of a poor man, advancing from indigence to ease; from oppression to freedom, from obscurity and contumely to some degree of consequency—not by virtue of any freaks of fortune, but by the gradual operation of sobriety, honesty, and emigration" (74). This was a parable for the aspiring middle class of course; "the rich," Crèvecoeur noted, "stay in Europe, it is only the middling and the poor who emigrate" (63). But "for men of middle stations or labourers," America held out infinite possibilities; this was the familiar vision which has endured down to today, and Crèvecoeur articulated its ethic with notable precision: "we are all animated with the spirit of an industry which is unfettered and unrestrained," he exulted, "because each person works for himself" (46).

That all this constituted a revolution in the politics of the individual and society was something which Crèvecoeur both understood and applauded. The American, he proclaimed, "is a new man, who acts upon new principles; he must therefore entertain new ideas and form new opinions" (50). Then why not a new nation? Curiously, given his enthusiasm over the newness of the New World and what must have been the currency of such speculations, this question seems not even to have occurred to Crèvecoeur until the Revolution was upon him. In other respects he was as visionary as any, rhapsodizing, for instance, that "Americans are the western pilgrims, who are carrying along with them the great mass of arts, sciences, vigour, and industry which began long since in the east; they will finish the great circle" (49). So his failure to imagine America's future as a separate nation is the more striking. Indeed, in retrospect, Crèvecoeur himself wondered how he could have ignored the larger issues of state and society for so long: "I lived on, laboured and prospered, without having ever studied on what the security of my life, and the foundation of my prosperity were established: I perceived them just as they left me" (204). Amid the ruins of that prosperity, he saw that he had given too little thought to its external guarantees. His personal life had occupied all his energies, because for him only the private world mattered. "The instant I enter on my land," he had written in happier days, "the bright idea of property, of exclusive right, of independence exalt my mind" (30). Too late, he came to ask himself, "what is man when no longer connected with society; or when he finds himself surrounded by a convulsed and a half dissolved one?"

But even as he expanded on this awakening social consciousness, he revealed in the terms by which he sought to define community why he had earlier overlooked it.

Man "cannot live in solitude," Crèvecoeur explained, because "men mutually support and add to the boldness and confidence of each other; the weakness of each is strengthened by the force of the whole" (204). But he still missed the point, able to envision a social model only as inorganic arithmetical linkage. Because personal worth for him was measured by autonomy, any area of mutual definition amounted to a sort of entail on the self. Thus all relations between free men were properly foreign relations and society had to do only with external affairs.

The problem of reconciling individual independence with mutuality was not Crèvecoeur's alone. It occupied his entire century and, for that matter, the next; we are still not clear what the concept of community means in a society of individualists. Moreover, this is an ontological question, and not merely an ethical one. For Crèvecoeur, the private citizen need be neither selfish nor unsociable. He himself was apparently the most benevolent of men. "I have at all times generously relieved what few distressed people I have met with" (217), he reported, judging this one of his proudest achievements. He considered neighborliness not only desirable but absolutely necessary. The Andrew parable in the third *Letter* cites prominently the unstinting aid of already established farmers. One of these employed the immigrant until he worked out his indenture, while at the same time disinterestedly preparing him for the day he would have his own farm; then others leased him land, lent tools and seeds, raised his barn, transported his crops. Andrew could not and should not have done it alone; like Jefferson, Crèvecoeur valued farming for the social bonds as well as for the independence it fostered. It is when Andrew is made overseer of the county road and serves on petty juries that we know he is successful. He has arrived at his goal himself only when the land surrounding his farm is also finally settled; "instead of being the last man towards the wilderness, [he] found himself in a few years in the middle of a numerous society." And the process was to continue, for "he helped others as generously as others had helped him" (90).

For Crèvecoeur, loners, as opposed to self-reliant individualists, threatened civilization itself. He condemned as the dregs of American society those isolated inhabitants of the wilderness become idle, licentious hunters who hated their neighbors and, living alone far from churches and schools, had themselves become wild, "ferocious, gloomy and unsociable" (57). Neither a Rousseau nor a Chateaubriand, Crèvecoeur sought to disabuse his European

readers of romantic notions about man in the state of nature. In the back-
woods of America, he told them, there reigns "a perfect state of war":

> that of man against man . . . that of man against every wild inhabitant of these
> venerable woods, of which they are come to dispossess them. There men ap-
> pear to be no better than carnivorous animals of a superior rank, living on the
> flesh of wild animals when they can catch them . . . (52)

and on pilfering from each other when they can't. So that when he regretted
his insufficient attention earlier to the social connection, he did not mean that
he had ever thought that men should or could live alone. Far from it: isolation
had always been for him not merely inconvenient, but a threat to his identity
as a rational civilized being. Finding himself cut off from his community by
the advent of the Revolution, he would become aware that the houses in his
settlement lay "at a considerable distance from each other" (204–5), and that
the wilderness, the "hideous wilderness" (222), was all about. In the contemplation of this wilderness he wrote poignantly, "I feel as if my reason wanted
to leave me, as if it would burst its poor weak tenement" (204).

To be human, one needs human ties; to be a man, one must be entirely independent. Crèvecoeur resolved this paradox to his own satisfaction through
his family. Having found farming dull in his youth, he came with maturity to
appreciate its solid virtues. He reported having for a time considered leaving
the land, but then

> I married, and this perfectly reconciled me to my situation; my wife rendered
> my house all at once cheerful and pleasing; it no longer appeared gloomy and
> solitary as before; when I went to work in my fields I worked with more
> alacrity and sprightliness; I felt that I did not work for myself alone, and this
> encouraged me much. My wife would often come with her knitting in her
> hand, and sit under the shady trees, praising the straightness of my furrows, and
> the docility of my horses; this swelled my heart and made everything
> light and pleasant, and I regretted that I had not married before. (28)

It is not what is included in this idyll that is striking, so much as what it leaves
out, which is any suggestion of going outward from the familial nucleus, of
ties or activities beyond the family. Instead, the economic sphere, for one, is
subsumed to the domestic; Crèvecoeur's wife is more often pictured coming
out to the fields than he home to her, the metaphorical point of these meet-
ings being to project the structure of his world and to measure its extent,

which world is amply coextensive with his family. Ideally society could be made up of such families related to each other by analogy and proximity while remaining separate and self-defined. To achieve this ideal state, those who are already established have a social duty, which works also in their own interest, to help others through temporary and reversible familial relations to achieve equal status, one mature family aiding another weak or fledgling as a father would his son. Such aid is a recurrent motif in the *Letters*. Andrew rises by being raised by parental figures who educate, equip, and stake him as he will do equally for the next "generation" of immigrants and for his sons. For America's brightest promise to the worthy is prosperity for their children, which "to every good man . . . ought to be the most holy, the most powerful, the most earnest wish he can possibly form, as well as the most consolatory prospect when he dies" (73).

Therein lay Crèvecoeur's social vision of a benevolent America which nurtured each immigrant to a fulfilled manhood he then manifested by nurturing his children in turn. It is important that this fusion of private and public realms in one code of personal behavior not invoke medieval associations. If there were signs in the eighteenth century of a feudal revival in America, Crèvecoeur would have had none of it.[5] For him, the private and the public came together not in any external common domain, but in the inner man, whence they were projected into a politics of private morality generalized. So the excellent Bertram of the eleventh letter, a botanist exemplifying Crèvecoeur's notion of the social good as validated by nature, is a kindly but firm father to his brood of children, women, and blacks, all of whom he will try to raise to fulfill their potentials. Conversely when the Revolution seemed to have destroyed all hope of peace and order, the farmer's survival plan was, by his lights, less quixotic than it might appear. Gathering his distraught wife and children, taking with him husbands for his daughters, he planned to settle among the Indians and there, reconstituting his family and even ensuring its descendance, he would regenerate a microcivilization. Civilization, in short, was the family writ large.

The contrast with Robinson Crusoe is compelling: when Defoe wanted to recreate society, he provided Crusoe with his man Friday; Crèvecoeur took a wife. Though there is a certain analogy between the captive worker and the subservient wife, the difference between them nonetheless has significant ideological implications. For Defoe, the world was a marketplace organized around the basic relation of propertied and propertyless whose hired labor enriches the former and maintains them in their status. Thus property owners benefit from the relative poverty of the lower classes. To put it simply, if Friday's share were to grow as fast as, or faster than Crusoe's profits, Crusoe would lose by it. He extends his holdings only when Friday gets back less than the wealth he generates. However productive, and whether or not beneficial for Friday or for society as a whole, this is an intrinsically competitive situation. But Crèvecoeur's relationship to his wife was not so overtly competitive. Indeed for his part, he perceived the relation as entirely complementary, between himself and just another aspect of himself. (How his wife saw it, of course, may be another story, or another history.) By the shift in Crèvecoeur's eighteenth-century world from the extended family to the individual as the unit of social identification, married women became more than ever identified with and through their husbands. It never occurred to Crèvecoeur that his wife might have interests other than his own, let alone competing interests. Thus there is a profound difference within middle-class thinking, between defining society in familial or in economic terms. In Defoe's world view, the economic model was all-pervasive and defined family relations well. But as a projection directly of the family, in the way Crèvecoeur envisioned society, that model appeared far less competitive, if also less dynamic, than it did either on Addison's Royal Exchange or in the shops of Franklin's Philadelphia. Both Exchange and shops, as well as Crusoe's island, would have appalled Crèvecoeur, whose social ideal reigned instead on another island, in peaceful, quiet, and cooperative Nantucket.

For a book about farmers, the *Letters* spend a surprising amount of time on Cape Cod. Five of the twelve are about Nantucket and Martha's Vineyard, and their repetitiveness suggests that their real meaning for him may have lain deeper than Crèvecoeur could quite articulate. Overall, he seems to have seen Nantucket as the essence of Americanness, as it abjured the corruption and decadence of Europe. "How happy are we here, in having fortunately escaped the miseries which attended our fathers," he exclaimed in the opening of the Cape Cod letters. He predicted that as the tyrants of Europe raged on, "this country, providentially intended for the general asylum of the world, will flourish by the oppression of their people; they will every day become better acquainted with the happiness we enjoy, and seek for the means of transporting themselves here. . . ." Now, if the theme is already familiar from other contemporary writings, its treatment was somewhat unusual, for Crèvecoeur's "asylum" was a rocky sandbar "barren in its soil, insignificant in its extent, inconvenient in its situation, deprived of materials for building. . . ." The significant point is that he regretted none of these shortcomings, on the contrary seeing them as the source of Nantucket excellence. It seemed to him that the island had "been inhabited merely to prove what mankind can do when happily governed." With "freedom . . . skill . . . probity . . . and perseverance," by their own "vigorous industry," unhindered but unaided, the people of Nantucket "have raised themselves from the most humble, the most insignificant beginnings, to the ease and the wealth they now possess." Crèvecoeur insisted on the arduousness of their effort, appearing gratified even that poor soil had kept them from farming. Instead of a nurturing earth, "they plough the rougher ocean, they gather from its surface, at an immense distance, and with Herculean labours, the riches it affords; they go to hunt and catch that huge fish which by its strength and velocity ought to be beyond the reach of man."

What they have shown is that nothing is beyond the reach of men free to pursue their dreams. This was Crèvecoeur's creed:

> Give mankind the full rewards of their industry, allow them to enjoy the fruits of their labour under the peaceable shade of their vines and fig-trees, leave their native activity unshackled and free like a stream without dams or other obstacle. . . . (94–98)

Such eloquence is far from his usual style, however, and he was at his most reserved in describing those rewards. Then he spoke of "decent plainness" (119), neatness, and simplicity, several times describing the dress and houses of Nantucket's Herculean laborers as "simple, useful and unadorned" (116). Earlier he had praised, as a happy contrast to the showy luxury of European houses, "the pleasing uniformity of decent competence [that] appears throughout our habitations" (46). Finally, this insistence on plain living comes to exceed the standards of middle-class prudence and we begin to realize that he objected not only to spending but to having as well: only the process of getting aroused his enthusiasm, the labor more than its fruits. He had no interest in superabundance, or in accumulation per se, were it of goods or profits; "living with decency and ease" in "plentiful subsistence" (95) was the decidedly limited goal of Crèvecoeur's model American, and his own:

> I have never possessed, or wish to possess any thing more than what could be earned or produced by the united industry of my family. I wanted nothing more than to live at home independent and tranquil, and to teach my children how to provide the means of a future ample subsistence, founded on labor, like that of their father. (217)

Thus despite unlimited willingness to work, and his rejection of any external limits to the self, Crèvecoeur might almost be said to have lacked ambition. He had enlarged his definition of subsistence and ease to the American scale, but he neither looked nor aspired much beyond the strict fulfillment of necessity. In speaking of the unceasing activity he saw all around him, Crèvecoeur referred to it approvingly as "restless industry" (19), a phrase with no progressive implications, projecting only continual hard work. With his family as his world rather than a home-base for forays *into* the world, Crèvecoeur's was a truncated, partial kind of middle-class ethos. According to this ethos, individualism manifests itself through independence and self-assertion but not (yet) in social power or accumulated wealth. (We should recall Crèvecoeur's context among Pennsylvania farmers whose sense of equality sprang from respective self-sufficiency, to appreciate how resonant this distinction between self-assertion and social power may have been.)

In Crèvecoeur's logic, equality had egalitarian implications, for how could a man be independent if he were not actually as well as potentially equal? But for all its idealism, this primitive individualism was necessarily transitory, for it became impractical in even the most fledgling of market societies. Indeed Crèvecoeur found all markets repugnant. They were inevitably theaters for theft: "if it is not (in that vast variety of bargains, exchanges, barters, sales, etc.,) *bellum omnium contra omnes,* 'tis a general mass of keenness and sagacious action against another mass of equal sagacity, 'tis caution against caution. Happy when it does not degenerate into fraud against fraud!" I cited earlier his description of the wilderness as a "perfect state of war . . . of man against man."[6]

In any case, the hustle and bustle of the marketplace had no charms for him, as his essay on "Manners of the Americans" makes very clear. It was not published in the *Letters* but with the more ambivalent *Sketches of Eighteenth-Century America*. Like the first letters, it depicts the evolution of an American settler from initial step into the wilderness to prosperous establishment as a foremost citizen of the region. But unlike Andrew and his kind, this farmer acts alone; no paternal neighbors help him and he has no intention of helping others. When he arrives at the point of selling crops or leasing land, he will drive the hardest bargain he can and not balk at a little cheating. He gouges interest and forecloses on mortgages; eventually he expands to become a general merchant, and "this introduces him into all the little mysteries of self-interest, clothed under the general name of profits and emoluments."

> He sells for good that which perhaps he knows to be indifferent because he also knows that the ashes he has collected, the wheat he has taken in may not be so good or so clean as it was asserted. Fearful of fraud in all his dealings and transactions, he arms himself, therefore, with it.

Crèvecoeur would have had difficulty with our nostalgia for the country store. "Very probably," he warned, the farmer-merchant will be "litigious, overbearing, purse-proud," and irreligious because religion is neither convenient nor useful; he cares only about himself, and in this setting, even his devotion to his family takes on an equivocal character. "To him," Crèvecoeur wrote, "all that appears good, just, equitable has a necessary relation to himself and his family."[7] He would have reversed the formula in describing farmer James or Andrew the Hebridean: all that was related to the welfare of their families *was* good, just, and equitable. The difference seems to lie between the self and the family in the noncompetitive, egalitarian terms of farming, and the same concepts qualified by the necessities of a mercantile context.

The figure of the farmer-merchant retrospectively highlights a peculiar aspect of the yeoman hero in the earlier letters. One wonders whether Crèvecoeur then had excluded all trading and market activities from his account of the farmer's life in order not to taint his ideal vision. Otherwise the lack of any commerce in the agrarian idylls of the *Letters,* where neighbors exchange goods and services, but never seem to sell them, remains puzzling. The issue is not money, which we would expect to be scarce in a rural economy, but profit. Crèvecoeur's model farmers achieve ease and plentiful subsistence, they gain respect and standing in the community, they earn their way, but they do not earn profits: for Crèvecoeur, this would have amounted to profiteering.

Thus anyway he argued in a sketch called "The American Belisarius," significantly written after the outbreak of the Revolution. The original Belisarius rose from the rank of servant to become the Emperor Justinian's chief general. He enjoyed something of a vogue in the late eighteenth century and was said by Sir William Temple to have been one of seven men in history who were worthy to be monarchs but weren't. The victim of endless intrigue, he reportedly refused to abuse his power to punish his enemies, while maintaining an unswerving loyalty to his Emperor. Gibbon was not certain whether the patience with which Belisarius endured his rivals' insults proved him more or less than a man; but for Crèvecoeur, the Roman's endurance and loyalty and withal the inherent superiority he refused to exploit—so that he lost his home and fortune finally without ever losing his temper—clearly made him the beau ideal of the American Loyalist.[8] His worthy American counterpart, S. K., had gone out to the frontier as a young man and built up a remarkably flourishing farm. As he grew rich, he did not forget his family, and duly settled his two brothers-in-law on neighboring lands where, with his help, they too were soon thriving. "Their prosperity, which was his work, raised no jeal-

ousy in him," wrote Crèvecoeur, finding it all a "pastoral and edifying spectacle: three brothers, the founders of three opulent families, the creators of
three valuable plantations, the promoters of the succeeding settlements that
took place around them." Here was the fulfillment of Crèvecoeur's ideal, the
family generating a community of equals who progress through the kind of
mutual assistance which leaves each one freely possessive of his own home
and hearth. With the coming of more settlers to the region, however, certain
complications do develop. "It was not to be expected that they could all
equally thrive. Prosperity is not the lot of every man; so many casualties occur
that often prevent it." How can the familial model deal with such casualties?
What can a democratic society do with its inevitable inequalities? S. K. again
points the righteous way. In hard times he opens his granary to his neighbors:

> he lends them hay; he assists them in whatever they want; he cheers them with
> good counsel; he becomes a father to the poor of this wilderness. They prom-
> ise him payment; he never demands it.

For Crèvecoeur what was most telling is his not demanding payment, for this
is the touchstone of S. K., morality. He refuses to enter the marketplace. He
has the largest stock of grain in the area, prices are soaring, and traders approach him with tempting offers, but he rejects them saying,

> "I have no wheat . . . for the rich, my harvest is for the poor. What would the
> inhabitants of these mountains do were I to divest myself of what superfluous
> grain I have?"[9]

We will pay you at once, they argue, while these poor will make you wait indefinitely. He answers that he cannot let his neighbors starve.

If S. K. will not sell, neither does he buy. At harvest time he requires no
hired help, for the grateful folk come from all around to gather in the "patriarchal harvest." S. K.'s patriarchism is in no sense feudal though Crèvecoeur's
use of traditional terms to suggest the deeper validity of this moral code may
obscure its antiaristocratic assumptions. But just as the Roman Belisarius was
a model *because* he was born a commoner, S. K. is called "princely" only to
suggest that none on earth is more deserving of the title than a "good substantial independent American farmer," such as he is and remains to the end.
His aim in helping his indigent fellows is not to earn their fealty but their
friendship, by freeing them into self-sufficiency. He is no better than his
neighbors except in the sense that he represents their common type at its

best, and when he rejects the merchants' offer, it is not out of a sense of noblesse but of common humanity. There is nothing contradictory to democratic thought in this stance as such. Familial patriarchs after all are as congruent with middle-class societies as a patriarchal nobility was with the feudal system, the modern family being essentially a small fiefdom, as the old adage has it that proclaims a man's home as his castle. What *is* unusual about S. K. is that he plays the role of noble father not only to his family but to the community at large. In this way he represents Crèvecoeur's democratic familialism, whose enobling patriarchism had neither the source nor the purpose of the feudal aristocratic variety. In modern terms, the alternative of such a kindly father would be neither wicked king nor faithless lord, but just such a gouging, thieving merchant as the one featured in "Manners of the Americans."

Indeed, Crèvecoeur's earlier list of the European evils that America has averted included, in addition to aristocrats, kings, and bishops, "great manufacturers employing thousands" (46). The old aristocracy was not the only one that he deplored. In a discussion of the unfortunate spread of tea drinking in America (when native herbs are plentiful and better for you), he shook his head over a newer breed of lords:

> It was necessary that our forefathers should discover and till this country in order that their prosperity might serve to enrich a parcel of London merchants who though but citizens in England, yet are nabobs in India; who though mighty fond of liberty at home for themselves and their children, yet do not choose that other people should enjoy these great benefits in their Indian dominions. The idea of merchants becoming sovereigns, lords and tyrants . . . but a poor American farmer must not say all he thinks.[10]

What he saw as best about America—or more to the point, what had been best about it before the Revolution—was that a good man could become wealthy without engaging in imperialism or even commerce: without having to deprive his equals of the substance he acquired.

Crèvecoeur's agrarianism may have been based on the view that only farming could produce wealth without exploitation. Like the Physiocrats by whom he was influenced, he believed that only the land produces value, so that all other means of acquiring it must amount to theft—hence the fraudulent merchant. Quesnay and the Physiocrats envisioned a stable, rationalized France of cultured farmers who leased their lands and derived a comfortable subsistence, with enough over to feed the minority necessarily engaged in nonagricultural tasks. But in the American context of expansion and open-ended growth, even the modest Crèvecoeur sensed that something more was needed. Though his aspirations were limited, they were still grander than those of his European counterparts. He recognized as much with satisfaction. He therefore modified the Physiocrat program by having American farmers eventually own their land, explaining that Europe was crowded and its lands long since taken up, but that the New World remained accessible to all.

But he knew too that this concept of "equal divisions of the land offered no short road to superior riches." To speak to the American situation, he needed to represent a possibility for even larger expansion which would still remain free of the mercantile taint. That is why Nantucket was so important to him. It seemed to embody a solution to the otherwise pervasively corrupt-ing paradox of equality and competition. For the sailors who "plough the rougher ocean" do have thereby a "short road to superior riches," which is as free from fraud as is agriculture. Like a plentiful harvest too, the sudden wind-fall of a good catch neither derives from nor generates pernicious social in-equalities. Among the people of Nantucket,

> the gradations [of wealth] are founded on nothing more than the good or ill success of their maritime enterprises, and do not proceed from education; that is the same throughout every class, simple, useful, and unadorned like their dress and their houses. (116).

But having an equal start and maintaining a relatively equal lifestyle does not yet comprise the fundamental equality which Crèvecoeur was after. He real-ized that this had to do more with the structure of the economy itself than with the way individuals entered into it. Not only do the free men of Nan-tucket begin their accumulation of property as equals, none having sig-nificantly more than any other, but the property they seek is such that it is continually accessible to each of them. The "necessary difference in their for-tunes" does not cause among Nantucketers "those heart burnings, which in other societies generate crime," because "the sea which surrounds them is equally open to all, and presents to all an equal title to the chance of good for-tune" (116–17). They get their riches from the sea, not from each other, so that no one person's income, however large, in any way lessens another's. Moreover, by using the limitless ocean to represent capital, Crèvecoeur avoided all the implications of scarcity, and could reconcile the inequalities generated by the unregulated individualistic enterprise that he considered the expres-sion of freedom, with his moral conviction that the means for such enterprise must be equally available. In Nantucket one doesn't need to engage in fierce competition in order to grow rich; one grows rich beside one's neighbors, working hard privately but in harmony with them.

This unique instance of transcendent enterprise, however, only underlined Crèvecoeur's general rejection of the commercial nexus. For him the marketplace did not make for a better product, but for the ferocities of the jungle. Just such a jungle (to return to the case of the unhappy American Belisarius) was what the Revolution seemed to Crèvecoeur to be creating in America. The story of S. K. ends sadly. Having rejected the blandishments of usurious commerce, and having sought only to mind his farm and to assist others in minding theirs, that good man still tries to keep his private counsel when the fighting breaks out. But privacy is no longer allowed; "as a citizen of a smaller society," Crèvecoeur wrote in the throes of the war, "I find that any kind of opposition to its now prevailing sentiments, immediately begets hatred" (207). The envious and greedy gather, S. K.'s brothers-in-law see an opportunity to vent their jealousy, local merchants want to see him forced to buy and sell, less advantaged farmers just want his land. Eventually he is driven from his burned-out farm into the wilderness. The leaders of the Revolution may have had more inspired motives, Crèvecoeur speculated, but the effect of their bid for freedom was to enslave everyone else. Shortly before he is totally despoiled, S. K. receives a group of local yeomen who come as usual to ask him for help over the long winter. Among them he recognizes some who have been persecuting him. They haven't wanted to, they explain, but what could they do? The weakness which has brought them to his door also makes them subject to all the petty tyrants the war has unleashed. S. K. understands their plight, and distributes the last of the grain.

What *we* come to understand is the necessity for a strong overall authority, equally restrictive of all to keep each man free of his equals. Crèvecoeur had hoped once that a benevolent environment would render its inhabitants equally benevolent. He had thought then that men might live together virtually without external authority. Again Nantucket represented the best of all governments, one which simply left people alone:

> solemn tribunals, public executions, humiliating punishments, are altogether unknown. I saw neither governors, nor any pageantry of state; neither ostentatious magistrates, nor any individuals cloathed with useless dignity: no artificial phantoms subsist here either civil or religious; no gibbets loaded with guilty citizens offer themselves to your view; no soldieries are appointed to bayonet their compatriots into servile compliance. (115)

The positive advantages of such governance are all negative, and Crèvecoeur would rather have done without it altogether. Unfortunately, even in the New World, many men have remained like those cattle who, "conscious of their superior force, will abuse it when unrestrained by any law, and often live on their neighbors' property" (237). Therefore, "the law is to us precisely what I am in my barn yard, a bridle and check to prevent the strong and greedy, from oppressing the timid and weak" (34). In Nantucket as everywhere, there are times when the weak must be protected from the strong, and thus "the law at a distance is ever ready to exert itself in the protection of those who stand in need of its assistance" (115).

"*At a distance*": the phrase was all-important to Crèvecoeur, it was the key to his outlook. If we recall that he defined personal identity entirely in terms of self-possession and property, it becomes evident that he must have viewed external authority per se as inevitably problematical. It had to be all-inclusive and absolute; it also had to be noninterfering, indeed nonengaging. Across a dangerous ocean, thousands of miles away, the crown of England was the best solution imaginable. It was "the law at a distance" incarnate.

Earlier Crèvecoeur had made the ideal explicit:

> Where is that station which can confer a more substantial system of felicity than that of American farmer, possessing freedom of action, freedom of thoughts, ruled by a mode of government which requires but little from us. . . . (28–9)

Pre-Revolutionary America, therefore, enjoyed the "general Happiness" which "proceeds from a government which does everything for us and requires little or nothing in return."[11] And Crèvecoeur's personal situation represented that blissful state perfectly: "I owe nothing, but a peppercorn to my country, a small tribute to my King, with loyalty and due respect" (28). If the Whigs found English intrusion in America unbearable, Crèvecoeur clearly did not share their view. A few taxes seemed to him relatively little compared to the secure freedom of the Nantucket sailors who ply the seas as they will:

> a collector from Boston is the only King's officer who appears on these shores to receive the trifling duties which this community owe to those who protect them, and under the shadow of whose wings they navigate to all parts of the world. (117)

His ideal government had little impact on the local activities of individuals; its role was global, and on that scale, absolute.

This notion that maintaining equal freedom requires a strong central authority did not originate with Crèvecoeur, of course. The case had long since been made by Hobbes, among others, whose account of man in the state of nature Crèvecoeur essentially echoed, while capturing also in his barnyard image the flavor of Hobbes' view of civilized man. Moreover, Hobbes was not alone in believing that this authority was best embodied in an absolute monarch. In the next century and in another country Giambattista Vico considered it only logical that societies desiring to institutionalize "natural equity" would be ruled typically by

> monarchs who have accustomed their subjects to attend to their private interests, while they themselves have taken charge of all public affairs and desire all . . . subject to them to be made equal by the laws, in order that all may be equally interested in the state.[12]

These founding theoreticians of modern liberal society thus projected a concept of monarchy which was neither that of feudalism nor that of the Renaissance. This monarchy is subject-centered, justifying itself as the guarantor of the subjects' rights. Such a concept in no way precludes liberal democracy. On the contrary, the extent of that democracy—its potential for including more and more people like Andrew the Hebridean, who work their way from indenture to a full-fledged property-owning selfhood—seems to depend on the monarch's being altogether absolute, and thus out of reach of manipulation: hence Crèvecoeur's enthusiasm for King George.[13]

It was Locke who introduced the possibility that a democratic society might instead govern itself. The base of that governance would rest on the ordering force of the market, now conceived as an arena of class rather than of purely individual activity. Having accepted the accumulation of larger amounts of property than one could use on the grounds that its translation into capital and subsequent reinvestment redounded to the general welfare, Locke foresaw this process generating a consensus among the investors which might be institutionalized contractually, and generalized into government. The participants in this consensus should be able to agree on the rules of the game.

This is where one sees the relationship between S. K.'s refusal to deal with the grain merchants and his vulnerability to the greedy mob. Crèvecoeur himself was only vaguely aware of this relationship, not quite seeing that S. K.

needs the King but that the merchants do better without him, their rights safeguarded by contracts, and by a contractual society whose law and order is suited to their entrepreneurial needs. Crèvecoeur's failure to understand the function of local laws and contracts was expressed more clearly in his hatred of lawyers. "What a pity," he exclaimed, "that our forefathers who happily extinguished so many fatal customs, and expunged from their new government as many errors and abuses, both religious and civil, did not also prevent the introduction of a set of men so dangerous" (146). They plagued America like the clergy did Europe. This was an acute comparison, lawyers being the interpreters of the new order as the clergy were of the old. Crèvecoeur, who had hoped that the world might at last be free of all impingements of personal freedom, but for a small set of permanent injunctions, saw lawyers reweaving entanglements all around.

The crux, then, of his disaffiliation with the Lockean compromise so well represented by the American Constitution was his rejection of the ethic of the marketplace. For the American revolutionaries, enlightened self-interest reflected the natural moral order, but to Crèvecoeur its mercantile expression was little better than theft. The sort of economic order he envisaged instead was evident in his appeal to American farmers to recognize the benefits of monarchy. Secure in your holdings and master of its fruits, he reminded the yeoman,

> thou needs't not tremble lest the most incomprehensible prohibitions shall rob thee of that sacred immunity with which the produce of thy farm may circulate from hand to hand until it reaches those of the final exporter.[14]

Once again, he defined freedom as being left alone; the right to trade is a "sacred immunity" from restraint. So might any merchant argue against restraints, but he would not do so just to have his product "circulate": what he would be after would be an increase in value at each transition, that *increase* not to be limited by "incomprehensible prohibitions." This view of the farmer's stake in the national economy translated the patriarchal-familial ethic into a paradoxical ideology we might term "monarcho-anarchism." Crèvecoeur was an anarchist in the sense that he carried the notion of the political integrity of the individual to its logical conclusion. His definition of self-determination was thus more radical or more absolute than that which is commonly implied by democracy, because he could see in the accommodations of majority rule no advantages but only a loss of freedom for each individual.

Both in this libertarian aspect and in its egalitarianism, Crèvecoeur's think-ing reflected his eighteenth-century agrarian experiences, but it might be seen also as a sort of prehistory to one important strain of nineteenth-century dissent. Populism invoked the yeoman ideal as the core of its program, associ-ating the vision with Jefferson as powerful validation of its Americanism; but a loyalist Frenchman the populists had probably never heard of would have been far more sympathetic both to their resentment of the rich and their con-viction that markets were where the rich became ever richer. Although histo-rians of the United States' War of Independence have long recognized that the patriots differed sharply among themselves about even the basic definition of democracy, by and large they have assumed that, as a group, those who fa-vored the Revolution were more democratically inclined than those who op-posed it.[15] The case of Crèvecoeur puts this assumption in doubt, and high-lights such findings as those of Jackson Turner Main, that the largest single group of Loyalists were, like Crèvecoeur, small independent farmers.[16] Yet these were the same "self-reliant, honest and independent" yeomen who be-came "the backbone of Jeffersonian democracy" and later "the common man of Jacksonian rhetoric."[17] Though such yeomen also swelled the Patriot ranks, some significant number of them rejected Jefferson's promise of a country of their own and, if Crèvecoeur is at all representative, they did so be-cause they feared it would be less free than colonial America, at least for their kind.

What all this indicates, I think, is a need to reconsider the structure of the Revolutionary debate that now represents the winners' assumptions. Crève-coeur's usefulness lies in his accepting none of these and yet still making per-fect sense. As a result he raises basic questions about the component values and ideas which the successful Revolution fused into one apparently organic whole. Crèvecoeur was independent while refusing to compete; a seeker after plentiful subsistence who rejected profits, and a supporter of the King because monarchy was for him the corollary of social equality. His opposition to the American Revolution was grounded in the principle that all men are created equal—and that so they should remain.[18] It was a basically localist, familial impulse which committed him to absolute monarchs. In these ways, he may be seen as representing an intermediate stage in the evolution of America's liberal political philosophy, or as a case in point for its paradoxical nature at any stage.

The nineteenth-century novel is quintessentially the genre of the middle class. Yet in quintessentially middle-class America the major authors, except perhaps for Henry James who wrote mostly in England, seem not to have written novels at all. Our writers spun tales of extravagant individuals in flight to the wilderness and beyond while, until recently anyway, the novel has explored the everyday lives of ordinary people at home. There have been various reasons suggested for this lack of sociability in American fiction: the greater allure of an adventurous frontier or the lesser fictional interest of a primitive social scene, even the callowness of a young culture seeking, as one critic put it, "to avoid the facts of wooing, marriage and childbearing."[1] But underlying these explanations and comparisons of the realistic novel with the romance (the latter being a term used originally by Richard Chase to describe America's nonnovelistic novels)[2] is a double assumption about the attitude to the real world that is implicit in each kind of fiction. It has seemed only logical to think that realism tends realistically to accept its material universe as given while the romance broods on metaphysical rebellion. But in fact the most characteristic examples of European realism are deeply, even radically critical of the world they depict, while however far away into the wilderness American romances take us, ultimately they find it an impossible situation and, whether out of commitment or by default, lead us back to society. For the self-reliant individuals, Natty Bumppo, Hester Prynne, Captain Ahab, Huck Finn, or Isabel Archer all fail in the end to create their private worlds, and their failure sounds dire warnings of the dangers of isolation and solipsism. Typically the American romance is the story of a *defeated,* a downed flight.

I use "flight" here in either or both its senses, as rising and as escaping. Both mean an attempt to transcend one's native condition and it is a remarkable irony that in the fiction of the New World such attempts are almost always stopped at an impassable frontier. Not that ambition is often successful in the English and French novel, but there the failure is of a different kind, not so automatic, more substantive. Julien Sorel and Emma Bovary, Dorothea Brooke or, for that matter, Clarissa Harlowe before them, are also downed but by real artillery, whereas the Americans must come down, as it were, just because they went up. Julien Sorel is broken by the power of an entrenched class and Clarissa by that of a rising class but when Ahab at last "strike[s] through the mask" he encounters—nothing. More precisely Melville stops writing about Ahab's thrust beyond this world at just the moment when it ostensibly happens. One minute Ahab, Melville, and the reader press forward together on the threshold of knowledge. Ahab hurls his challenge: "*Thus* I give up the spear!" and

> The harpoon was darted; the stricken whale flew forward; with igniting velocity the line ran through the groove;—ran afoul. Ahab stooped to clear it; he did clear it; but the flying turn caught him round the neck, and voicelessly as Turkish mutes bowstring their victim, he was shot out of the boat ere the crew knew he was gone.[3]

From the grandiloquent periods of the Captain's last defiance in the paragraph preceding the one just cited ("Ho, ho! from all your furthest bounds, pour ye now in, ye bold billows of my whole foregone life, and top this one piled comber of my death!")[4] the language itself retreats to the status of impartial recording, noting physical details with careful precision and quite declining to interpret anything. As for Ahab, why is it that in a book otherwise intoxicated with rhetoric and himself the greatest orator of all, he goes to his death mute?

On one level, of course, the answer is obvious. Melville could hardly follow his hero into the Other World. But the real point lies in the very locating of Ahab's goal, of his vision of freedom and self-realization in a realm that is not only unattainable but even inconceivable. In *Moby-Dick* one lives here or nowhere.[5] The Nantucket shore and the Pequod represent the concept of society itself and the open sea its blank negation. Similarly Hester Prynne could choose in America only between Puritan Boston and the wild woods; and as he drifted down the Mississippi, steering clear of both its shores, Huck Finn would try to escape not only Hannibal but all civilization. In contrast, as we will see, the European novel more easily envisages alternative societies or at least their theoretical possibilities. Other systems than the contemporary are not there so literally unthinkable.

The source of the difference lies, I think, in the different ways in which the middle class achieved its hegemony in Europe and in America. This issue of hegemony was discussed by Raymond Williams, who cited Gramsci's stress on ideological hegemony as a totality "which is lived at such a depth, which saturates the society to such an extent" that it "even constitutes the limit of common sense for most people under its sway."[6] But Williams himself wanted to examine the inner complexity of hegemony and to describe the constant changes that it undergoes: its dynamic rather than static nature. To this end he distinguished between "the dominant culture" in the society and certain other "practices, experiences, meanings and values" which are "alternative" to the dominant culture or even "oppositional" to it. He distinguished further "between *residual* and *emergent* forms, both of alternative and of oppositional culture." One might put it another way, that the content of alternative or oppositional cultural forms is lent by either residual or emergent ideologies. Now this is where the American experience has differed from the European which in modern times became to charged by a sense of history that both residual and emergent cultures could achieve a remarkable degree of immediacy. In America, on the other hand, at least through the nineteenth century the dominant culture seems to have been able to co-opt alternative and oppositional forms with unusual effectiveness, to the point of appearing to preclude even their possibility. Residual values here are associated with the Old World and thus rejected by the very process of national emergence. As for notions of still further emergence, these are also essentially precluded by that same peculiarly ideological origin in America which identified nationhood itself with a specific vision of both nation and state.

America, in other words, was conceived not so much in liberty as in liberalism. It was a new home that the middle class built for itself according to a design it deemed not only desirable but natural. What is generally recognized as a lack of historical sense in the national consciousness means just this: the idea that the Founding Fathers, building on the wisdom of the ages, erected a structure which was so well suited to the basic needs of men and societies that with an addition here and there, it could accommodate all likely futures. Less capable and well-destined peoples, of course, constantly had to redo their societies, but not America which, having begun with a revolution, need never revolve again. History, in this view, is an affliction brought on by a poor Constitution and America's growth is seen instead as the unfolding realization of its inherent form and meaning. Paradoxically the middle class's faith in a progressive history had thus achieved an annihilating apotheosis in the conviction that all progress led to America. Indeed even those who have taken class struggles in this country seriously have usually shared in the millennial vision. As C. Vann Woodward observed, much of the persuasiveness of Southern populism, for example, derived from its claims to more truly represent the *real* America. The inherent fundamentalism of American dissenters is notorious; how else to explain the accusation of the trustbusters that monopolies are un-American?

In Europe, on the contrary, the rise of the there insurgent middle class was associated with an attack on such static absolutism, whether personal or social. Personality and history both came to be seen as continuous processes and capable therefore of only relative and mutable definition. And reflecting the individual's loss of given, a priori identity, his now problematic sense of self, the protagonist of the European novel is born already an existential outsider, self-generated in Georg Lukács's terms, as "the product of estrangement from the outside world."[7] For Lukács this condition reflected the personal alienation inevitably inflicted by bourgeois society. Unlike the members of older "integrated civilizations" each one of whom knew himself for a part of the organically cohesive whole, people were now thrown back on themselves, on "the autonomous life of interiority" for values and meaning in a universe become subjectively anomic. No longer able to identify *with* their society, in short, men and women in a bourgeois society identified themselves in terms of their existential distance from it. In an age "in which the extensive totality of life is no longer directly given," writes Lukács, "in which the immanence of meaning in life has become a problem yet which still thinks in terms of totality . . . the novel seeks, by giving form to uncover and construct the concealed totality of life."[8] Quentin Anderson put it with admirable brevity: "God dies and Stephen Dedalus goes to work."[9] Hence we note the novel's concern with plot continuity and development and with the inner coherence of its characters, all being structural components of the teleology it seeks to create. Or of its theology, as J. Hillis Miller thought, seeing "the fundamental theme" of Victorian fiction as "an exploration of the various ways in which a man may seek to make a god of another person in a world without God."[10]

•

The crux of the matter for these and other critics of the novel, the basic factor they have seen in its development, is the absence of transcendent order or unifying purpose in the novelist's bourgeois culture. (To use Williams's terms one might talk about a fatal relativism in the dominant culture which causes it to appear no longer so natural or commonsensical.) I would suggest that it was a contrary sense of order so pervasive as to seem inescapable that generated the American romance. Miller's thesis that the novel seeks God surrogates may be applied conversely to the romance: when God left Europe he came to America and went to work for Ben Franklin, which is why blasphemy is the darkest sin American fiction can envision. In Lukács's terms, middle-class America *was* an integrated society, I am suggesting, like Athens and Renaissance London, and very unlike nineteenth-century London and Paris.

But this integration was paradoxical. What American writers assumed by the terms "Human Nature" and "Society," those principles writ large in the New World cosmology, were nonetheless characteristically middle-class in describing the universe as essentially a natural marketplace. (Not that all writers sought to corner the market—Thoreau, for instance, wanted none of it— but they did take it for granted as the inevitable setting for the development of personal identity.) Indeed one has only to compare the Americas of Cooper, Hawthorne, and Melville to Chaucer's or Shakespeare's Englands (the latter being comparably absolute paradigms), to see how ideologically particular American ideals really were. Even Cooper's fussy elitism does not make him an aristocrat but only a conservative burgher; it is a natural, a competitively viable meritocracy that he envisages and that is not at all inconsistent with notions of equal opportunity. At the other end of the political spectrum, neither is the "Spirit of Equality" which inspires Melville to invest in "meanest mariners, and renegades and castaways . . . high qualities, though dark,"[11] proletarian. Its "august dignity" requires "no robed investiture" it is true, and it can be glimpsed radiating from "the arm that wields a pick or drives a spike," but it does not the less imply the transcendence of a unique Best One. "Thou great democratic God!" Melville intones,

> who didst not refuse to the swart convict, Bunyan, the pale poetic pearl; Thou who didst clothe with doubly hammered leaves of finest gold, the stumped and paupered arm of old Cervantes; Thou who didst pick up Andrew Jackson from the pebbles; who didst hurl him upon a warhorse; who didst thunder him higher than a throne! Thou who, in all Thy mighty, earthly marchings, ever cullest Thy selectest champions from the kingly commons . . .

Melville's democratic hero nurses at the common source of individualistic ambition only to rise the higher above his fellows.

Indeed one key middle-class assumption that Cooper, Melville, and their colleagues shared was of the naturalness of individualistic ambition. The self, in this view, is an autonomous entity one makes oneself and therefore makes as powerful as possible. But here is the special dilemma of American writers, and the source of tragedy in their works: the self-made, self-regulated man is only viable in the context of an open future, of an evolving social history that yields him the wherewithal to create. His identity is, precisely, a matter of "residual" or "emergent" cultures. What happens when such an individualist inhabits instead a world structured by the absolute necessities we associate with theology or myth, is the story of Ahab. Or, if the individualist bows to necessity, it is the story of Hester Prynne. It can also be the story of Huck Finn, if he simply abandons the quest. But for any of these actually to realize the power of their individualism is taboo, implying as it would an un-American mutability. It is almost inevitable then that however glorious the "Spirit of Equality," its incarnation in the Captain of the Pequod must become Satanic. I do not mean to interpret Ahab simply as a heroic rebel. But for better and for worse the Captain of the Pequod represents individualism and the assertion of total free will. Indeed only in the context of possibility for substantive change could the "Spirit" have taken a Promethean form.[12] But the myth that American liberalism allows for all possible surface adjustments in the system and thus obviates the need for basic ones, was too strong, even for the national heroes, and especially for the historical dialectic they would have energized.

This is not the place for a discussion of philosophical dualism or its absence in American thought but I want briefly to refer to Emerson as representative in his urge to monistic resolutions of conflict and his sense that the dualities which may arise at any stage of understanding are only apparent and thus capable of being transcended by rising another level toward the ultimate abstract One. The concept of the all-pervasive Oversoul in which oppositions and contradictions dissolve is, of course, familiar. But more specific to my concerns here is Emerson's sense that there is no necessary contradiction either between the individual and society. (He would have capitalized both and made the principle absolute.) "Speak your latent conviction," he urged each fellow citizen, "and it shall be the universal sense."[13] And should society seem for a time to have departed from this universal sense, then, it would be due to a flagging "self-trust" among those who constitute its "delegated intellect."[14] The difference between this "self-trust" as a focus for individual political judgment and Lukács's previously cited "autonomous life of interiority" is crucial. The latter is born of the recognition that the individual is inevitably separate from society while Emerson affirms their underlying identity of interest. Thus Emerson's famed uncompromising individualism unto himself never needed to place him in opposition to the doctrines and laws of a properly constituted society, as he thought America to be at bottom. If he proclaimed that "the only right is after my constitution; the only wrong what is against it,"[15] the point is that he considered the right defined by his constitution as really, objectively right. What was right for Emerson was happily right for the nation. And this because the world was made so, with individualism generating public morality as surely as free enterprise in the marketplace did the general welfare.[16] The neoclassical conservatism of this has been noted before but what I want to stress is Emerson's assumption of a snug at-oneness with the universe, and also with his local township. By this I do not mean, of course, that he necessarily approved of all its policies. "I know that the world I converse with in the city and in the farms, is not the world I *think,*" he writes in the America of 1844–45.

> But I have not found that much was gained by manipular attempts to realize the world of thought. Many eager persons successively make an experiment in this way, and make themselves ridiculous. They acquire democratic manners, they foam at the mouth, they hate and deny. Worse, I observe that in the history of mankind there is never a solitary example of success,—taking their own tests of success. I say this polemically, or in reply to the inquiry, Why not realize your world? But far be from me the despair which prejudges the law by a paltry empiricism;—since there never was a right endeavor but it succeeded.[17]

(This ultimate triumph of good is assured for him by the fact that "power is in nature the essential measure of right.")[18] He begins here with the recognition that the actual condition of the world is not what he thinks it should be. But he treats this as a pseudocontradiction about which not only can nothing be done, and then not only *need* nothing be done but even nothing *should* be done lest the goal be lost in the attaining. For it is "in the solitude to which every man is always returning, [that] he has a sanity and revelations which in his passage into new worlds he will carry with him."[19] And in this last the contradictions of thought and action, of individual and society, and of ideal and reality have been resolved or, rather, dissolved in that single higher Reality which is already complete and will in its own time manifest itself.

Even Melville apparently came to feel that dualism was a wicked rationale for detaching oneself from the world with the intent to control it. Ahab's last speech bristles with dualities he has himself created out of his blasphemous ambition. In focusing on his monomania itself critics have overlooked its effect, which is to set up gratuitous oppositions between the self and the world. Insisting on his vision of such fatal contradictions, Ahab becomes a polarizing presence that threatens, if indeed he achieves his transcendence, a progressive dialectical episode. With his death, however, the dualities he has generated are rejoined. When finally the Pequod founders and the ocean rolls over the "Pole-pointed" ship which, in a last defiant affirmation of duality, has dragged down into the depths of the sea "a living part of heaven," Ishmael is left to reconcile land and ocean, man and society, and life and death, all of which, washed clean as lambs, we now recognize are one in the bosom of nature.[20]

It is worth comparing to Ahab's the last speech of Stendhal's Julien Sorel (about whom more later) who asserts his Napoleonic ambition to the last, drawing the lines of class conflict tight between himself and his persecutors.[21] But unlike Melville, Stendhal confirms his protagonist's vision of contradiction so that his execution in no way resolves the conflict but indeed affirms its inescapable reality. There is even something prophetic about Julien's last challenge suggesting the possibility of other outcomes sometime in the future. If other outcomes than defeat are ever projected in American fiction it is in the form of Hester's vision mentioned late in Hawthorne's book of "a new truth [which would] establish the whole relation between man and woman on a surer ground of mutual happiness."[22] But Hester learns Emerson's lesson: like his, her new world can be delivered only in the fullness of time, and then entirely from within the body of the old. Above all, she comes to understand, no one who has ever placed herself in radical opposition to her society can hope to assist in its transformation. For such a one has denied America, much, one feels, as Moses did God, for which, it will be recalled, he was barred from ever entering the Promised Land.

Emerson's version of better days coming is similarly apocalyptic. "There is victory yet for all justice," he proclaims, "and the true romance which the world exists to realize will be the transformation of genius into practical power."[23] I hesitate to give much weight to his use of the term "romance" here, and yet it is suggestive. That "transformation" it will record is really the unfolding realization of an innate being: this is not an event about which one could write a history, for histories in the modern Hegelian sense focus on the creation of new conditions that negate the old. It needs "romance" to depict the timeless and agentless comings-about that constitute Emerson's sense of the American future. Agentless because as we noted earlier any attempt to enact the desired state hopelessly compromises it. Hence Emerson's notion of social responsibility which is fulfilled in the furtherance of one's own best interests; morality and identity, in short, are for him entirely intrinsic. Which is indeed how Richard Chase described the abstract characterizations of the "heroes, villains, victims [and] legendary types" who people American fiction and whose self-contained and self-defined careers led him to conclude, citing Henry James, that "'the disconnected and uncontrolled experience'. . . is of the essence of the romance."[24] A central thesis of this chapter is that the anti-historicism and the disengaged, abstract concept of personal identity which characterize the romance, like those same aspects of Emerson's thinking, are ideological and ideally suited to the maintenance of a specific society, that individualistic "nation of men" which Emerson envisioned as America's special destiny. So that William Gilmore Simms's comparison of the romance to the epics of the ancient world was very precisely apt. Like the epics, the American romance makes heroic myth out of the ultimate efforts of characters to conquer structural constraints of a hermetic cosmos. No one in epic or romance believes he can overcome, but all have to try.

Still, if it ultimately generated the anomaly of a bourgeois yet tragic vision, the ideological triumph of America's middle class also had a positive, even an inspirational aspect. The task which Emerson set before American scholars (chiding that "events, actions arise, that must be sung, that will sing themselves")[25] was truly epic, at once elevating and celebrating a civilization with which the writer identified deeply. Even those American writers, perhaps the majority, who were less pleased with America than Emerson, did feel privileged to be in at the second coming of Western Civilization and inspired to, godlike, create a new literature. The astonishing power and range of the best American writing was likely sparked by this, generated out of that terrible tension between imperial arrogance and the terror of blasphemy which also not infrequently drove American writers mad. And there is a sense in which the absolute hegemony that the middle class was able to claim in America, despite its paradoxical nature, also enabled a more complete ideological development than was attained in Europe. Perhaps it is to its American avatars that one should look for the real fulfillment of individualism—and therefore to such as Melville—for the most telling critiques, exposing at once the enormous creative potential and the appalling destructiveness it renders possible. So if Melville is less tolerant of romantic rebellion than his European counterparts he is also probably better aware than they of just what it can entail.

The contrast I have been sketching between the European novel and the American romance, whereby the former takes the internal organization of society as its "problem" and the latter, accepting the status quo as simply natural, focuses instead on the difficulties of individual conformity, may be clarified by more detailed examples of each genre. I want to stress again that basic assumptions are involved in creating the difference and not any conscious choices of subject. There is nice evidence for this basic divergence of vision in an introduction to *Madame Bovary* written by Henry James. This is his summary of the plot:

> A pretty young woman who lives, socially and morally speaking in a hole, and who is ignorant, foolish, flimsy, unhappy, takes a pair of lovers by whom she is successively deserted; in the midst of which, giving up her husband and her child, letting everything go, she sinks deeper into duplicity, debt, despair, and arrives on the spot, on the small scene of her poor depravities, at a pitiful, tragic end. She does those things above all, while remaining absorbed in the romantic vision, and she remains absorbed in the romantic vision while fairly rolling in the dust.[26]

For James who, ironically, criticizes his compatriots for their inadequate treatment of social experience, Emma Bovary is nevertheless to be understood in universal, abstract terms. She is thus merely an abject everywoman living anytime, anywhere. And since the predictable career of an ignorant, foolish, flimsy, unhappy, even if pretty housewife is of scant interest, James finds himself puzzled by the inconsequence of the novel and forced to conclude that it reveals a certain "defect of mind" in Flaubert himself. "Emma Bovary," James regretfully decides, "is really too small an affair." In France, of course, she was either a national scandal or an international triumph but no one seems to have doubted her significance. Indeed for one French critic writing at about the time James did, *Madame Bovary* said everything. But then he summed it up differently. "To find a way at once to express all romanticism's hatred of the bourgeoisie, and all the resentments of the bourgeoisie against romanticism," he noted with relish, "that makes a lovely stew."[27]

Instead of abstract romantic visions, the French critic sees nineteenth-century Romanticism embattled with the bourgeois ethos and perceives in Flaubert's small affair the representation of a very large social theme. Moreover it seems clear that for Flaubert himself, Emma's situation, which James passes over as merely the dust in which she rolls, is of paramount importance. Unlike the American who at once focuses on Emma and then sees nothing but her, the French novelist opens his story with the supporting cast. We first meet a young schoolboy who will someday be her husband, accompany him through his first marriage, the beginnings of his career as a country doctor, his loss of his first wife, and finally arrive at the eve of his second marriage where at last the heroine enters the story. It should be noted that she is in fact the third Madame Bovary to appear on the scene, and by the time we understand that it is she to whom the title refers, the stage is set and she can only assume a name and place she never made.

In this Flaubert is not so deterministic as pessimistic, for Emma's environment molds her less than it prevents her from molding herself, but even in the stuff of her most escapist fantasies, she remains inextricably involved with history and society. Madame Bovary's "self" is therefore more extensive, more socially encompassing than James, writing from within a social structure he tacitly approved, or anyway accepted, was prepared to see. The problems that essentially define her were simply not problematical in his eyes; but neither did James quite acknowledge that, barring the rebel's engaged and thereby limited morality, the "finely civilized consciousness" which alone interested him could be developed only by someone who was very successful in just the civilization that made poor diminished Emma so boring.

One can imagine James comparing her deprecatingly to his own vibrant, perceptive Isabel Archer; but unfairly, for the world is very good to Isabel, bestowing on her just what Emma dies for lack of, the financial means to "gratify [her] imagination."[28] If this bounty has unfortunate consequences, it is because Isabel herself is not wise enough to profit from it. Neither would Emma have been, of course, but the point is that she never has the chance to try, and this represents the great difference between the world of Flaubert and that of James. For the American writer's fictional universe is, especially by comparison to Yonville l'Abbaye, truly a land of opportunity where a woman may, and only therefore must, call her soul her own. James's America may not be altogether a free country but it is as free as any society can be. Flaubert's France is horrendously unfree: so much so that his villains can only just barely be blamed for their sins. Even the village usurer only acts out the logic of his social role. We can reproach him for personally accepting that role but not blame him for the very introduction of evil, as we can his counterpart in *Portrait of a Lady,* Madame Merle. When the romantic Isabel sees the world clearly, she acquires the freedom to choose on universal moral grounds; romantic Emma can come only to see that she has no choices. Ultimately it is her society we blame rather than any of its members and we readily imagine another society, drawn according to the precepts perhaps of the compassionate and aristocratic Docteur Larivière, in which Emma and her life would be entirely different.

That James should have missed the point of *Madame Bovary* is the more significant in that he and Flaubert were in other respects virtual counterparts. They would not have differed much about the politics of literature. Both cared most about form and language, and insisted that art be valued primarily for its own sake; both might well have been accused before the popular bar of a fastidious and most undemocratic snobbery. But while Flaubert despairingly viewed the French bourgeoisie as the most dire threat yet encountered by civilized values, James actually saw their best hope among the reigning elite of middle-class America. For Flaubert it was a historical catastrophe that France had become bourgeois. For James the coming of America offered the possibility of transcending both class and history.

Another illustration of the difference in world view that underlies the difference between the novel and the romance: both Melville and Balzac, as it happens, based characters explicitly on Shakespeare's Lear. That archindividualist, of course, exaggerates both man's cosmic status and his domestic role as a father. Indicating no awareness that there was another side to his character, Melville and Balzac elaborated opposite facets of the king's fatal arrogance: Ahab acknowledges no mortal limits and the père Goriot aspires to ideal fatherhood. And the worlds each defines in his own image are also opposites. "Justice is on my side, everything is on my side, natural affection, and the law as well," the neglected Goriot protests. "Society, the whole world, turns on fatherly love, everything falls to pieces if children do not love their fathers."[29] But Ahab cares nothing for the world: he aspires to the throne of heaven, or hell.

Thus Goriot, Lear's novelistic avatar, is realistically defined by a precise sociology and also by the details of a rich internal life that enables us not only to believe in him but also to feel that we know him personally. We know very little about Ahab personally and, if anything, less and less as the story progresses. He is mysterious, archetypal rather than socially typical, abstractly conceived, perhaps universal but certainly not of the everyday world. And the ideological assumptions which I suggested earlier were implied by each fictional form, are in fact evident in *Le Père Goriot* and *Moby-Dick:* the French novel enjoins defiance of a corrupt society while the American romance warns urgently that the wages of blasphemy are death. In short, judging by their respective interpretations of Lear, the American writer is, contrary to the usual expectations, *less* aggressively individualistic than the French.

For Melville, whose alienation from American society is only too painfully evident, still cannot reconcile himself to being alienated, while Balzac actually overstates his disaffection. Melville actually apologizes for conventional society through Starbuck, who is a man of delicate moral sensibility whose concern for the financial success of the whaling expedition expresses only devotion to his duty and not greed. Generally, indeed, the case for social constraints, for law and order, for conformity to conventional roles, is powerfully argued throughout American fiction, and particularly in those very works of the first part of the nineteenth century which are usually cited as evidence of America's intractable commitment to individual freedom. For it is in these writings, of Hawthorne and Melville especially, that the representation of such freedom is most tense and guilt-ridden, and its exercise most often sinful and/or fatal. Of course such freedom is also tantalizing. But like Milton who harbored passions that enkindled his Satan without therefore enlisting on the side of Hell, Melville never suggests that even the most limiting social compliance absolutely precludes personal integrity. And so Ishmael, the wisest character in *Moby-Dick,* who avoids institutional entanglements as scrupulously as cosmic confrontations, remains nevertheless on congenial terms with New England—and New England in turn readily accords him a reasonable degree of freedom, even, at intervals, to drop out. Moreover Ishmael's few active principles are more at variance with Ahab's behavior than with Starbuck's. For Ishmael believes in being companionable and survives largely for reasons embodied in his "marriage" to Queequeg, a relationship whose real interest has been unfortunately obscured. At the end, as we noted earlier, Ishmael sounds a last note of harmony with all of nature and with men too, represented by the whalers who rescue him. And the peace he has achieved is apparently attainable by anyone who can acknowledge the lure of total freedom yet recall that his mortal state requires that he still be social, even sociable.

This conclusion would have amazed Balzac who ends his novel with a declaration of war against a society he likens to an ocean of mud splattering one on mere proximity. Standing high on a hill overlooking Paris (as in the crow's nest which Ishmael warns us against for its dangerous isolation), Eugene Rastignac divorces himself from the "humming hive" of the city below 1and vows to avenge the death of the old man who had tried to be something of a queen bee. From the beginning Balzac juxtaposes the incipiently rebellious, ambitious Rastignac to the ultracompliant and self-sacrificing Goriot (as Melville makes a reverse comparison between Ahab and Ishmael); and Goriot's final agony destroys Rastignac's last feelings of obligation to conventional values, exiling him in a moral autonomy that Cooper, Hawthorne, Melville, Howells, James, and even, it can be argued, Mark Twain would have deemed dangerously akin to blasphemy. But Balzac has few qualms, for Rastignac's ethics are at least superior to those of Paris, in all of which there is not one Starbuck. Thus the basic thrust of *Le Père Goriot,* which considers Lear's family to be the most problematical situation he faces, is the opposite of *Moby-Dick's,* in which Melville depicts how cold and deadly can be the universe beyond the glow of the homefires.

The necessity therefore to live, as it were, within the city limits, is the recurrent motif of the work of Hawthorne. In fact in *The Scarlet Letter,* where he grants rebellion its strongest case by embodying it in his most compelling character and at the same time depicting society at its worst, the right and wrong of the matter are never even so much in doubt as they are for Melville. Hester Prynne presents a total contrast to Goriot, being initially as delinquent a wife and mother as he is the perfect paterfamilias, while in the end, when he dies disillusioned, she becomes not only personally reconciled to her role but its proselytizer toward other women. Of course her progress is not easy, nor is Hawthorne himself uninvolved in her trials. Her first appearance, cradling the innocent fruit of her sin, evokes disturbingly mingled associations: she is a madonna demanding sole custody. But all the more does it seem in the end, when she pledges her exceptional creativity to legitimacy and order, that she has reversed the course of the primordial rebellion.

Actually her whole career is relevant to this discussion. Before the start of the novel, Hawthorne tells us, she had lived in England as a seventeenth-century Lady Chatterley married to an aging scholar. She comes to the New World with the wrong expectations for, finding herself temporarily free of her husband, she defies all laws and commits adultery with the minister of her new community, subverting it to its very soul. By making the outlaw a woman who realizes the full implications of her sin when she bears a female child who could therefore continue to propagate anarchy, Hawthorne interprets Ahab's rather abstract defiance as an immediate threat to social order. For Hawthorne, the savage in man and especially in woman, is never noble, and individualistically to indulge it is to undermine at once civilization and one's own higher humanity. When the lovers meet in the forest to plan their escape somewhere they can live together openly, their child spurns them and, in pursuit of some wild fantasy, runs dangerously deeper into the woods. But later in the antithetical scene in the middle of town, she is said to weep her first human tears standing quietly between her humbled parents. For the minister, the adulteress, and their child, at last a family and fully compliant to the will of the Protestant god and the laws of Boston, have become the real emblem of America's safe passage out of the wilderness.

It is a road traveled by most of the major American fictions, whose characters initially separate themselves from society but come back to it in the end. Even Huckleberry Finn's unique refusal sadly lacks conviction. But, as we saw earlier, Emma Bovary, Julien Sorel, and Eugène Rastignac (whose stories are among the first to come to mind when one thinks of the French novel) sketch out a contrasting paradigm, trying first to realize themselves within society and failing, becoming outcasts and even subversives with the approval of their authors. Julien Sorel struggles from Verrières to Paris wanting only to become a man of the world. He will abide by its rules, adopt its principle, adapt himself to its tastes, if only the world will have him. But when it won't, in pointed contrast to *Billy Budd,* for instance, he goes defiantly to a rebel's grave. American characters seldom die victorious, the deaths of such as Ahab and Hawthorne's Zenobia being used instead to prove a rightful subjection to higher laws.

It may be well to repeat that I do not claim that American writers were placid apologists for higher laws or for those of the state either, but rather that for a lack of a sense of a world elsewhere, this indeed being the world elsewhere, the malaise was guiltily exorcised; and once Hester Prynne voluntarily resumes the emblem of sin, once Melville consigns Ahab to the devil and Huck Finn drifts past Cairo, a certain imaginative vitality seems also extinguished. Indeed the frustratingly few real achievements which too early exhaust some of the greatest American writers may well represent their utmost attempt to establish an independently critical stance. It has been a persistent pattern, tracing a relatively rapid rise to a major defiant, sometimes demonic work and a subsequent painful retreat. At the end of *Absalom, Absalom!,* Faulkner's most critical and powerful work written midway in his career, a disillusioned Quentin Compson cries out in agonized denial, "I don't. I don't! I don't hate [the South]! I don't hate it!"[30] But of course he does, and also loves it too much or is too loyal, too frightened, or too dependent to admit his revulsion. At any rate, it is not to society but at the possibility of active dissent that Quentin hurls the thunderous no. After this, Faulkner created more relaxed protagonists who confronted a less objectionable South and he found them easier to reconcile, but his writing suffered notably. A century before, Hawthorne also retreated after *The Scarlet Letter.* The descendants of the dangerously dualistic Hester come in allegorical pairs, a dark lady and a fair, a sexy one and a chaste, a rebel and a sweet conformist. The dark rebellious self need not be then overcome or absorbed: she can be exiled, excised. Only Melville tried to return to the fray in *Pierre,* albeit at the remove of an ambiguous irony.

Pierre's is probably the most radical critique in the contemporary litera-

ture. What he uncovers beneath the triumphant legitimacy of his family's social dominance, gnawing at the roots of his family tree, is a variant of Hester's
subversion: a bastard child that his father never recognized. But whereas in
Hawthorne's treatment legality and the definition of legitimacy are not at
issue, only how an individual should relate to them, Melville questions the validity of both and, by extension, of the social order they preserve. Pierre's
father who figures as a god of the ancestral estate and its ultimate law, had
himself violated the most important law of all and the result has been potentially revolutionary. Instead of a legitimate heir, his eldest child is an illegitimate heiress; and thus personal morality and even the integrity of the law (of
primogeniture) are hopelessly at odds with the preservation of the status quo.
In contrast, Hester found her salvation in a right accommodation with a society whose shortcomings were stylistic rather than structural. And we need no
political sociology to explain her temptation. Pierre's problems, on the other
hand, are not properly his own but society's and society's not in manner but in
substance. In short, Melville's is almost uniquely an internal political analysis.
And, though he renders them abstractly, the structures of social life familiar in
the European novel are for once at the center of an American work: the intricacies of the family, an urban setting (once Pierre realizes that life is not a pastoral idyll) and the rigors of economic survival. (*Absalom, Absalom!* has virtually the same plot as *Pierre*, the illegitimate eldest child whose existence must
be denied being translated in Faulkner's southern idiom into a black son.)[31]

It is worth explicating the plot of *Pierre* further to see how fundamental
Melville's attack really was. The appearance of an illegitimate sister evokes for
Pierre an alternate family shadowing his own: the castaway mistress, the dark
sister, Isabel, and the father whose alter-ego might quite overwhelm the
super-ego he had always been to Pierre before. That family, Pierre now sees,
has prior claim to all his worldly estate; he and his queenly mother are usurp-
ers who can only atone by acknowledging the old injury and reinstating its
surviving victim. Since his mother and the powers vested in her will never accede to this, Pierre must exile himself with his sister and suffer with her since
she cannot rejoice with him. They will become outcasts together. Of course
the good and the bad of the situation are not altogether as clear as I am suggesting. Just as toward the rebellious Ahab, Melville was ambivalent toward
Pierre whose selflessness might well mask a towering, blasphemous egoism;
we can never be sure. The angelic Isabel may be fallen; moreover legitimacy
and convention have a powerful advocate in the unequivocally sainted Lucy,
whose own attitude toward Pierre's sacrifice is finally undecipherable. Still,

when they all three die (in the deepest dungeon of the dark city they fled to out of their Fallen Eden) leaving as heir a cousin whose very duplicity has been the key to both personal wealth and the preservation of the family, we have come very close to the state of mind with which Rastignac sets out to do subversive battle—only our battlers then commit suicide.

In this light, *Billy Budd* may be seen as the account of the suicide itself, a masochistic probing of the fatal wound, that irrevocable glimpse of a real opposition between the law (the structure, the institutions, and the norms of society) and a true morality. Unable to imagine another world (the American blasphemy), Melville becomes both Captain Vere, representing the social order that can no more be set aside than that of God, and Billy Budd, the moral vision that is henceforth inarticulate except, in its agony, to praise its executioner. The impact of *Billy Budd,* as of *Moby-Dick* and of *Pierre,* may be to make *us* rebel but it is against Melville's despair rather than in response to his vision. For even Melville had blinded himself rather than see beyond America.

Most American writers are at least reticent, and their allegiance, anomalous for the period and the hemisphere, was the main force shaping American fiction at least through the nineteenth century. The principles of the bourgeois family, as the heart of middle-class ethics, are consistently upheld in American writing and, not at all paradoxically, they have inspired the strident masculinity, even the celibacy of its heroes.

One of the important signs of the inadequacy of the unregenerate individualists in American fiction is their inability to form familial and social attachments. The significance of this should be clear: indeed in a middle-class society the family is the crucial institution that counters the disruptive and centrifugal potential of individualism. Hester Prynne's sins in this regard are evident as well as the source of her redemption, but Isabel Archer's recognition of the sacrosanct character of marriage, the doom inherent in Natty Bumppo's failure to marry, and the moral triumph of Huck's filial relationship to Jim, not to mention the "marriage" of Ishmael and Queequeg, are all examples of an identification of family and social morality. The same ideology can be shown to have brought about that scarcity of adult women and of sexuality, the adolescent repression that worried Leslie Fiedler and appalled D. H. Lawrence and which Hawthorne explained clearly through Hester and Zenobia. Individualist women were to him intolerably subversive because they undermined the very institution by which individualist men might yet cohere into a moral community. It was Hawthorne too who saw most clearly

that sex is the wilderness within while American literature is a saga of colonization. American fiction has been willy-nilly an ally in that colonization.
Indeed, it seems doubtful that a jury composed of American writers would
have or could have been much more lenient with Stendhal's Julien Sorel than
the "bourgeois indignés" who demand his head.

If slavery had not actually existed in the United States, it seems unlikely that any novelist could have invented it. Imagining slavery in a nineteenth-century novel would involve a fatal contradiction, between the terms that engender modern characters and plots and those that authorize modern slavery. The form of bondage that developed in the American South differed significantly from its ancient models by defining not only the political and economic status of the enslaved but their organic nature as human beings. When slaveowners in columned houses cited Aristotle's dictum that some were born to be masters and others slaves, they meant something different than he had, for ancient slaves retained their species equality though they belonged to a conquered or even a despised nation. African slaves in the United States were considered inferior in kind; their actual or potential slavery was organic to them.

This additional insult was hardly gratuitous. Indeed it was the ground for justifying a practice which otherwise violated the most basic precept of the prevalent ideology, the idea that human beings as a condition of birth possess themselves inherently and inalienably. Therefore to deprive a human being of self-possession is tantamount to murder, an indefensible act of aggression—unless this ostensible human being is of a kind that is not quite human. Unfit, therefore, for citizenship not only in a republic but in a novel whose primum mobile is precisely its characters' capacity, born of self-possession, for self-direction. This capacity is often thwarted, it is true, and the failure of characters to control their lives generates more plots than their successes. But just as republican theory after Rousseau and Hobbes cannot encompass a social category of slaves, for the same reason the novel after Richardson cannot envision a being lacking potential autonomy and incapable of choice. Modern republic and novel alike depend on the assumption that it is in the nature of individuals to be able to at least try to govern themselves.

It is as an aspect of his very being rather than of his character that the modern protagonist is able to speak for himself. Melville's *Benito Cereno* dramatizes this assumption in the character Babo who, having defined himself a protagonist by refusing to be a slave (indeed by turning out to be his owner's master), then refuses to speak when he is returned to bondage. Babo exits the story mute: "His aspect seemed to say," Melville's narrator conjectures, "since I cannot do deeds, I will not speak words."[1] That conjunction of the commands of self and of language was prohibitive for the novelistic portrayal of slaves.[2]

Obviously, in the real world real slaves—enslaved men and women—spoke quite eloquently and, in this way among others, manifested a capacity for autonomy not different from their masters'. That reality emerges in novels written by slaves, but not without also posing formal problems. The special problem novelists who are slaves confront has to do not with their characters, whose full humanity the novelists derive from their own, but with themselves, with their own authorship and authority. In fact, the assertion that the story has been written by a slave and draws on personal experiences, is a characteristic and nearly universal feature of slave fiction;[3] and to the contrary of similar claims made by Moll Flanders or Captain Gulliver (claims one has to recognize as fiction in order to understand the story), this one needs to be believed as fact for the fiction to work. The assumption that this assertion of authenticity tries to counter is the same as the one tending to preclude slaves as characters. Slave authors need to establish through writing the competence to write with which free authors are endowed from their literary birth; a slave author is a contradiction in terms in the same way as a slave character.

The improbability of slave characters is moreover compounded by the racial character of American slavery which offers the possibility for a white writer to be opposed to slavery but still believe that blacks are an inferior people, that they possess diminished selves, or less of the quality of individualism. Antislavery and racism were quite compatible; indeed they were joined in much of Abolitionism. As they can be associated politically in a single program, so they can come together in individual characters. Novelistic antislavery has a wide range, from characters whose claim to equality is more evident to God than to man, to others who might almost as well be white. At the core, however, any representation of a slave as a feeling and reflecting character (not a mere prop) is contradictory and potentially unstable. There are in fact very few.

Uncle Tom's Cabin is the extraordinary exception.[4] Harriet Beecher Stowe constructed a novel about slavery which is on one level a triumph of conventional form, setting out the most widely accepted concepts and values. Her characters issue from the standard repertory of sentimental fiction and her moral and political philosophy mostly articulates the abiding creed of the established middle class. Yet her novel was at once recognized as an overwhelming challenge to the existing law and order and in the first weeks after its publication it had already begun to change the world. This paradox, however, is its own explanation: it is precisely through the juxtaposition of the conventional and the incongruous that *Uncle Tom's Cabin* works and generates its transcendent power. To the novel's fundamental belief in individual self-possession, Stowe holds up characters who are the property of other characters and are therefore themselves also entangled in irreducible contradiction. And before her readers' axiomatic belief in the liberal individualism of the free market, the author displays the travesty of the marketplace of men and women. In the end the impossibility of these juxtapositions is Stowe's irresistible point.

To reach that end, however, she has to travel a somewhat circuitous route, for impossible adjuncts thrown up against one another make incoherent stories. *Uncle Tom's Cabin* has an exact contemporary in Melville's *Pierre,* a masterpiece of incoherence in which the armies of convention and radical reform clash their way into impenetrable night. Stowe finds ways of negotiating her chasms. First, instead of taking the novel at its most individualistic, in the mode of Hawthorne and Melville, she interprets it in the attenuated terms of sentimental fiction;[5] and rather than the self-sufficient self-reliant individualism that makes a nineteenth-century American man a man, she invokes individualism's complementary female form as deployed in the ideology of domesticity. The world she ultimately reconstructs does not therefore feature an altered hierarchy; white men pursuing the rewards of self-reliance are still the world's rightful masters. "Master," however, has a newly moralized meaning, an individualistic integrity whose achievement has crucially required the assistance of wives and mothers. Masters regain their heroism and slaves become characters in *Uncle Tom's Cabin* through the agency of women, a revolutionary change that is intended to restore both the novel and America to itself.

Actually the task is not to restore but to create a more perfect nation, since slavery was already part of it at the republic's founding to which it made an ominously paradoxical contribution. Edmund Morgan has argued that the establishment of American democracy, far from being contradicted by slavery, actually depended on it. Many of the wealthy, Anglo-Saxon, Protestant founders, according to Morgan, feared that the general extension of democratic rights could in time threaten their hegemony, should the population grow too large and too disparate. The permanent employment of slaves on Southern plantations, which were the only enterprises at the time that required large numbers of workers, removed the need and the opportunity for a too abundant immigration. Slavery would prevent the emergence of an important and potentially challenging class of propertyless laborers.[6]

After 1789, however, the economic and social base of ruling class politics broadened considerably to a point where the old homogeneity ceased to be even a useful fiction. By the middle of the nineteenth century, European immigration and expansion westward had vastly complicated the class structure and concomitantly the character of the political process. With these developments, the paradox that had linked democracy with slavery grew into an increasingly sharp contradiction, and one that was inextricably economic, political, and moral. The Fugitive Slave Law bespoke this contradiction unmistakeably. Forcing non–slave owners to participate in the maintenance of slavery, it confronted them inescapably with their own complicity. The nation's growing guilt and apprehension is tangible in the overwhelming response to *Uncle Tom's Cabin*.

Harriet Beecher Stowe projected a radical solution which at the same time sounded deeply familiar themes. The first installment of *Uncle Tom's Cabin* appeared in the moderate Abolitionist newsletter in 1851 subtitled "The Man Who Was a Thing." This installment introduces the slave George Harris as the inventor of a hemp-cleaning machine comparable to Whitney's cotton gin, and concludes, "He was possessed of a handsome person and pleasing manners . . . nevertheless as this young man was in the eye of the law not a man but a thing, all these superior qualifications were subject to the control of a vulgar, narrow-minded master" (22). Stowe's readers could readily see that Harris's situation was doubly unjust. Or more precisely, they understood the injustice of his enslavement in terms of a second deprivation which, while perhaps less outrageous, was also more immediately resonant to a middle-class audience. Besides suffering the theft of self (of his handsome person and pleasing manners), Harris has also been robbed of the chance at self-improvement, of his rightful place as not just the peer of his vulgar[7] master, but as his superior. Stowe here articulates the all-important corollary of self-possession, the one that sets it in motion; for self-possession is not a static but a dynamic condition fulfilled in an ever-growing increase of status and property. George Harris is unfree not only in situ, within himself, but in his movement through society where another man denies him ambition. Politically Harris is deprived of his birthright to become himself; in novelistic terms, he is denied his own plot.

A brief episode early in the story illustrates the coherence of these deprivations. Some time after his own successful escape, George returns to arrange that of his wife and son. Traveling in disguise, he arrives at a tavern whose occupants are just then engaged in reading a bill offering a reward for his capture. Far from recognizing George as the advertised runaway, the rude backwoodsmen take him for an aristocrat. The reader's pleasure in this reversal is twofold, for George has not only escaped discovery as a slave but more positively he has been recognized for the remarkable man he really is. His *invisibility* as a slave would have made the antislavery point by itself, since his passing for any sort of man invalidates his treatment as a thing. But the way he *is* seen fulfills a larger program, for the escaped slave can not only pass for white, he is better than at least these whites. True, these are not the very best whites, not gentlemen, so that appearing a gentleman in comparison with them does not yet make him the equal of the real thing. Still, gradations like these are immaterial in this episode, while what is at issue is fundamental to both the novel and its contemporary world—the principle that individual worth is what one makes it, an entirely personal value realized in competition with others.

Thus the best of the slaves in *Uncle Tom's Cabin* are models of upward mobility. Before being sold downriver, Uncle Tom is his master's right-hand man while his wife Chloe is the best cook in the county. The power of these characters as fictional constructs is identical with the power their author ascribes to them as people. Slavery may do its worst in breaking up families but a close second is its denial of social advancement. George Harris's most bitter plaint might have been voiced by Benjamin Franklin. When his jealous master withdraws him from the hemp factory where he has distinguished himself, George loses heart: "What's the use of our trying to do anything, trying to know anything, trying to be anything? What's the use of living?" (27) Given the opportunity, however, as he is in Canada, he immediately moves to the top of his trade as a mechanic. George Harris is the sort of man whom one predicts will be president, perhaps of Liberia (where the Abolitionists around Stowe expected the emancipated slaves to emigrate).

In the nearly white, well-spoken, and ambitious George Harris, Stowe presented her white, educated, and ambitious audience with an embodiment of their most basic ideological beliefs. George Harris towering above the vulgar slavers in the tavern is followed by a scene in which he manifests the other part of the power of the manly individualist, his familial side. The wife he has returned South to rescue is Eliza who in the best-known scene in the novel herself escapes with her child across the frozen Ohio. When, in a development to which I will return, the family is reunited, George has an opportunity to express the rest of his middle-class philosophy. "Sitting with his child on his knee, and his wife's hand in his," Harris muses, "'O! Eliza, if these people only knew what a blessing it is for a man to feel that his wife and child belong to *him!* I've often wondered to see men that could call their wives and children *their own* fretting and worrying about anything else'" (220).

The phrase "belong to *him*" cannot be inadvertent and if it is idiomatic, its idiom has become self-reflexive and consciously provokes scrutiny. The fact that in the slave system one person does materially belong to another, renders the entire image of people belonging to one another newly resonant. Its female expression will emerge more clearly when it comes up again at the end of the novel in the story of Cassy. At this point it is the male version that concerns Stowe, who here archetypically redeems an expression of individualist power from its perversion in slavery. George is now the complete American middle-class man; he is ambitious and likely to succeed, he cherishes his family and wants them his. It would be difficult to argue against these absolutely standard desires, and why would we?

One reason might begin with the recognition that although George has middle-class aspirations, he is more accurately described as a laborer. In that case not only does he seem less easily absorbed into the existing order of things, but also his deprivations may appear less clear-cut. The role of raising this complicating caveat is given to Augustine St. Clare who gives the most persuasive possible articulation to the common Southern defense that its slaves were only the counterparts of the North's industrial workers, and perhaps better off. In a long embittered diatribe addressed to his cousin Ophelia, a Northern Abolitionist, St. Clare cites his brother's view that there will always have to be a lower class. When she objects that "the English laborer is not sold, traded, parted from his family, whipped," he replies more or less irrefutably: "He is as much at the will of his employer as if he were sold to him. The slave-owner can whip his refractory slave to death,—the capitalist can starve him to death. As to family security, it is hard to say which is the worst,—to have one's children sold, or see them starve to death at home" (269). Hard indeed, and Stowe does not try, or not directly.

Rather than attempt to defend Northern industrialism, Stowe moves the argument back to the Southern slaves themselves, dropping the examination of their connection to northern laborers instead of concluding it. But this is somewhat less evasive than it may appear, in that it also reflects the transformation of American society since the Revolution. Agricultural workers in the South and industrial workers in the North were no longer equivalent entities, though the South wanted to maintain the comparison. The relations of the Northern middle class, for which Stowe spoke, to its workers were now actually complicated by the existence of slavery.[8] As industrial production overtook agricultural production in the half century following the Revolution, there developed a growing demand for free workers who would gravitate toward the areas in which they were needed; in other words for a free labor market. It was widely believed that when these workers were not needed, as territorial expansion also accelerated, the workers would move themselves west.

In the context of this accelerating mobility, St. Clare's vision of starving laborers, however accurate, is less definitive than it might be. Referring to the poor as the "lowly" (rather than as laborers), Stowe is able to translate rigid class categories into mobile relativities more likely to inspire the less propertied to emulate their betters than to threaten them. If, as Morgan argues, the patricians who led the Revolution feared the mob enough to ratify its enslavement, the ideology and mythology of Stowe's post-Jacksonian America disperses the mob into ambitious individuals, each one an aspiring patrician. As for St. Clare, his despair over the plight of workers North and South appears to reflect his own problems more clearly than those of the world. St. Clare would rather brood over a cosmic destiny than "do what one man can do." "Why didn't you free your slaves?" Ophelia asks him. "Well," he answers, "I wasn't up to that" (271). And that is finally where St. Clare's long speech comes to rest, in an exposition of his own impotence. In some ways the ideal novelistic character, St. Clare has become as incapable of advancing a plot as a slave.

If in George Harris we have the model entrepreneur paralyzed by the slave system, and in St. Clare (an aristocrat who calls himself a democrat) the equally exemplary gentleman also paralyzed by the slave system, how is either history or the novel to move forward? The answer lies in Ophelia's question, "Why didn't you free your slaves?" That is, it lies in the capacity and the tendency to ask that question which is in fact deceptively simple. For until she poses this most transitive of questions—implying an action comparable in its effect to the divine gift of life itself—St. Clare has spoken only reflexively, only with reference to himself. In that self-absorption indeed lies much of his novelistic interest, but it connotes a historical impasse nonetheless. Ophelia's laconic brusque query cuts across St. Clare's introspections; we follow her pointing finger to examine his impact on others. *Why* didn't he free his slaves?

From the first scene in the novel when two men, one evil and the other good, negotiate the evil of Uncle Tom's sale, such female interventions are in fact the way the novel advances. Tom's kind owner, Shelby, is helplessly indebted and hopelessly manipulated by the trader Haley. Mrs. Shelby, appalled when she learns that not only Tom but the small child of her maid Eliza have both been sold, begins the process of feminine activity when she effects the failure of the chase after the escaping Eliza. In time a widowed Mrs. Shelby will take over the plantation, restore it to solvency without ever selling another slave, and pass it on to her son George, explicitly his mother's and not his father's son, who will be seen later finally emancipating the slaves. When he does, however, the ease with which this world-changing event is accomplished will echo the question of the last paragraph, why didn't St. Clare or any right-thinking Southern planter free his slaves?

Conversely, how do the women do it? Indeed so empowered are the women in *Uncle Tom's Cabin* that a number of critics have suggested, citing as well the novel's denunciation of the slave market and through St. Clare of market society as such, that Stowe despaired of the patriarchy and advocated a matriarchy. But in fact although they are virtually the only ones able to cause things to happen (to forward the plot), women in *Uncle Tom's Cabin* do not even try to run the world. Their contribution is not only more circumspect, circumspection is its cardinal principle, even its goal. It is not Mrs. Shelby who frees the slaves. That possibility is never broached, does not figure in the story.

The major scenes of female power occur appropriately at home. Once Eliza has astoundingly carried her child across the icy river, essentially walking on water, she finds her way to her first feminine refuge. The diminutive Mrs. Bird, wife of a Senator who has supported the Fugitive Slave Law, proves a formidable defender; when the Senator returns from the voting to find Eliza in his parlor, his wife persuades him not only to shelter the runaway slave but to conduct her to the next station of the underground railroad. This second refuge then measures the utmost heights of feminine power, but as well its limits. Eliza reaches the farm of the Quaker Rachel Halliday as she might have entered Heaven, this being a female Eden where maternal love makes the most arduous housekeeping "like picking up the rose-leaves and trimming the bushes in Paradise." Representing the antipode of ideal femininity from little Eva, the plump middle-aged Rachel is not at all ethereal. Seated in her rocking chair, the largest in the house, or moving about the kingdom of her bright kitchen, Rachel Halliday commands and orders the whole domestic universe. (In a corner of the kitchen, her husband can be seen engaged in what Stowe dubs a touch irreverently "the anti-patriarchal operation of shaving.") Chaos never threatens and the kitchen is immaculate all through the "complicated and multiform" culinary consummation of an Indiana breakfast. "Busy girls and boys . . . mov[e] obediently" at Rachel's bidding and the very "chicken and ham had a cheerful and joyous fizzle in the pan, as if they rather enjoyed being cooked than otherwise" (170).

In the radiant circle about Rachel, it is possible to think that the world would be a better place were it renovated into one large kitchen. But no sooner has Eliza's child little Harry had his fill of griddle cakes than his father appears and we realize that this has been only an interlude. Eliza herself has in fact dreamed away half her time there, and she awakes to find her husband by her bedside. There follows the scene described earlier in which George expresses his gratitude for the restored order of his family which now at last *he* possesses. The immediate impulse for his escape had been in fact the denial of his family; when his master ordered him to abandon Eliza and take up illicit housekeeping with another woman, he had to run away in order to preserve a manhood which begins at home. Conjugal mastery is doubly sanctified here, first by the plot which celebrates George's husbandly sway in the unambiguously happy reunion of the tormented family, and second precisely by the setting of Rachel Halliday's home whereby it receives the blessing of the ideal and very powerful matriarch. There is no ambiguity here and no regret: what Rachel Halliday blesses is the restoration of patriarchal power to the slave whose manhood is inextricably a matter of self-possession and of the possession of others, of *his* wife and child.

By extension, white men in *Uncle Tom's Cabin* have failed and worse, and the problem confronted by white women will not be solved by their staging a simple gender-coup. For such women as Mrs. Shelby, Ophelia, and Rachel Halliday, taking society over would seem easy. Getting men like Mr. Shelby and St. Clare *not* to give it up is the difficult task.

It will have to be done, however; the necessity of restoring men to the right conduct of society is incarnate in the novel's very plot. The family homes in which the story unfolds are readily controlled by women, and even when they are not (St. Clare's is not, which generates a large part of his angst), they should be. But to reach these homes and to link them into a society, one

must undertake a series of journeys that Stowe cannot imagine women taking on their own, still less leading. It is for men to free America's byways.
When George, Eliza, and little Harry leave the Quaker refuge, George takes
up a gun to fight off highwaymen who would not only rob but steal them.
Claiming his family in the Halliday bedroom has been a rite of passage into
the manly condition of armed combat through which he will enter into an
order of things based in the family but extending abroad into the embattled
territory where men realize their individual worth in competition with other
men.

Stowe's argument against slavery follows this same path. It begins with a
denunciation of slavery for its corruption of the familial heart of American
society. Struggling against this corruption, appropriately, are the several
women, starting with her master's wife, who help Eliza escape. They demonstrate a private, domestic form of liberal morality which has survived its public downfall. Once the Harris family is restored, however, Stowe moves with
it toward a new reconciliation of home and market. By realizing his possession of himself in possessing his family, George has renovated the slave's cabin
as a free man's castle. Pursuing the same logic, he goes forth to rebuild free enterprise. Stowe imagines him eventually on the horizon of her story, a free
man taking passage beyond India and building his own world, a redeemed
American republic in Liberia's green and pleasant land.

George's young son Harry is the type of a purified but rigorous entrepreneurial individualist. At the kitchen table in their Canadian home, Harry announces that he has done all his homework. "I did it, every bit of it, *myself*, father; and *nobody* helped me!" To which his proud father responds, "That's
right, depend on yourself, my son. You have a better chance than ever your
poor father had" (498). This homely scene would have worked just as well to
propound the more cooperative values of domesticity by showing the father
instructing his son, as he could not when both were slaves, or more poignantly
still, by having little Harry teach his deprived father. But this would be to present domesticity as the goal when Stowe intends it to be the means to an individualist integrity nurtured by mothers but embodied in independent sons.

In a parallel way, the goal is not to replace the market with the domestic
economy but to achieve integrity in commerce. The opening scene in which
the deal for Tom and little Harry is struck suggests in fact that the reform of
commerce, its emancipation from the curse of slavery, is the first priority. The
thrust of the scene is to make distinctions. Between trader and planter to begin with, sharply juxtaposing the odious Haley to the ineffectual but well-
meaning Shelby. Having told us that only one of these men is a "gentleman,"

Stowe (who must have been reading Dickens) has Haley boast of his "human-ity." At times slaves upon being separated from their families will threaten sui-cide, he tells Shelby. But he knows how to handle them and in fact loses "as few as any man in the business. . . . And I lays it all to my management, sir; and humanity, sir, I may say, is the great pillar of *my* management" (16). With this, Haley takes his place at the very bottom of the novel's moral ladder, becomes the pure embodiment of slavery's inhumanity. And with this also, Stowe while not altogether exonerating Shelby, distances him from slavery's inhumanity by the considerable extent of his distance from Haley.

The distinction between Haley and Shelby extends into one between two kinds of markets. Shelby has been driven to trade on the slave market by his failures in legitimate commerce, the latter badly distorted in the Southern economy by the former. But precisely by exposing their promiscuous interac-tions, Stowe intends to establish their radical difference. Mrs. Shelby will refuse to trade on the slave market and thrive on the free. Her son will abolish the slave market and replace it with the free. "I shall pay you wages for your work," he tells his just emancipated slaves now employees, "such as we shall agree on" (509). To George Shelby, not accidentally sharing the name of George Harris, is given the actual task of redeeming the nation's political morality and purifying its economy.

In this and other ways, he is the reverse of St. Clare. St. Clare's inability to achieve any of the social changes he so brilliantly and feelingly envisions re-sults from the way he represents a conventional type of male protagonist trag-ically divided by the familiar paradox that individualism encounters in serving as a collective ideology. On one hand the individual defines himself by the way he recreates the world in his own image. On the other, the very auton-omy which gives him the capacity to rebuild society seems to imply separa-tion from the world. An individual can bear witness to his political convic-tions, as Thoreau did, but the realization of these convictions in concerted social action would tend to compromise precisely the sense of personal inde-pendence that inspired the action.

The definition of a slave as a being unable to be a character in a novel seems to have an equally prohibitive corollary: the inner freedom that makes St. Clare an excellent character essentially prevents him from freeing others. The problem embodied in St. Clare is that even uncompromised as it was by its pact with American slavery, individualism in its masculine individualist mode offered the *reason* for Emancipation, but not any *way* to achieve it. St. Clare's cousin Ophelia, however, is not similarly stymied and, having made him sign Topsy over to her in good time, she saves her slave when St. Clare dooms his. Ophelia, as fierce an individualist as any, represents its female domestic mode whose terms not only permit but enjoin such interventions. The nature of female individualism had been described more than a decade before *Uncle Tom's Cabin* by Tocqueville when he extolled American women for the voluntary gift of their independence to fulfill their husbands' self-sufficiency and the country's. The vitality of American society, Tocqueville wrote, depended on its women who, after an exceptionally free girlhood, became as exceptionally devoted wives. Like the men, the women of the New World were newly self-reliant, yet they demanded less independence in marriage than the women of the Old World. On the contrary they lent all their considerable energy to their husbands' progress. They did much of the work of democracy, therefore, but above all they made democracy work.

I said earlier that the assumption that wives were aboriginally self-possessed was essential to the metaphorical meaning of their belonging to their husbands. This assumption is basic also to the political meaning of conjugal possession which augments men precisely because women are free others who volunteer to be auxiliary selves. As according to the Natural Law philosophers the worker owns his labor and thereby the right to sell it, a woman must possess herself to give herself away and, in becoming what her fond husband may call his most precious possession, she proves she was first her own. In the modern world, women are a kind of metaproperty, and at the same time the reverse, the ground of property rather than property itself. They must be potentially individualists themselves before they can be the wives and mothers of individualists.

But in voluntarily becoming wives they reveal an aspect of individualism that is not evident from their husbands' perspective, although it is precisely the aspect that renders individualism collectively viable. A white man, St. Clare represents for Stowe the political paralysis which the dominant male form of individualism can produce; a black woman demonstrates the potential for action in individualism's domestic mode. This character, Cassy, is St. Clare's counterpart also in her elaborate interiority, for Cassy alone of all the characters is as fully realized as St. Clare.

We meet her as Simon Legree's slave mistress. One night she tells Uncle Tom her story. Born of a slave mother, she was raised in luxury by her white father who "kept [her] dressed like a doll" and provided her with a convent education. He gave her everything but her freedom, however, and when he died the nice young lawyer who came to arrange the affairs of the estate listed her among its goods. She did not know this and was not suspicious when the lawyer brought another nice young man to meet her. She thought him the handsomest I had ever seen. I shall never forget that evening. I walked with him in the garden. I was lonesome and full of sorrow, and he was so kind and gentle to me; and he told me that he had seen me before I went to the convent, and that he had loved me a great while, and he would be my friend and protector;—in short, though he didn't tell me, he had paid two thousand dollars for me, and I was his property,—I became his willingly for I loved him. . . . O, how I *did* love that man! How I love him now,—and always shall, while I breathe! He was so beautiful, so high, so noble! He put me into a beautiful house, with servants, horses, and carriages, and furniture, and dresses. Everything that money could buy, he gave me; but I didn't set any value on all that,—I only cared for him. I loved him better than my God and my own soul; and, if I tried, I couldn't do any other way from what he wanted me to. (423)

All the pieces of Stowe's argument come together in this extraordinary passage. First, in its bitter parody of conventional romance, it repeats the recurrent theme of human relations poisoned by slavery at the source. Parody from one perspective; however, from *hers* at the time, Cassy's love is real and, like Uncle Tom's refusal to run away when he learns that he has been sold, manifests the humanity of the slave in the teeth of its denial. But although Cassy feels love, she cannot express it, all the terms of its expression, the terms of giving and wanting to please, having been taken from her. And when her master deprives her of the power to give, he is himself deprived of the gift: by looking at it from the perspective of the slave (who has been by the form of the novel deeded with the selfhood to act a part of her own), we now see slavery as not only an act—the violent deprivation of one person's freedom by another—but an interaction that acts on both.

The sentence "Everything that money could buy, he gave me" fuses parody and pathos to describe the mutual annihilation of master and slave. Its radical reach derives characteristically in Stowe's writing from its absolute conventionality turned inside out into the negation of the convention's most fundamental value. The sentence begins by telling us that Cassy's lover expressed his transcending love for her by buying her the world; and that way measures the all-negating abomination of his having for exactly $2,000 bought *her*.

But the real genius of the passage lies in its perception that there is more at play here than a hideous perversion of human relations. For the ease with which the language expresses both relations, of lover and of master, reveals that they are after all not absolute opposites; had she been free, his gifts would in a sense also have bought her. He would have "possessed" her; she would have been "his." "Everything that money could buy, he gave me," pointing to the interaction of buying and giving in man-woman relations even outside the context of slavery, measures neither a transcendent love nor yet an infernal lust. Instead its radical ambiguity reveals its dualistic origin in a dialectic whose female term is not less active for being negative.

Cassy abandons herself to her love actively, or she would had she a self to abandon. Her lack of such property to give away renders the entire transaction void, and the master who would become her lover is unable to just because he already owns her. Later in the story we see the converse of the master's powerlessness in the slave's equally helpless power over him; Cassy has "an influence over [Simon Legree] from which he could not free himself" (432) and which is precisely the influence of his denial of her freedom retroactively denying his own. With Cassy Stowe has fully elaborated the implications of George Harris's paean to a man's possession of his wife. Until the phrase "a man's wife belongs to him" can be read metaphorically because it has no literal reality, the self-fulfillment of men in the self-abandonment of women will be impossible. Thus the Revolution's unholy marriage of slavery and freedom has to be dissolved because it has invalidated marriage for all the citizenry. And without marriage and the kind of fulfilling interaction it models, the self-reliant individual man, the ideal American, Stowe's no less than Emerson's, cannot be.

Translated into the terms of erotic romance, the most intimate version of domesticity, an individualism that in its male mode implies laissez-faire comes to demand engagement. Harriet Beecher Stowe's major achievement in *Uncle Tom's Cabin* was this, to identify the emancipation of American slaves with both individual and national destiny. It is no accident that this crucial identification which permitted the claim that the Civil War completed the Revolution, emerged so clearly and forcefully first in a novel written by a woman. Individualism in the writings of Stowe's masculine contemporaries, Hawthorne and Melville, seems to mean an absolute personal social disengagement that tragically moves their protagonists to reproduce the founding dilemma. To free herself, Hawthorne's Miriam enthralls one man into murdering another, and Holgrave forbears from similarly sacrificing Phoebe at the explicit cost of abandoning efforts to change society. To free himself, Melville's Captain Ahab usurps the very soul of his crew, and Pierre kills his entire family to redeem his and their past. Domesticity offers an alternative definition of the individualist self according to which the self realizes its freedom in connection with an other whose own ontological freedom is essential to the self's fulfillment.

This formula has a certain Utopian cast and may appear to resolve more problems than *Uncle Tom's Cabin* raises; but the altruism it offers has its limits. For one thing, its concepts of "self" and of "other" are neither anonymous nor interchangeable. Stowe's notion of the self is generically male and of the gentleman class. A female self is possible but only on sufferance and never realized in competition with a man, hardly even in his company.

The converse of this principle is equally active and the male self cannot realize itself in domestic terms or even with too pronounced an admixture of domesticity's otherwise admirable values. George Shelby illustrates this converse, and demonstrates in the process that Stowe does not envision men adopting a domestic mode of self-definition, only that they will allow themselves to be influenced by the values that attend their wives' and especially their mothers' aptly described selflessness. For despite his wonderful moral and political effectiveness, Mrs. Shelby's son is unfortunately not a very interesting character. He fails to thrive as a protagonist for the reason that makes St. Clare work so well as a character though so badly as a social actor. St. Clare we saw was introspective to a fatal fault. George is defined entirely by the external imperatives of his mother's, and Uncle Tom's, domestic ideology. Not being a woman, he cannot derive personal substance from that and therefore remains a cipher, an instrumental allegory of the social fusion of men and women which cannot and should not occur personally. Ideally a man would be wholly masculine but married to an excellent woman instead of one like St. Clare's selfish and ambitious wife Marie (selfishness violates a woman's most basic value); and the influence of his wife would confirm the abiding sway of his still more excellent mother.

In relation to issues of self-fulfillment, women mostly play the role of other. As for blacks *qua* blacks (George Harris nearly transcends his race) they are constitutionally other, defined through the moral and social problem they pose for whites. *Uncle Tom's Cabin* seeks to end slavery, not racism or sexism. Harriet Beecher Stowe invoked conventional feminine values and concepts to urge men to be truer to themselves. *Uncle Tom's Cabin* constitutes a feminine pastoral in which men of good will who are failing to govern (abdicating to slavetraders like Haley) are morally renewed by journeying through a domestic Forest of Arden of which Rachel Halliday's kitchen is the heart, and thereby regain the fortitude and rectitude to rule the world.

Both conservative and revolutionary, therefore, Stowe's novel differs in its definition of both terms from the picture drawn by recent feminist critics of women's writings, in which ostensible acquiescence in the plots of female submission is subverted by the heroine's appropriation of narrative power. Indeed, while in current historicist or cultural criticism, authors and characters generally are seen to navigate between poles of subversion and complicity, feminist critics have tended to find their authors and characters grouped about the pole of subversion.[9] In even the most conventional women's fiction, these critics have uncovered an unsuspected independence from the established patriarchal ideology, a critical distance from it or a zone of criticism within it that provides a staging area for autonomy.

But this is not the case in *Uncle Tom's Cabin,* which appropriates the patriarchal ideology only to force it to repossess itself, seeks not autonomy but reconciliation and, in time having achieved its patriarchal reform, becomes a Western classic. For it matters that *Uncle Tom's Cabin,* whatever academic critics thought of it, became a classic alongside the novels of Dickens and Robert Louis Stevenson. The status of classic bespeaks a primary and direct relation to the dominant culture which is the counterpart of this novel's primary and direct relation to the historical process. In both areas Stowe's novel contributed significantly to major change, and in both areas it was also a force for keeping things as they were: freeing the slaves to be both novelistic characters and citizens while maintaining and even strengthening existing social and cultural hierarchies.

There is nothing surprising in any of this except perhaps the exceptionally clear picture it offers of a kind of women's writing whose subversions, if any, are somewhat paradoxical. Stowe's literary feat worked a sort of Darwinian mutation on American society. As much as any individual including the men who made the Civil War, she helped America evolve from its relatively oligarchic beginnings into a middle-class republic. But she did not seek to advance the cause of women's self-rule; in fact she reaffirmed their feudal placement, at the same time establishing an equivalent place of subservience for blacks. Harriet Beecher Stowe envisioned a second American revolution much like the first which left existing hierarchies of power and property essentially intact, in fact preserving them through strengthening reforms. The end of slavery was an unmitigated good, an indisputable gain for all humanity. Still, one can discern in the Civil War the genius of American politics which, as many have observed, has been the ability to make changes that seem only to confirm the basic order of things. While the Civil War is certainly not what is generally meant by the femininization of America, it may give one pause to reflect that such preservative action, capable of great violence in its protectiveness, has traditionally been the work of women.

As the home of Emerson, Thoreau, Hawthorne, and the Al-
cotts, the very name of Concord, Massachusetts, connotes
sophisticated literary dissent. Yet a month after the publication of *Adventures of Huckleberry Finn*,[1] the committee in
charge of Concord's public library voted to remove the book
from its shelves, fearing that Huck Finn's irreverence would
undermine the morals of young readers. In full agreement,
Louisa May Alcott proposed a more radical ban: "If Mr.
Clemens cannot think of something better to tell our pure-
minded lads and lasses," she advised, "he had best stop writing for them."[2] Jo March would not be allowed to play with
Huck.

Thus far, the banning of *Huckleberry Finn* is a familiar sort
of ironic anecdote whereby Alcott and the cultural guardians
of Concord reveal their moral timidity, their literary obtuse-
ness, or both. But the story does not end here with the self-
exposure of an ostensibly enlightened authority. *Adventures of
Huckleberry Finn* did go on, of course, to become *the* American classic, and generations of children were duly made to
read it. What makes this turnabout remarkable, and unlike the
elevation of, for instance, *Madame Bovary* after it too was to be
banned or, nearer home, the ascension of *Pierre* into a classic
and a cult, is that the canonization of Twain's novel has not involved significant rereading. The *Huckleberry Finn* celebrated
as the archetypal American novel is acclaimed precisely for
being, as the Concord critics charged, "rough, coarse, and in-
elegant," and especially for featuring a hero who lies, uses profanity, and steals besides, a boy who everyone agrees is, as to

class and culture, the "veriest trash." When Bernard DeVoto declared *Adventures of Huckleberry Finn* the preeminent American novel (maybe approached but certainly not surpassed by *Moby-Dick*), he took it as generally understood that jettisoning elegance and refinement through a vernacular narration was the novel's most spectacular achievement.[3] "It is the one book in our literature," Leo Marx noted, "about which highbrows and lowbrows can agree."[4]

Hemingway, announcing that "all modern American literature comes from one book by Mark Twain called *Huckleberry Finn*," dismissed the other possible ancestors—"Emerson, Hawthorne, Whittier, and Company"—for their lack of vulgarity: "All these men were gentlemen, or wished to be. They were all very respectable. They did not use the words that people always have used in speech, the words that survive in language. Nor would you gather that they had bodies. They had minds, yes. Nice, dry, clean minds."[5] Besides Mark Twain, according to Hemingway, there were two other "good writers," Henry James and Stephen Crane. Stephen Crane "wrote two fine stories" but died too young to play a substantial role in the American tradition. Linking James and Twain (never mind that Twain once declared he "would rather be damned to John Bunyan's heaven than read *The Bostonians*")[6] is more than mischievous; for while failing to explain how James escapes the imputation of respectable language, Hemingway consolidates an American way of writing in the image of Mark Twain. Real American writers use real people's real words to tell the down and dirty of carnal lives.

This image of the quintessential American writing as not really literary goes along with a vision of the great American novel as not really literature but rather a sort of spontaneous telling of unmediated experience. In the same passage Hemingway explains that he has never been able to read Thoreau for being unable to read "literary" naturalists, only those who are "extremely accurate." "There ain't nothing more to write about, and I am rotten glad of it," remarks Huck at the end of his story, "because if I'd knowed what a trouble it was to make a book I wouldn't a tackled it and ain't agoing to no more" (912). And the famous last two sentences of the novel complete the picture: "But I reckon I got to light out for the territory ahead of the rest, because Aunt Sally she's going to adopt me and sivilize me and I can't stand it. I been there before." "I been there before" looks straight at the Concord Library Committee. The gentlemen and ladies of the committee have not got it wrong: Huck sets himself against respectability not in boyish innocence but knowingly, in fact like Hemingway.

How does a work justly seen to reject the achievements and values of high culture come to be the high culture's favored self-representation? It happens all the time that works of art are reviled when they are produced and later celebrated. But these recuperations turn on transformed understandings. The avant-garde looks iconoclastic to its age but the next recognizes it as, on the contrary, a reformation. The icons were false idols; their smashing purified the faith. A 1993 retrospective essay on Roy Lichtenstein's Pop painting observes: "That those very early pictures in his signature style had anything to do with high style wasn't, at first, easy to see. They just looked like comics."[7] But Mark Twain's comedy always looked seriously defiant of high style.

While latter-day readers, careless of Huck's profanity and even of his tendency to "borrow" the occasional chicken and watermelon, differ that way from his contemporaries, Twain's audiences overall have always held to the literary faith. Unlike Huck, who lost all interest in Moses upon learning that the baby in the bulrushes was long grown up and gone, readers of *Huckleberry Finn* generally take great "stock in dead people" (626). The issue here is not the rejection of the traditional culture of books, this being a common motif of modernist writing. "What would we really know the meaning of?" asked Emerson sweeping aside the long descent of erudition. "The meal in the firkin; the milk in the pan; the ballad in the street; the news of the boat; the glance of the eye; the form and gait of the body."[8] Though he was indubitably "very respectable," Emerson anticipated Hemingway's preference for a quotidian and experience-based speech by a century. But Hemingway was probably right in implying that the sage of Concord would not therefore have embraced the style of *Huckleberry Finn*. For the simplicity and directness of idiom Emerson recommended and sought in his own writing was an ideal that actual vernaculars fulfilled little more than did conventional formalities.

In short, neither enlightenment nor retrospection elevates the style or the philosophy of *Huckleberry Finn*'s narrator into the high culture that has placed the work itself at its pinnacle. It might be argued that Huck's cultural authority is limited in that readers often exactly reverse his judgments—for instance, his judgment of the humbug Colonel Grangerford, who mightily impresses the naive Huck. But even as we overturn Huck's misunderstandings, we nonetheless endorse his more fundamental morality, which, indeed, eventually inspires his disillusionment with the whole senselessly violent Grangerford clan. Huck's lapses in authority thus do not mitigate the force of his challenge to the high culture, nor the puzzle of the high culture's embrace of his challenge. Let us be clear about this: Dickens wrote popular classics; the vernacular *Huckleberry Finn* is better described as a *populist* classic, a work animated by its defiance of high culture.[9]

It is possible that its anomaly is the source of the other peculiarity of

Twain's novel, the fact that, despite its established status, it has been exceptionally controversial. *The Scarlet Letter, Moby-Dick* (once people learned how to read it), *Portrait of a Lady, Absalom, Absalom!*, to name four works likely to appear on any list of great American novels, are about controversial issues but have not been particularly controversial in themselves. Controversial at its publication, *Huckleberry Finn* is again today, and has been for the past twenty years. Indeed, it is undergoing a second period of banning, this time for conforming too much to convention in a racist portrait of the slave Jim. *Moby-Dick* and *Absalom, Absalom!* contain similarly offensive characters and events but they have not been cited. Perhaps *Huckleberry Finn's* racism is more flagrant; but its targeting, given the rich possibilities for identifying racist writing among the classics, probably responds also to its availability.

Moby-Dick clearly refers to *King Lear* and *Absalom, Absalom!* to the biblical story of the son of David. These are elevating references that lend authority to everyone concerned by identifying the authors, the novels, and their audiences with high culture. The burlesque Shakespeare in *Huckleberry Finn* does require its readers to know enough to recognize that the speeches recited by the duke and the dauphin are a senseless pastiche (of *Macbeth* and *Richard III* along with *Hamlet*), thus to be themselves and to recognize that the novel is of a higher culture than Huck.[10] At the same time, any burlesque lowers its object. Twain's work *is* irreverent, and its lack of respectability is more precisely a lack of respect. It is perhaps only fair that its readers take their cue from it and treat *it* without reverence. No one feels compelled to grant *Huckleberry Finn* artistic license, as many do, for instance, *The Merchant of Venice,* with even Jews interpreting Shylock as an exposure of anti-Semitism rather than condemn Shakespeare.

Huckleberry Finn's lack of respect seems to have rendered it less sacrosanct than is common with classics; yet it has achieved, in Jonathan Arac's term, a state of "hypercanonization."[11] Its banning is no surprise and not unreasonably, but simultaneously it is the country's official text. What does it say about America that is so telling, and how does its peculiar dissonant voice enter into what it tells?

• • •

I want to propose that dissonance *is* the message of *Huckleberry Finn.* On one level, this message is intentional or conscious and represents Mark Twain's understanding of the world of Hannibal, Missouri, and late-nineteenth-century America. Much of nineteenth-century literature projects a similar vision of contradictions in the national culture. But Twain's novel is not only about contradiction, it is itself radically contradictory—so dissonant, indeed, that it finally fails to represent the contradictions it means to address. At a deeper level than Twain controls, the great American novel is itself literally incoherent. *Adventures of Huckleberry Finn* sounds the contradictions of American culture so deeply that the novel drowns in them, collapsing at the end into embarrassing slapstick and bad writing.

This final collapse has received considerable critical attention, which we will look at shortly. But before considering the explanations that have been offered, let me point to just the experience of reading through *Huckleberry Finn* and into its drastic decline. While the plot ends comically, the degeneration of the work evokes in the reader, on the contrary, something on the order of tragedy. One feels oneself in the presence of an artistic fatality. And since it is the work in itself that ends tragically, there is no catharsis: having exposed contradiction to an ultimate clarity, *Huckleberry Finn* stands witness to the impossibility of any acceptable resolution. It is, I think, this experience of artistic fatality at the close of the novel, following on the brilliant life of the preceding pages, that has rendered Twain's classic the most widely compelling of American classics and at the same time the most frequently and harshly attacked. *Huckleberry Finn* has been throughout its history peculiarly unsettling for being itself so unsettled.

It is unsettled, of course, for good reason, over issues its readers can no more resolve than could Mark Twain, for at the core of the contradictions that finally rend *Huckleberry Finn* is the ideal of individual freedom. The conflict between this ideal, which is fundamental to the nation's founding philosophy, and the founders' tolerance, in some cases their endorsement, of slavery needs no explication. *Huckleberry Finn* is about that conflict. It was written, however, not while that conflict was still clearly inscribed in the law of the land but after two events had greatly obscured it. First, the Civil War legally emancipated the slaves and in the judgment of many redressed the founding error; then Reconstruction failed to establish the conditions that would realize this emancipation, so that the former slaves returned to a servitude from which it would require a different sort of intervention to free them than any declaration. This new intervention would have to be positive, not only severing the bond of slavery but reconnecting the former slaves and masters in mutually responsible relations. Social responsibilities, however, tend by the definition of self-reliant individualism to come into conflict with both the theory and the practice of personal freedom. *Huckleberry Finn* is not only about slavery and the nation's compromised past but also, and in my view principally, about the contemporary dilemma of Reconstruction.

In a sentence, the two principal characters, Huck and Jim, represent the two sides of the dilemma: Huck strikes out for an absolute freedom, while Jim requires, in order to gain his own freedom, that Huck qualify his freedom by entering into the pursuit of Jim's. Signs that these two definitions of freedom pull the story in different directions are evident from the beginning, but their opposition becomes unmistakable at a fork in both the novel's plot and its physical terrain, as if the author had prefigured the trajectory of the work's own unfolding or were producing, along with his story, an allegory of its writing.[12] The fork, of course, is the meeting of the Mississippi and the Ohio where, I will now try to show, individual freedom for Huck reveals itself to be as different from what it is for Jim as North differs from South.

• • •

Very briefly, at the beginning of the story, freedom appears to be a single concept, in fact one that can unite individuals as different as black and white. And at this point, social engagement, defined globally as living inside society, is also a single concept that joins quite disparate persons in a generalized servitude. That civilization imprisons is not an unfamiliar theme in American literature, nor is the complementary theme of running away into nature. Escaping, Huck from family and Jim from society, they come together on the island and for the next six chapters forge an alliance of free individuals so without contradiction that it even recuperates the benefits of social engagement without its burdens. For in the first chapters, Jim and Huck have freedom in nature and live at home too. Forgotten are the tensions that had begun to emerge at the start of the story when Tom and Huck played practical tricks that shamed Jim. Instead, on an evening soon after they join forces on the island, with thunder rolling overhead and the rain coming down in sheets, Huck observes, "Jim this is nice, . . . I wouldn't want to be nowhere else but here. Pass me along another hunk of fish and some hot corn-bread." They have "got home all safe" (674).

Moreover, the next two chapters prove Jim's and Huck's home-bond solid *and* proof against society, as when Huck famously rushes back from reconnoitering the situation back in St. Petersburg to join Jim in his runaway status, "Git up and hump yourself, Jim! There ain't a minute to lose. They're after us!" (685). And when they set out downriver, the raft is itself an idyllic home for which the river and the farms along its shores provide a cornucopia of waterfowl, chickens, watermelons, mushmelons, pumpkins, corn, and other "things of that kind" (689). But already a complication is emerging in the simple opposition between nature (natural human relations) and society. To

Jim, a wrecked steamboat in their path seems best left alone; he cites the wisdom of heaven in support of his own down-to-earth good sense: "We's doing' blame' well, en we better let blame' well alone, as de good book says"
(690). But Huck answers to another authority: "Do you think Tom Sawyer
would ever go by this thing? Not for pie, he wouldn't. He'd call it an adventure . . . and he'd land on that wreck if it was his last act. . . . Why, you'd think
it was Christopher C'lumbus discovering Kingdom Come." "I wish," concludes Huck, "Tom Sawyer *was* here" (690). The problem is that Tom Sawyer
is there, in spirit, a spirit difficult to reconcile with the spirit of Jim and Huck's
antisociety.

Something new becomes apparent in this dispute: Huck's entire acquiescence, for all his social discomfort, in cultural conventions. Up to this point,
only his rebellious side has been visible. Now Huck reveals what will become
fully evident (in his admiration, for instance, of the Grangerford's parlor) as a
totally uncritical acceptance of the established culture. A conventionalism as
instinctive as his rebellion, as well as the way this duality endangers Jim,
emerges in the incident of the wreck. Huck wins this argument and boards
the wreck, placing Jim, whose flight from society has nothing to do with adventure but with its opposite, survival, in dire peril.

This first time, however, the peril passes. Although Huck's tomfoolery
briefly loses them the raft, the two runaways soon regain it and their unity,
which grows even stronger. They now make Cairo the goal of the voyage; at
this town on the river fork, Huck explains, "we would sell the raft and get on
a steamboat and go way up the Ohio amongst the free States, and then be out
of trouble" (704). Associating legal freedom with being out of trouble implies
a newly political interpretation of Huck's rebellion, of course, and here the
novel briefly adumbrates an internal social critique rather than a blanket rejection of society as such. As long as Huck and Jim have a common goal, the
novel is inevitably political and cannot restrict itself to styles and mores.

The raft on which Huck and Jim float naked frees Huck from the itchiness
of new clothes and Jim from shackles. The larger significance of Huck's bid
for freedom in this first part of the novel comes willy-nilly from its association
with Jim's escape. Withdrawing from slavery is not like withdrawing from the
world, which leaves the world unchanged. A successful escape from slavery
defeats it in that instance and in that way changes the world. The two runaways don't just leave Hannibal; as Huck guiltily realizes when Jim, anticipat-
ing his own freedom, begins to plot the escape of his two children, helping
Jim subverts Mississippi society internally. Involvement is unavoidable: there is
no world elsewhere, not the raft or the island to which Huck escapes with a

cache of supplies and the dispossessed Jim with nothing. In the first part of the journey, the raft is not yet an alternative world but a world in opposition, instrumental to a political act and something to sell in exchange for still more useful steamboat tickets; nor is the Mississippi yet Nature but a particular river set in a political geography and to be left for the better-sited Ohio. Up to this point, therefore, until Huck and Jim run past Cairo, their escape connotes something very like a revolution.

In his classic essay entitled "Mr. Eliot, Mr. Trilling, and *Huckleberry Finn*" and addressing the problem of the ending, Leo Marx argued that when the raft floats past the mouth of the Ohio, the novel begins a long moral and political retreat from the rebellion that had inspired it and suffers a "failure of nerve." The trip downriver, Marx stresses, is "*away* from St. Petersburg," home of slave owners, pious hypocrites, petty tyrants, and abusive fathers. The road to freedom starts off down the Mississippi but takes a sharp left at the Ohio. When they miss this turn, Huck and Jim are heading due south, toward the heartland of slavery. It is only logical, Marx goes on, that at the end of *this* journey, Huck reconnects with Tom and surrenders both his moral and common sense to Tom's extravagant but entirely conventional fantasies. The political realities that had driven Huck and Jim to escape St. Petersburg fade out to be replaced by a hodgepodge of romances whose single unifying theme is the glory of Tom the Hero. To that glory, Jim's dignity is the first sacrifice and his very life could at any moment follow. Huck's dignity too is forfeit and, for Marx, so is the novel's when it ends in duplicity.

Now, there is little to dispute, I think, over the political offensiveness of Jim's reenslavement on the Phelps farm. This is especially apparent to a current reader, but insofar as the preceding chapters have revealed Jim's full-fledged manhood, his humiliation at the hands of the increasingly idiotic Tom must have made unpleasant reading at any time. Indeed, Jim's diminution thins the very fabric of the novel in that his reduction to an object of the two boys' connivance saps a linguistic agency that has been a major part of the novel's verbal wealth. In the often-cited dispute that ends with Huck's withdrawal because "you can't learn a nigger to argue," the essence of the humor and of the linguistic agility from which it arises comes from the reader's recognition that Jim has in fact won the argument. His syllogism proving that it makes no sense for a Frenchman to speak French demonstrates an exemplary logic. The premise is that all men speak English. "Is a Frenchman a man?" Jim asks. The answer being yes, then "why doan' he *talk* like a man?" (703). The premise is false, to be sure. But this is merely an error, not a fallacy; like Jim's superstitions in general, and unlike the prejudices of St. Petersburg worthies, the wrong premise reflects a superficial ignorance and does not impugn Jim's good sense. The incident reveals Huck's inability to argue, not Jim's.

But once returned to slavery, Jim seems incapacitated on even the most obvious points. His cabin filled with a slapstick assortment of rats, spiders, and snakes according to Tom's ideas of romantic imprisonment, Jim protests feebly and always in vain. For that matter, Huck is no more persuasive himself, as when he fails to carry an argument with Tom that there is no need to saw off the leg of the bed to free Jim's chain when it is perfectly easy to lift the bed and slip the chain off. The only absurd measure not taken is called off by Tom himself, who upon reflection decides not to saw off *Jim's* leg because "there ain't necessity enough for it" (859). The destruction of Jim is complete when at the end of one chapter devoted entirely to Tom's harebrained schemes, Jim finally rebels only to apologize when "Tom most lost all patience with him": "So Jim said he was sorry, and said he wouldn't behave so no more" (884). The problem is that, entirely submissive to Tom, Jim no longer exists *for the novel* anymore than he does for himself; and Huck is not in much better shape.

But how did Jim and Huck slide to this ending from that beginning? We saw the first slip earlier in the incident of the wreck, which revealed a conflict between Huck's quest and Jim's, the former being to escape society, the latter to escape to a better society. The components of the conflict as they emerge at the wreck are, on one side, Huck's acceptance of Tom Sawyer culture, this in tandem with his impulse to free himself from culture as such and from the set of life paths that culture projects, in short from all plots, and, on the other side, Jim's need to plot his life in minute detail, so that stepping anywhere to the side of his life path, for instance onto the wreck, is potentially fatal. At Cairo this conflict comes to a head and shows itself more radical than any political disagreement: Jim's path diverges not from Huck's path but from his *pathlessness.*

The incidents at the river fork are well known. Just as the raft's occupants are reluctantly admitting that they may have missed Cairo in the fog, a monstrous steamboat bears down on them coming upriver from the South. That a huge "black cloud" suddenly appears on the raft's horizon and resolves into a behemoth armed with "a long row of wide-open furnace doors shining like red-hot teeth" (717) just at the plot's moment of truth requires no comment. Twain, the novel, and the characters are all headed toward a potentially fatal crisis: one or the other of the two *Huckleberry Finns* currently drifting along together will have to be sacrificed, either the story of Huck's escape or the story of Jim's. When the boat smashes through the raft, therefore, "Jim went overboard on one side and I on the other" (717).

As this moment of truth approaches, Huck is in an agony of indecision.

Moments before, Jim's happy cry that they have reached their destination "went through me like a shot, and I thought if it *was* Cairo I reckoned I would die of miserableness" (711). He feels "so mean and miserable I most wished I was dead" at the thought that he has now done it—he has helped Jim steal himself from a "poor old woman" who had "tried to be good to [Huck] every way she knowed how." He is tortured by the sense that at Cairo he becomes irremediably *engaged:* Jim is now talking about returning to St. Petersburg later, possibly to steal his children from slavery, "children that belonged to a man I didn't even known," "a man," Huck broods guiltily, "that hadn't ever done me no harm" (712). His better instincts prevail, of course, and immediately thereafter he finds himself protecting Jim from slave hunters. When Jim, from his fundamentally different perspective, thanks Huck and calls him "de ole true Huck; de on'y white genlman dat ever kep' his promise to ole Jim" (712), he identifies Huck's problem exactly, namely that the association with an escaping slave is turning Huck into a reformer, a true white gentleman in a false genteel society.

But the hunters go off and Huck returns to the raft "feeling bad and low, because I knowed very well I had done wrong" (714). He is not a reformer; on the contrary, his rejection of society as such undercuts any more local criticisms. He performs all his brave acts on behalf of Jim out of his own desire for absolute freedom, not out of any antislavery conviction. The humor and pathos in the passage depend on the reader's recognition that Huck has done absolutely right. That he has done right while confronting an overwhelming social force for wrong is heroic; but it is also indecisive. He has succeeded in keeping things in suspense, with Jim and himself still runaways. Huck's unaware moral rectitude is also a state of suspense, however we may approve it, for at least part of our approval devolves on his personal disaffection while what it implies about social action remains uncertain. Huck's insurgency never aspires to establish itself; it wishes not to become established. Huck has no ambition to change the world; he just cannot live in it.

The fork of the Mississippi and the Ohio in *Huckleberry Finn* represents an archetypal American choice between uncompromised individualism and responsible citizenship. Or more precisely, it forces the recognition that there is an absolute choice to be made between the two, that, contrary to some accounts of individualism at work for the improvement of society, one cannot be both. Huck's pursuit of individualism takes him into the deep South in the company of a runaway slave he has therefore failed to help free. The steamboat that smashes the raft at Cairo is headed right back to St. Petersburg. The pastoral idyll is over, and Jim and Huck are no longer bound on a common quest.

Huckleberry Finn is Huck's book, not Jim's. It starts out as a comedy, an "As You Like It" with a hero drawn from the bottom of society rather than the top. But whereas the Forest of Arden is to be the setting for the reform of society, the world of the raft becomes an alternative to St. Petersburg, not its better self. While "As You Like It" implies, in the journey away from a corrupt court, a restorative return, *Huckleberry Finn* would imagine returning, either north or south, either toward freedom or slavery, only as defeat. Thus, it threatens to end as a tragedy. The ending, which returns Jim to slavery and Huck to the domesticity of the Phelps household and his role as Tom's sidekick, replaces a possible tragedy by a second version of the comedic beginning. This then concludes the same way as the first beginning, with Huck's escape and in fact Jim's as well. The circle overcomes the threatening line of the river plot, which can only lead in the South to tragedy and in the North to a social involvement that would be equally annihilative for Huck. Hemingway's praise for *Huckleberry Finn* extended only to the point of Jim's recapture; the rest, he thought, was "just cheating." It is cheating, in that Jim's prior emancipation obviates the thorny problem of freeing him in the South. It is also probably a failure of nerve and even a defeat, as Marx contends, in its abandonment of the challenge to racism. But through those very failures, the ending reaffirms the morality of an individual commitment to freedom in the face of society's entrapments and to transcendent truths against the world's inevitable duplicities.[13]

Moreover, the ending is disturbing because it is all three: a cheat, a defeat, and an affirmation, and makes their connection too evident for philosophical comfort. Through this ending rather than despite it, *Huckleberry Finn* uncovers a contradiction that is not as visible in other major novels. It is not absolutely clear that Ahab *has* to drown the entire crew of the *Pequod* to fulfill his individual vision; and it is the less clear in that he is himself drowned. But the necessity of sacrificing Jim's freedom to Huck's independence is inscribed in the novel's very geography, in the river fork that heads one way to Jim's emancipation and the other to the continuation of Huck's outsider status. When in the end Jim too is freed, this further frees Huck, for Jim's reenslavement would have embroiled his friend in continuing guilt. Freed through no act either of his own or of Huck's, Jim embroils Huck in neither history nor future obligation.

• • •

The steamboat comes crashing through the raft in full symbolic throttle and elicits a commensurately resonant reaction: "I dived," Huck explains, "and I aimed to find the bottom, too, for a thirty-foot wheel had got to go over me, and I wanted it to have plenty of room" (717). From this dive he resurfaces alone and drifts with the current, which now heads toward shore. Landing near a log cabin, he feints a continuation of his flight but it is for now at an end: "I was going to rush by and get away but a lot of dogs jumped out and went to howling and barking at me, and I knowed better than to move another peg" (718). Huck has reentered the world and, contrary to Hemingway, Marx, and the tradition that sees the ending as a sudden debacle, his encounter with the society centered in this log cabin already marks his return to the world of St. Petersburg.

This version of St. Petersburg centers on male violence but as the complement, not the opposite, of female domesticity. The Grangerfords greet Huck with guns at the ready until they determine that he is not associated with their arch-enemies, the Shepherdsons, whereupon they embrace him as family. Calling off dogs and guns, the Grangerford patriarch "told me to make myself easy and at home," and home is the province of the Grangerford matriarch, "the sweetest old gray-headed lady," who takes over: "The poor thing's as wet as he can be," she chides her husband, and "it may be he's hungry." The Grangerford girls are made to run around and get him something to eat while Buck, a boy just about Huck's size, age, and name, is instructed to "take this little stranger and get the wet clothes off from him and dress him up in some of yours that's dry" (720–21). Huck is back with Miss Watson and Tom, with a twist: the murderous father is no longer the outcast pap but a magisterial colonel. This father does not threaten his own son, but he kills sons he designates as enemy as ruthlessly as ever pap did. In fact, Grangerford is only more successful in bringing about the death of his sons: three of an original six have already been killed in the family feud. The opposite of pap, the Colonel is also pap come back as his own ideal fantasy.

"Col. Grangerford was a gentleman," Huck begins his description. "He was well born, as the saying is, and that's worth as much in a man as it is in a horse, so the Widow Douglas said, and nobody ever denied that she was of the first aristocracy in our town; and pap he always said it, too." As prepossessing in his linen suit "so white it hurt your eyes to look at it" as pap was disreputable in his rags, Grangerford has perfected the art of the menacing temper. He gets the kind of respect in seconds that eludes pap in hours of rampaging: "When [the Colonel] turned into a cloud-bank it was awful dark for a half a minute and that was enough; there wouldn't nothing go wrong again for a week" (728). Grangerford is also a drinker, starting at breakfast when his two eldest sons mix him his first glass of bitters. As irrational and deadly in his hatreds as pap, the Colonel is far more dangerous. The society in which Huck lands just the other side of the Ohio fork is a corrected version of St. Petersburg, its flaws perfected and made fully operative. So once again fleeing for his life, Huck regains the river, the raft, and Jim. Drifting down the Mississippi, they hang up their lantern and celebrate exactly as they had earlier. Jim cooks up "corn-dodgers and buttermilk, and pork and cabbage, and greens . . . and whilst I eat my supper we talked, and had a good time." They've gotten away again. "We said there warn't no home like a raft, after all. Other places do seem so cramped up and smothery. You feel mighty free and easy and comfortable on a raft" (739).

Except that every minute the raft floats deeper into slave territory. As the journey proceeds, the best Jim and Huck can hope for is not to arrive anywhere; it is now that life on the raft becomes idyllic. Jim and Huck go naked and lie about dangling their feet in the water, smoking their pipes and talking "about all kinds of things." To avoid being apprehended, they travel at night and tie up days under sheltering banks in an Edenic landscape of "song-birds just going it," cool breezes, and sweet smells. In the midst of a lyrical description of this enchanted world, Twain suddenly pulls back to caution that the smells wafting from land are not always sweet "because they've left dead fish laying around, gars, and such, and they do get pretty rank" (740). This touch of realism only underlines its suppression as the runaways run toward their prisons.

But the idyll does not last. While Twain seems to keep his eyes averted from the Deep South looming ahead as determinedly as Jim and Huck, he is nonetheless clearly worried. The duke and the dauphin are commonly taken to represent Twain's increasingly uncertain hold on his story.[14] At a loss about how to restore some sort of reasonable purpose to the journey downriver ("Goodness sakes, would a runaway nigger run *south?*" retorts Huck when queried about Jim's status), Twain, according to this reading, gave up on Jim and Huck as captains and handed the tiller to two new characters who would at least provide new topics of conversation and occasion some diversionary adventures. The duke and the dauphin do qualify as replacements in that they too are runaways; in fact, when Huck first hears the sounds of the chase he is certain he is himself the target, "for whenever anybody was after anybody I judged it was *me*—or maybe Jim" (742). The new escapees, however, have been forced to flee by their own duplicity, not society's, and they bring this redoubled duplicity to the raft.

Already in the Grangerford episode, Twain had focused on fakery. The gentlemen in that episode kill one another without reason and the ladies weep as senselessly, both acting out a debased cultural script. The duke and the dauphin are the proper poets of such a society. Emmeline Grangerford's odes to death expose the superficiality of the conventional culture but not the corruption in its depths. To plumb those depths we need a longer fish line, as it were a measure for measure, a standard in the measure of the outrage: the quintessential standard, Shakespeare. The duke and the dauphin make their first fraudulent foray from the raft bearing a sham Shakespeare. Hamlet's soliloquy is the classic of high writing in Anglo-American literature. Bilgewater explains to the king, who has never heard of it, "Hamlet's soliloquy, you know; the most celebrated thing in Shakespeare. Ah, it's sublime, sublime!" (757). The English classic of classics is appropriately invoked in the American classic of classics—invoked and burlesqued, which brings our discussion back to the issue of *Huckleberry Finn*'s irreverence.

For while the counterfeit soliloquy exposes Bilgewater's own falseness, the burlesque inevitably bleeds onto the real thing. It is difficult after reading the duke's speech not to laugh a little at Shakespeare's. By a sort of Gresham's law of literature, parody has a tendency to drive out the authentic, or at least to demote it. Once the duke has taken hold of *Hamlet* and shown that the tragedy of moral compunction can be adapted to the purpose of a comic imposture, the demolition of conventional and traditional culture begun in St. Petersburg with Huck's telling commentaries on the Old Testament, continued in the Grangerford parlor (where Huck sums up *Pilgrim's Progress* as being "about a man that left his family it didn't say why" [724], an accurate and devastating account), is complete. In this work of literature, finally, there is nothing to be hoped for from literature.

Not surprisingly, the episode of the Shakespeare burlesque also contains what may be finally the most disturbing incident in the novel, although oddly, as Forrest Robinson, who has dealt with it at length, points out, it has received little critical attention.[15] Huck and his companions land at a small town called Bricksville to hold a "Shaksperean Revival!!!"[16] Bricksville is the grimmest of the river settlements Huck visits. Little luxury has been displayed elsewhere, but the houses of St. Petersburg, for instance, had a certain snugness and comfort. In Bricksville, "the stores and houses was most all old shackly dried-up frame concerns that hadn't ever been painted"; a failure at mastering the accoutrements of civilization, the town is no better at harnessing the energies of nature: "The houses had little gardens around them, but they didn't seem to raise hardly anything in them but jimpson weeds, and sunflowers, and ash-piles, and old curled-up boots and shoes, and pieces of bottles, and rags, and played-out tin-ware." In front of the stores that have produced this sterile refuse, the people lounging are even more blighted than their town. Long conversations unfold on such themes as chewing tobacco, as follows: "'Gimme a chaw' v tobacker, Hank.' 'Cain't—I ain't got but one chaw left. Ask Bill.'" These exchanges can wax witty, as when the donor of a "chaw" considers the quantity returned and quips: "Here, gimme the *chaw*, and you take the *plug*." Twain's humor is here particularly agile in turning on the feebleness of the joke. At the same time, nothing is more damning to a character in a work of wit than displaying his lack of it. The inhabitants of Bricksville are the dregs of a never impressive world.

One of the few entertainments life in Bricksville affords is the monthly drunken spree of old Boggs, a cantankerous but wholly harmless codger everyone even in that town takes humorously. Huck encounters Boggs lurching about threatening to kill everyone he meets but especially Colonel Sherburn, the owner of the biggest store in town and "a heap the best dressed" as well. When Boggs begins boozily to insult Sherburn, the Colonel unexpectedly takes it all seriously and threatens to kill the drunken fool if he does not cease his rantings forever after one o'clock that day. Out of control with drink and stupidity, Boggs is quite unable to quit and Sherburn carries out his threat, Boggs pleading, "O Lord, don't shoot!" a pathos reinforced by the cries of Boggs's young daughter, who runs weeping to throw herself on her dying father.

All this naturally riles up the lethargic populace, who now threaten to lynch the murderer. Contemptuously facing this mob, Sherburn delivers an oddly ambiguous speech. The Colonel begins ("slow and scornful," observes Huck): "The idea of *you* lynching anybody! It's amusing. The idea of you thinking you had pluck enough to lynch a *man*. . . . Why, a *man's* safe in the hands of ten thousand of your kind—as long as it's day-time and you're not behind him." As he warms to his harangue, the remarkable thing is that Twain clearly does too, to the point that Henry Nash Smith suggested Sherburn is the only character in the book besides Huck with whom Twain seems to identify, animating the speech with his own sentiments.

> Do I know you? [Sherburn asks the crowd.] I know you clear through. I was born and raised in the South, and I've lived in the North; so I know the average all around. The average man's a coward. In the North he lets anybody walk over him that wants to, and goes home and prays for a humble spirit to bear it. In the South one man, all by himself, has stopped a stage full of men, in the day-time, and robbed the lot. Your newspapers call you a brave people so much that you think you *are* braver than any other people—whereas you're

just *as* brave, and no braver. Why don't your juries hang murderers? Because they're afraid the man's friends will shoot them in the back, in the dark—and it's just what they *would* do.

There is more in this vein until, having declared that "the pitifulest thing out is a mob," Sherburn waves it away and "the crowd washed back sudden, and then broke all apart and went tearing off every which way."

Sherburn's speech (the murder seems to be just its pretext) enters the story without preamble and ends without aftermath. It seems disconnected from the plot, a sort of rupture in the narrative as if some impulse that could neither be contained nor translated into a plausible addition to the story had overtaken Twain and he had blurted it out. This impression is strengthened by the fact that the speech rings with conviction and is, against one's expectations and principles, entirely persuasive. When he delivers this attack on the cowardice of the average man, Sherburn has just killed a helpless buffoon. He does not defend this murder; he does not even mention it. Instead, he accuses the mob of being unable to carry out its own murders. An incident in which a rich and powerful man has claimed and exercised the right to kill at will anyone weaker than he ends with his denouncing his inferiors; and the novel approves of him.

I would read Sherburn's speech as a soliloquy inspired by the proximity of Hamlet's, and the Nietzschean accents of Sherburn's speech as a response to the decadence of cultural value represented by the duke's travesty. Hamlet, who also lives in a corrupt world, finds conscience a source of cowardice, reflection an impediment to action. Sherburn denounces a world where an absence of moral conviction makes cowards who are indecisive only because they wait for others to tell them what to do. Hamlet shies from "enterprises of great pitch and moment" out of an excess of complexity; Sherburn kills his man, not a fratricidal king but a foolish lout, in simple rage. Nothing in the universe of the duke's travesty or in the degenerate village that is to be its stage can command humanity or even common decency. In that context, untrammeled and unmediated by any traditional system of values, Twain speaks through two characters, one an outcast, the other a strongman. This is another side of the same contradiction that paralyzes Twain at the fork at Cairo, between a vision of uncompromised personal integrity and another of moral effectiveness in society.

Sherburn is a merchant and a military man, a double pillar of society—but in a society that does not deserve to be supported. On the contrary, it merits being brought crashing down, for all the reasons Huck has been exposing through the incidents of his journey. This is not a reformable society; one can only curse it and leave. Sherburn curses it and stays, and Twain finds himself approving the cursing and not knowing what to think of the staying. Does he see something of his own situation in Sherburn's furious isolation among idiots and knaves? Sherburn, moreover, is not merely an inhabitant of society; as storekeeper and military man, he is presumably one of those who shape it. In Huck, Twain depicts on the contrary someone who has no power at all. Homeless and a child, soon an orphan, Huck is a complete outsider. The real question is not whether he will leave society but whether he will enter it and to what end? From his ontological distance, Huck looks at the world of men with natural detachment. At his most critical he feels "ashamed of the human race" (784). Instead, Sherburn sets about shaming the damned human race, inveighing against an odious weakness to its face, hating its inescapable presence. The murder of Boggs, who is in Sherburn's eyes the lowest representation of humanity, expresses that hatred: he tells Boggs to be gone, but Boggs stays and Sherburn can't stand his presence another moment. What Sherburn cannot do is himself leave, so as to be, like Huck, peacefully and even compassionately ashamed of the human race—away from it.

Robinson treats the Sherburn episode as an instance of acute bad faith in which the townspeople abandon their moral responsibilities to the ferociously individualistic Sherburn. His speech, according to Robinson, is a jeremiad and to that extent proffers certain truths. Bad faith, however, is reciprocal and Sherburn for his part seeks from his audience confirmation that he is beyond them. I disagree only on this last point. The bad faith of the Bricksville mob is evident, but Sherburn's may not be. There is too little dramatic development in the scene to indicate that he is drawing his self-image from the mob. Indeed, as Robinson observes, critics have generally dealt with Sherburn by complaining that his speech is aesthetically unintegrated into the novel. The harangue stands out by its departure from Huck's idiom, although he is presumably its reporter. This failure to translate Sherburn's speech into Huck's language seems to me to reflect an incompatibility between the two. Nor is Sherburn as a character any better able to enter *Huckleberry Finn*. Instead, the speech and the Colonel bespeak an authorial position outside the novel from or against which the novel may be written but which cannot itself be encompassed. As a part of the novel's world, Sherburn's position, that since the average man is a petty coward sneaking about in fear of his worthless life, killing one is good riddance, would invalidate Huck's moral dilemma and collapse the novel into a diatribe.[17] Indeed, Sherburn's town of Bricksville owes its extreme dreariness, beyond not only the necessity but also the possibility of mockery, I would suggest, to the extremity of Sherburn's vision.

It is also impossible in the Mississippi River towns through which Huck and Jim journey to imagine being a hero. This in turn makes Sherburn a cold-blooded killer and Huck a saint (and Tom a fool). Let me repeat that as a saint, however, Huck is no more bent on social reform, no more optimistic about it, than is Sherburn. That is, his radical liberalism, not unlike Emerson's, is also conservative. He never reacts to social iniquities by imagining them reformed; they appear to him natural, ineluctable parts of a system as fixed as the system of nature. You either stay inside the system, bathe every day and wear tight collars, or you leave. Colonel Sherburn has stayed inside and the recognition that the bathwater is dirty causes him unendurable disgust. In Sherburn's soliloquy, irreverence has turned to bitter revulsion.

Though extraneous, the Sherburn episode marks a turning point. The Shakespeare fraud does little overt harm to anyone in the story. It is a second-degree fraud, an opportunistic deceit exploiting real and therefore more dire vulnerabilities in the people it cons. To Jim's astonishment that "dese kings o' ourn is regular rapscallions," Huck explains calmly that "it's in the breed. . . . all kings is mostly rapscallions." Huck has read history: "Look at Henry the Eight; this'n 's a Sunday-School Superintendent to *him*. And look at Charles the Second, and Louis Fourteen, and Louis Fifteen, and James Second, and Edward Second, and Richard Third, and forty more; besides all them Saxon heptarchies that used to rip around so in old times and raise Cain" (775). Compared with these, he concludes, the duke and the king "ain't nothing" (776). But their next exploit, as if this one had been an overture, *is* something and sets its own standard.

The Wilks family are good people; though others have been good to Huck, like Miss Watson and the Grangerfords, they have been clearly implicated in bad things. One touchstone of the Wilkses' real goodness is their grief at the sale of their slaves. Twain never undercuts Mary Jane's sincerity when she tearfully tells Huck that "she didn't know *how* she was ever going to be happy . . . knowing the [slave] mother and the children warn't ever going to see each other no more" (807). "Miss Mary Jane," says Huck, "you can't abear to see people in trouble and *I* can't—most always." The humor comes from Huck's wry self-awareness and implies no qualification of the girl's kindness.

On the other side, the king and the duke wax seriously evil; indeed, the long Wilks episode is not funny. Had a lawyer named Levi Bell, a precursor of Puddn'head Wilson, not intervened, the outcome would have been dark in the measure of Sherburn's misanthropy—darker, in that in Sherburn's world there are no good people to be ruined. In the Wilkses' world, however, the good people are as powerless as the cowards in Bricksville. The helpless lambs offer no hope of betterment; they only measure its absence. Huck and Jim had left St. Petersburg with high hopes of freedom that are badly set back at Cairo. The Wilks episode ends in the utter defeat of these hopes. There seems to be no way to escape the duke and the king, who now on the contrary complete their takeover by turning in Jim. The rest we have already discussed. Jim's captivity is paralleled by Huck's in thrall to Tom.

It is on the very verge of collapse of all possibility of freedom that Huck places his highest bid for it. Indeed, Jim has already been recaptured when Huck finds himself at last making the decision Twain had not been able to make at Cairo: "It was a close place," he realizes. "I was a trembling, because I'd got to decide, forever, betwixt two things, and I knowed it. I studies a minute, sort of holding my breath, and then says to myself: 'All right, then, I'll *go* to hell'" (834–35). Let us say the obvious: Twain has chosen the route of social engagement when it is too late in the story to take it. Huck has decided he is willing to go to hell, but the harder decision was whether to go to Ohio.

Though he never makes this harder decision, though indeed he evades it in a way that implies he would have been unlikely to choose the Ohio route—unlikely, that is, to write the story so as to indicate this was the right direction—the fact that it emerges as a decision already distinguishes *Huckleberry Finn* from its cohort of great American novels. *Huckleberry Finn* represents the characteristic American theme of the conflict between the individual and society more penetratingly than its peers do: more commonly, the conflict of individual versus society appears only as it does at the very end of *Huckleberry Finn,* not as it does earlier at the fork of the two rivers. Why does *Huckleberry Finn* go deeper? My suggestion has been that precisely its irreverence—the reason it was banned in Concord—uncovers for it a conflict *within* society that is more or less invisible in works such as *Moby-Dick.* The chapter in Melville's novel entitled "Knights and Squires" raises the issue of intrasocial differences but makes nothing of them to qualify the global representativeness of Ahab and Ishmael. The formal, aesthetic, as well as thematic premise of *Huckleberry Finn* is that class difference matters, that in the course of their lives individuals continually encounter forks where their own fate is inextricably joined with that of others they either succor or sacrifice.

For the centuries since it was written and in all the European-engendered cultures of which America's may be the ultimate embodiment, Hamlet's soliloquy is the ideal representation of heroic self-scrutiny and of the examination of one's life in the world. Hamlet, Prince of Denmark, queries his soul in a way that speaks directly to many souls, but not everyone's. One has to be able, reading it, to imagine oneself apart, therefore free to choose one's way of being, yet at the center of things and thus able to choose: a self-image that is actually available only to a minority of people. This limitation is not evident when one reads the soliloquy. On the contrary, reading it at all, one reads it as universally applicable; otherwise one does not read it. One can emerge from the reading in despair at the state of things, disgusted with the world and especially with one's own role in it. But this response is not as radical as it seems or may feel, for the very act of reading and thus manifesting one's place in the community of Hamlets provides a considerable consolation. Reading and understanding *Hamlet* brings one to doubt the world; by the same token, in the same process, it also earns the reader a certain dispensation from resolving those doubts. One simultaneously, dialectically escapes, by reading *Hamlet,* the truths revealed by it. This power to partly absolve or at least console is embedded in the very language of the play, which makes transcendent order out of disorder.

The burlesque soliloquy in *Huckleberry Finn* disorders the Shakespeare text and leaves its readers with no dispensation, no escape, nothing to mediate their recognition of Denmark's rot. Worse, the burlesque does not just remove it; it mocks the dispensation others have found in the soliloquy. Colonel Sherburn's soliloquy is one result of the fall to the very bottom that results; the conflict of individual and society appears in his speech as absolute and hopeless. Worse yet, the burlesque enacts an aspect of Hamlet's speech that is otherwise invisible, the fact that it is class-bound. This is a concrete effect. The distance between the real text and the travesty is the distance between the educated individual who knows the real text and the populace that does not. My point will have become evident: the burlesqued soliloquy exposes the myth of universal individualism in nineteenth-century America. Or perhaps it does something a little less absolute: it opens up the question of universal individualism and enables us to look deeper to where that question arises in a context of social relations.

I am using the parody of Hamlet's speech, of course, to represent the relation of the novel generally to high culture. That relation, which has been seen widely to render *Huckleberry Finn more* universally resonant, while it makes the work more broadly accessible, tends almost in the opposite direction to give it more social specificity, to bring to the surface the ways in which universality is socially specific. When this specificity surfaces, it brings with it something we have already traced out in the plot, the recognition that the universal individual is not only a limited being but a dependent one: Huck will get to light out once more for the territory only by *not* going up the Ohio with Jim—in general by not involving himself in his society. His individual freedom is not simply an evasion of social engagement; it involves a negative engagement, a sacrifice of Jim because Jim would implicate him, and elsewhere a conservativism that precludes other implications. Sherburn's creed of the superman is the other side of this coin.

The end of *Huckleberry Finn,* which has disturbed and continues to disturb virtually everyone who reads it, is neither cheating nor a failure of nerve. It presents the ugly truth that to be Huck Finn and stay Huck Finn you have to let Jim be returned to slavery. Mark Twain found this truth as unbearable to acknowledge as anyone, so (here is the cheat and the failure of nerve) he freed Jim anyway. But this evasion actually deepened his critique of individualism by revealing how much it depends on political quietism, for in order to save Huck, Twain has to depict the slave society as relatively humane and quite capable of self-reform. There is no need for a civil war in St. Petersburg—nor for reconstruction.

A recasting of Huck's vernacular voice has identified it as in fact black.[18] Shelley Fisher Fishkin has argued that Huck's dialect is taken not from Tom Blankenship, a poor-white boy on whom Twain wrote he had modeled Huck, but from Jimmy, a black child who waited on the author at a hotel supper. The conclusions Fisher Fishkin draws from her discovery are, first, that the roots of American writing are sunk deep in African-American culture and, second, that *Huckleberry Finn* is "multiracial and multicultural." But while the first seems undeniable, the second does not necessarily accompany it. It is Mark Twain and by projection Huck Finn who speak in Jimmy's accents, not Jimmy; and an impersonated voice does not speak in its own words or express its own thoughts. Is Twain's novel "multicultural" or does it represent a culture that has successfully appropriated a multitude of accents into its own language? It seems important that despite the central place of Jimmy's voice in constituting the story, the black character Jim could not be imagined as narrator. Huck's narration of Jim's story in Jimmy's idiom only extends Huck's cultural power: Twain controls poor-white Huck, who controls black Jim/Jimmy. This is of a piece with Huck's moral breakthrough at the moment Jim is reenslaved: it is Huck who is made better and stronger by deciding to go to hell rather than turn Jim in, not Jim. I can sum up the preceding discussion in terms of this rereading of *Huckleberry Finn* by suggesting that if in fact Huck speaks with Jimmy's voice, Jimmy's voice, like Jim's freedom, has been sacrificed to Huck's enlarged democratic persona.

• • •

Why is *Huckleberry Finn the* American classic? Because almost uniquely it probes the lowest and most sensitive layer of the American mind, where individualism takes a first purchase on the world in some degree cognizant that the community will have to pay for it. Classics typically mediate a culture's founding contradictions. The *Iliad* celebrates and abhors war. *Huckleberry Finn* celebrates and abhors individualism. Other American classics share that ambivalence, of course, but perhaps none see the contradiction between the generals and the soldiers in the individualist war as clearly as Twain, who, perversely, made his individualist general someone who should have been cannon fodder and then had him enlist his own sacrifice. Not all readers see that this is cause for despair, as Twain ultimately did, but that this funny book for boys has glimpsed the heart of the national darkness is, I think, generally felt; and one essential power of a classic is to see in the dark.

Literary fictions can no more transcend history than can real persons. Although certainly not universally acknowledged, in the current criticism this truth has replaced the former truth that literature is a thing apart. Once banned from the interpretation of books for violating the integrity of the imagination, considerations of race and sex (and of class) have entered into even the most formalist readings.[1] Race and sex are now found organic to problems of organic form. As a result, those problems have become vastly more complicated than when a literary work was thought to invent its own sufficient language, for then the task of the critic, although complex, was also simple, it was to show how everything within the text worked together, taking coherence as given. A poem or story was a puzzle for which the critic could be sure that he or she had all the pieces and that they dovetailed.

Neither assurance is any longer available; one cannot be certain a work seen as engaged in history is internally coherent, nor that the issues it treats finally hang together. This development is not altogether congenial to literary critics, who mean to analyze works, not to dismantle them. But if we take literature's link to history seriously, we will have to admit that it renders literature contingent, like history itself. My case in point is *Pudd'nhead Wilson,* the writing of which posed problems that were made impossible to resolve by the history of racial and sexual thinking in America. The ideologies of race and sex that Mark Twain contended with in this novel were finally not controllable through literary form. They tripped the characters and tangled the plot. *Pudd'nhead Wilson* exemplifies the tragedy of the imagination, a literary kind that, ironically, only a historical criticism can fully appreciate.

Pudd'nhead Wilson builds its plot upon a plot. The subversive schemer is a young slave mother named Roxana (Roxy), who is thrown into panic one day by her master's casual threat to sell some of his slaves downriver into the inferno of the Deep South. Reasoning that if he can sell these, he can as readily sell her baby, she first determines to kill herself and the child rather than lose it to the slave market. Then she finds another way. Being not only a mother but the Mammy of her master's child, she simply switches the infants, who look so much alike that no one suspects the exchange. In contrast to their perfect resemblance as babies, the two boys grow up totally unlike. The black child taking the white's name of Tom (for Thomas à Becket Driscoll), becomes a treacherous, cowardly thief; the white child, assuming the black name, Valet de Chambre (Chambers), is gentle, loyal, honest, and brave. Tom's path of petty crime leads eventually to murder, and his victim is his putative uncle and guardian, the much-loved benevolent Judge Driscoll. A pair of visiting foreign twins are wrongly accused of the crime and are about to be convicted when Pudd'nhead Wilson, a local sage in the tradition of shrewd Ben Franklin, uncovers the real murderer who is, coincidentally, the real black. The amiable foreigners are vindicated, the real white man is freed from his erroneous bondage and restored to his estate, and the murderer is punished. He is not hanged because—not being really a gentleman but a slave—he has to be punished as a slave: he is sold downriver into the Deep South.

Twain starts off simply enough with a farce whose characters' opportunistic prevarications expose established lies. The lie Roxy exposes when she successfully replaces her master's child with her own is that racial difference is inherent. As the ground for slavery, this racism is unambiguously false, its inversion of human truth dramatized in Roxy's dilemma: she can jump in the river with her baby or live in daily peril of its being sold down the river. Given those alternatives, her stratagem appears righteous and even fair despite its concomitant enslavement of the white baby. Without condoning this but simply by focusing on Roxy and her child, the story enlists the reader wholly on their side since the failure of the scheme can mean only the sale of mother and child, no doubt separately, or their common death.

But then things take an odd turn, which in fact will culminate in an about-face, the reversal ultimately going so far as to transform the exposure of Roxy and her son into a happy ending that rights wrongs, rewards the good, punishes the bad, and restores order all around. When, at an eleventh hour, Pud-

d'nhead Wilson unmasks Tom and justice is done, the reader is actually relieved and gratified. If by this intervention the story does not exactly celebrate
the return of the escaped slave to bondage or his sale to the demons of tide-
water plantations, neither does it regret these events. Roxy's broken spirit and
the double defeat of her maternal hopes are pitiable sights to be sure, but there
is a consolation prize. In *Pudd'nhead Wilson's* finally rectified moral economy,
Roxy's punishment is quite moderate. Not only are the legal authorities of
the town of Dawson's Landing forbearing, but also "The young fellow upon
whom she had inflicted twenty-three years of slavery continued [the pension
she had been receiving from Tom]."[2] Exemplary generosity, to be sure, but
also a startling turnaround. Roxy, who once was so helplessly enslaved that her
only recourse was suicide, is now being represented as herself an enslaver.
Adding insult to injury, the pension her victim bestows upon her makes her
appear still more culpable. Roxy and her baby exit as the villains of a story
they entered as the innocently wronged.

Twain recognized that this about-face required explanation. One reason
Tom turned out so badly and Chambers so well, the narrator suggests, is because they were brought up in opposite ways. "Tom got all the petting, Chambers got none. . . ." The result was that "Tom was 'fractious,' as Roxy called it,
and overbearing, Chambers was meek and docile" (18–19). Slavery is made to
counter racism here much the way it does in *Uncle Tom's Cabin* and not to any
better effect except that the black man made Christlike by his sufferings is really white, so that in the absence of real blacks similarly affected the case is not
fully made. All that these distortions of character argue is the evil of human
bondage, not the equality of master and slave, and even less so when we know
that the master is a member of the slave race. For Stowe, countering racism
was incidental, indeed she had only a limited interest in doing so, up to the
point of establishing the humanity of the slaves in order to argue her central
case, which was against slavery. But this is not Twain's situation when he published *Pudd'nhead Wilson* in 1894, thirty-two years after Emancipation. In fact,
his novel and its story of the baby exchange has little to do with slavery: the
plot does not follow Chambers the white slave in order to depict the horrors
of his condition, but Tom the black master and the crimes he has all his freedom to perpetrate. In appropriate contrast to *Uncle Tom's Cabin, Pudd'nhead
Wilson* is only peripherally concerned with the atrocities of the slave system.
Although Chambers is sadly disadvantaged by his years of servitude, his debil-
ity has too little force to motivate the novel, nothing much comes from it or
is expected to. On the contrary, everything comes from Tom's ascension to
power, all of it bad.

Nothing in the original premise of the story predicts this sad development, so the obvious question is, Why does Tom, the former slave, turn out so villainous and dangerous a master? The most congenial explanation—that Tom has been fatally corrupted by his translation into the class of oppressors— omits too much of the story to serve. Twain offers it only half-heartedly, presenting the true white planters as a decent lot, often absurd in their chivalric poses and inadequate to their ruling tasks, but on the whole men of integrity, faithful to their "only religion," which is "to be a gentleman . . . without stain or blemish." Even their slave owning seems less evil than careless. The description of Pembroke Howard as "a fine, brave, majestic creature, a gentleman according to the nicest requirements of the Virginian rule. . ." (4) mingles affection with mockery, and although his dash is balderdash, there are worse things—Tom for example. His sale of Roxy treacherously and symbolically downriver is transcendingly evil, branding him an unnatural son and a denatured man. To underline the exceptional quality of his betrayal, Twain shows Tom prepared to sell his mother twice over, for when she escapes and seeks his help against pursuing slave hunters, only her threat to repay him in kind prevents him from turning her over.

It is more than a little perverse that the two characters who actually traffic in slavery are both black. Percy Driscoll's threat to sell his misbehaving slaves is the novel's original sin responsible for Roxy's desperate deed. But having the sale itself take place offstage and specifying that, unlike Tom, the judge only sells to his relatively humane neighbors and not to the Simon Legrees of the Deep South, attenuates our sense of the planter's guilt. On the contrary, the story pointedly reports Tom's plan to sell his boyhood companion Chambers, a plan foiled by Judge Driscoll, who buys Chambers to safeguard the family honor: "for public sentiment did not approve of that way of treating family servants for light cause or for no cause" (22). Tom's corrupting environment, therefore, does not explain why the disguised black is both more deeply and differently corrupted than his fellow slave owners, a development that is the more startling because it reverses the initial expectations of virtue inspired by his first appearance as a hapless babe.[3]

But if no explanation emerges directly from the novel, consider its historical context. The year of its publication, 1894, was the eve of McKinley's election and a period of accelerating racism marked by the bloody spread of Jim Crow. The formative experience of *Pudd'nhead Wilson*'s era was the defeat of Reconstruction, not the end of slavery. In that context the story of the replacement of a white baby by a black has a local urgency we may miss at this distance. And its progress from a good thing to a bad as the black boy grows up to murder the town patriarch who is his uncle and to rob, cheat, and generally despoil the whole village, as well as plunge his mother into a worse state than she had been in before, makes as much sense in history as it fails to make in the story.

In the story, Tom's villainy appears only arbitrary. As much as Twain justifies Roxy's revolution by appealing to the transcendent motive of maternal love, making her insurrection finally inevitable and in no way a sign even of inherent rebelliousness, he damns Tom from the start as "a bad baby, from the very beginning of his usurpation" (17). So the good black is a woman; the bad, a man. The good woman, complicated enough within herself to act badly while remaining herself good, is black; the bad man, lacking interiority and simply expressing a given identification that is barely an identity, is also black. With this formula, *Pudd'nhead Wilson* emerges as a remarkable exploration of the anxieties aroused by a racist social structure, as a literary locus classicus of one modern (in its integration of individualist concepts of identity) paradigm of race, and perhaps most strikingly, as the exposition of the relation between the racial paradigm of race and a modern paradigm of gender. The conjunction of race and sex is more often pictured as an intersection but here it is an interaction. Moreover, this interaction does not simply join, but combines, race and sex so that in certain pairings they are more stringently limiting than when taken separately.

When Twain associates the black race with the female sex, he represents racism in the uncontroversially repugnant form of slavery. Roxy's force and shrewdness work to disprove stereotypes of servility. Her sovereignty over the children extends naturally to the story of which she is a sort of author. She achieves the highest status available to a fictional character when she and the narrator are the only ones who know what is going on and can truly identify the participants. The white baby's mother is dead, and his own father fails to recognize him. Roxy alone knows who he is—and what. Further, the way she knows this bears its own antiracist implications; because both babies have flaxen curls and blue eyes, her discrimination can have nothing to do with physical characteristics. Thus as she identifies, them, in her own image, *who* Tom and Chambers are is entirely independent of *what* they are. They embody the American ideal belief that a man is what he makes of himself, which is potentially anything he determines.

Consonant with this liberal view, *Pudd'nhead Wilson* initially defines black character in universal traits as benign as Roxy herself. If Roxy at times falls prey to the lure of unattended objects, "Was she bad?" Twain muses. "Was she worse than the general run of her race? No. They had an unfair show in

the battle of life, and they held it no sin to take military advantage of the enemy—in a small way." He insists, "in a small way, but not in a very large one"
(11). Even as Twain writes this, Roxy takes the very large military advantage
of exchanging the infants. But the petty thievery, in this case not even her
own, that has called down the wrath of her master and thus precipitated this
ultimate transgression was a very small crime. If Roxy's pilfering turns to pil-
lage, the novel suggests that this is not her fault, hardly even her doing, but that
of a criminal society that monstrously deforms not only marginally guilty relations, but also purely innocent ones.

The night of the exchange, Percy Driscoll, whose threat to punish theft by
selling the thief has raised for Roxana the specter of her child's own com-
modity status, sleeps the sleep of the just. By contrasting her master's smug
oblivion to her anguished wakefulness, through which she becomes for this
moment the story's consciousness, Twain condones and even endorses her
crime. The novel continues to side with her when it is not Roxy but Percy
Driscoll who enforces the children's inequality, permitting the ostensibly
white boy to abuse the child whom he fails to recognize as his son (19). In this
representation of the political economy of slavery in terms of the family, the
author's voice speaks against the regnant patriarchy, espouses the oppressed,
and applauds subversion. Fathers in Mark Twain are not a nice lot, and boys
are frequently abused. A black woman enslaved by white men is the natural
ally of white boys. Would that all boys had mothers like Roxy!

Tom's becoming a man, however, rearranges this scheme radically. His passage into manhood, marked by his return from Yale, seems to start the story
over. At Yale he has been a desultory student but has acquired a number of
grown-up problems. His indifferent intellect has prevented any deeper penetration, but Tom has acquired the superficies of elite culture, its dainty dress,
and its mannered ways. The local youth naturally scorn such refinements, but
when they set a deformed black bellringer dressed in parodic elegance to follow Tom about, the young popinjay is debunked more profoundly than anyone in the story suspects. And it is unclear just what is being satirized: is it simply foppish pretension, or rather some special absurdity of black foppery?
Because the characters are unaware that their parody of Tom possesses this additional dimension, it becomes a joke shared by the narrator and the reader, a
joke with a new target.

Twain had already mocked black dress when he described a despairing
Roxy adorning herself for her suicide. Her ribbons and feathers, her won-
drously gaudy dress, certainly reflect on her race, but the butt of the joke is not
race as such. Being black is not given as ridiculous, although blacks may be-

have ridiculously. In the later episode being black is itself absurd: the private joke we share with the narrator is the very fact of Tom's negritude, that while pretending to be a high-falutin' gentleman, he is really a "Negro." Here, the novel begins its turnaround from the initial view implicit in the identical babies, that human beings are potentially the same, to the final dramatization in the Judge's murder, of black duplicity and violence as inherent racial traits.

Tom's grown-up inferiorities in fact make his spoiled childhood irrelevant. He cannot have acquired his fear of dueling, for instance, from being raised a Southern gentleman. While his overexcited peers in the Dawson's Landing peerage fall to arms at the least imagined slight, Tom turns tail at the first sign of a fight. This is only one of a constellation of traits that define Tom as a different sort of beau ideal, the very type of the upstart Negro of post-Reconstruction plantation fiction: cowardly, absurdly pretentious, lazy and irresponsible, a petty thief but potentially a murderer. Born the generic, universal baby, Tom has grown into a very particular sort of man, unlike both his white and black fellows; on the white side, he is not capable of being a master, and on the black, he has been dangerously loosed from the bonds that keep other black men in check.

I want to stress the next point because it is central to the racial/sexual paradigm developed in *Pudd'nhead Wilson*. The white man who has taken Tom's place might have been expected, in the context of the novel's increasingly essentialist view of race, also to manifest an essential nature. He does not. "Meek and docile" in adaptation to his powerless state, Chambers yet does not become a white man fatally misplaced among blacks, as Tom is a black man fatally misplaced among whites. This asymmetry embodies that of racial typing that applies only to the inferior race. The superior race, when defining itself in the terms of modern individualism, claims not a better type, but the general norm—universality or the ability to be any type and all of them.

Unhappily for Chambers, however, universality imparts only potential, a capacity to become rather than an already defined (therefore limited) being. That is, what characterizes the norm embodied in the superior race, instead of a particular set of traits, is universal potential. Such potential realizes itself in relation to environment: ironically, the white "Chambers" is far more vulnerable to the shaping force of the exchange, for had Tom remained a slave he would have unfolded into essentially the same man, although a crucially less powerful one and for that reason a less harmful one. So Chambers, unlike Tom, adapts to his sad situation and is shaped by it. In one important respect his adaptation represents one of the novel's most basic if unacknowledged issues. As I suggested earlier, in Roxy, Twain endorses a black woman's subversion of the white patriarchy, whereas in Tom, he rejects a black man's takeover. The fate of Chambers begins to explain why Twain distinguished so sharply between mother and son by revealing the stake in his relation to the latter.

That stake is manhood. Through Tom's usurpation, the white community of Dawson's Landing risks losing its manhood. A black woman exercising the authority of motherhood in a white society may call in question the domestic ideology of white womanhood. In *Pudd'nhead Wilson* this domestic ideology means the genteel sentimentalism of aunts and widows. Had it been only a question of Roxy's passing off her child as the child of a white lady, the baby switch would have been a disturbing but limited affair. But the far more encompassing event of a black man occupying the place of a white man, wielding the same power, usurping (Twain's repeated term) the authority of white fatherhood connotes a global reversal that, instead of emancipating the iconoclastic boy who typically articulates Twain's abhorrence of genteel culture, literally emasculates him. The subversion in Tom's usurpation of white identity turns Chambers into a woman, for feminization is the lasting result of that unfortunate man's slave upbringing. Once a black slave, he can never take his place among his real peers: "The poor fellow could not endure the terrors of the white man's parlor, and felt at home and at peace nowhere but in the kitchen" (114). Note that Chambers's loss of manhood is clearly regrettable only because he is white. A black man may be improved by the attenuations of femininity, as is the case elsewhere with Twain's motherly Jim. One stereotype of the black man threatens violence and uncontrollable sex. The other has him contemptibly effeminate. Black men are seen simultaneously as excessively male and insufficiently masculine. Inextricably entangled in these ideological contradictions, Tom is incoherently both. Although his final act is a stabbing, earlier in the story, disguised as a woman, he robs houses. The witnesses who fail to recognize in a dress the man they know as a white gentleman are actually seeing the real Tom, who thus shows himself one way and another not a real man.

By the logic of the different *kind* of identity that real men develop, a black mother can be the ally of rebellious boys, but a black father would rob them of their very selves as heirs to the mantle of universal (white) manhood. We stand with Roxy when she defies the social order to save her boy-child. But when this child grows up, he embodies a revolution which has displaced the erstwhile ruling children, usurping their manhood. Once this implication has been realized by the story's unfolding, even the benignity of Roxy's crime seems retrospectively less certain. On the last page of the novel, the story finally represents the exchange not as freeing the black child, but as enslaving the white.

That ending was implicit all along in the slave situation, which stipulated that the only way to free Tom was to enslave Chambers. This unhappy reciprocity, however, was not manifest in the story so long as it focused on mothers and children. The maternal economy is a welfare state. Its central concern is not production but distribution, and even when it is unfair, it has primarily to do with giving, allocating privileges and goods among the more or less undifferentiated members of a group who seek more not from each other but from the mother/state. But production, not distribution, was the chief care of the market-capitalist economy of the United States in the late nineteenth century; and in that context, distribution was a matter of competitive acquisition.

Much has been written about the relation of these two economies that in some respects confront and in others complement each other.[4] The peculiar slant of *Pudd'nhead Wilson* comes from presenting them not, as usual, synchronically, as simultaneous dimensions of one society, but diachronically, the market economy following the maternal. Thus sequentially related, with each one in its time defining the fictional universe, their contradictions emerge more sharply, along with the way that the hierarchy of family and state, private and public, gives the market the last word. It certainly has the last word in *Pudd'nhead Wilson,* as we will see. Although a mother may take something from one child and give it to another who needs it more but not deprive the former, in an economy in which personally recuperable profit is the bottom line, taking away and giving must show up on the ledger ultimately. And when self-sufficient individuals—men and fathers—possess unequal amounts of power or wealth, reallocation, however equitable, does mean deprivation: one gets only by taking away from another. At the point at which the story of Tom and Chambers leaves the nursery and enters the marketplace, Tom, who as a baby was the innocent and even rightful recipient of the freedom he unjustly lacked, becomes a usurper; Chambers is seen to have been robbed.

The maternal and market economies which in their turn dominate the plot of *Pudd'nhead Wilson* do coexist to a degree. Although the story starts out in Roxy's control, the market wields overwhelming force from the first because the power of whites to sell blacks to other whites inspires the exchange of the babies. But at this point, even though in Roxy's world slavery functions as a harsh necessity that will ultimately deprive her of all power, the market as such is not yet the primary setting. Indeed, when this necessity first manifests itself, she resists successfully, temporarily returning her world to its prior order

and keeping both babies. All through their infancy and childhood she administers her welfare system, taking care of both of them as fairly as she can under
the circumstances despite the fact that her own child is in the master position
and would be favored if she were to fully implement the unfairness of the
slave system. When Tom is no longer a mother's child but his own man, however, he takes over the fictive universe and administers it his way. Because he
is a man, whatever the quality of his administration, it participates directly in
the patriarchal economy and in this new context the baby exchange realizes
its meaning in the trade of Chambers's white manhood for Tom's black impotence, and vice versa.

Because the asymmetries of race and of sex are parallel, Roxy's innate
character as a mother is congruent with her innate nature as a black woman.
Paradoxically, even ironically, this very limit permits Twain to endow her as a
character with a considerable degree of transcendence, the way that Flaubert,
for example, endows Emma with much of his own sense of self without ever
questioning the nontranscendence of female selfhood as such.[5] Roxy, a black
woman, actually approaches individualist selfhood while her son is denied it
altogether and is depicted as capable of achieving self-creative powers only by
the outright usurpation of whiteness. On the other side, Chambers's failure to
achieve manhood, in dramatizing the transcendence of white identity which
defines itself by going beyond nature, also points up a terrible vulnerability
that springs from the very quality that makes white men superior. To be capable of making oneself and one's world is a very fine thing, but that ability has
its price. The price of white men's power of self-creation is the risk of failing
not only to achieve but also to be, whereas women (as such though not always
as fictional characters) and blacks are essentially and thus invulnerably what
and as they are born. And this inequality of vulnerability counterbalances
racial inequality, coming first, in the ideological and psychological universe of
Pudd'nhead Wilson, to equate the plights of blacks and whites then finally to
make blacks appear stronger, or at least more threatening.

An essentialist identity requires, for the good of the community, more social control; it is too little vulnerable to be allowed as much freedom as identities that carry their own constraints in their vulnerability. It is generally recognized that the ratio of self-making to being determines the status of
modern individuals, so that the more a man is his own author the higher he
ranks and the more authority he wields. The converse is less often articulated,
that an essentialist identity not only brands the socially inferior but also ne-
cessitates their submission. In one scene of *Pudd'nhead Wilson* this logic almost
begins to justify slavery.

In this scene, Chambers has just revealed to Roxy that her errant son is a dissolute gambler who at the moment owes the huge sum of $200. Roxy is stunned: "Two—hund'd—dollahs! . . . Sakes alive, it's mos' enough to buy a tollable good second-hand nigger wid." Now the irony, indeed the wit, here lies in the fact that the $200 Tom has gambled away are $200 *he* would fetch, being himself "a tollable good second-hand nigger." But the possibility of buying and selling human beings, which up until this point has implied such intolerable violations of natural law as the separation of mothers and children, has become, astonishingly, a way to measure and *preserve* genuine value: Tom's worthlessness as a white man is measured by his gambling away his worth as a slave. Lest we not grasp this point fully, Twain spells it out in the ensuing dialogue. Chambers's report that Tom has been disinherited for his scandalous conduct infuriates Roxy, who accuses her supposed son of lying, calling him a "misable imitation nigger." Chambers retorts, "If I's imitation, what is you? Bofe of us is imitation *white*—dat's what we is—en pow'full good imitation, too . . . we don't 'mount to noth'n as imitation *niggers*" (35). But Chambers *is* an "imitation nigger," being really white. He is also really honest and good, as he shows by openly declaring his purported blackness, unlike the true blacks in the story who lie about race. Once again the reader of *Pudd'nhead Wilson* understands a scene by knowing better than the characters and the better knowledge is the reality, the truth, of race.

The preceding scene plays directly to the concealed switch of Tom and Chambers and exactly negates its original thrust that whites and blacks can be exchanged because in *fact* blacks can be essentially white—read: universally human. Now on the contrary, the exchangeability of physically resembling blacks with whites represents the way apparent likeness can mask real and profoundly different beings. Initially, clothing and social status were seen as hiding real human resemblance. These same superficial differences have come to mask real difference, and the bodily likeness of Tom and Chambers that first expressed their common humanity now renders their total opposition invisible. People may *appear* equal, it says, but they are really not.

What matters in this scene is the real difference between Tom and Chambers while what had mattered about them at the start was their real likeness. Coincidentally in the same episode, Roxy herself sadly dwindles as the narrator ascribes her anger at Chambers for reporting Tom's disinheritance to her fear of losing "an occasional dollar from Tom's pocket" (35). This is a disaster she will not contemplate, the narrator laughs. But earlier, Roxy defined herself in relation to a larger disaster, not the loss of a dollar but the sale of her baby. And when two pages later Tom actually does refuse his mother a dollar, the novel's shift of perspective is complete: where the injustice of racial in-equality was first measured by the violation of Roxy's natural motherhood, now inequality will be justified by the spectacle of the emancipated and em-powered Tom's unnatural sonhood. Roxy's subsequent threat to expose him articulates his falseness; the "truth" about Tom is that he is false, that he is not who he is or should be. Henceforth the story of *Pudd'nhead Wilson* is not about interchangeable babies irrationally and unjustly rendered master and slave, but about a black man who has taken a white man's place. Roxy herself, who first identified Tom as a universal baby—who revealed him as "white" as any baby—now dubs him a "nigger."

The first name she had bestowed on her child was the name of a servant, Valet de Chambre. The fine sound of it appealed to her, Twain explained, al-though she had no notion what it meant. But we do, and when we first laugh at it we do so out of affectionate condescension. When later Roxy exchanges this name for that of a lord, Thomas à Becket, we begin to see that both names have their serious implications: they project a spurious identity that yet deter-mines what each man becomes. In the end, however, we find that we have been wrong twice, first when we took the names lightly, but second when we took them as seriously damaging misnomers. Valet de Chambre was all along the correct identification of a man born a servant and for a time dangerously misnamed a master.

Thus Roxy's final renaming of Tom does not merely exchange one name for another, but redefines the very nature of his identity. When she called her son Tom and thereby made him the equal of whites, it was on the ground that in himself he was indistinguishable from whites. Scrutinizing his golden babyhood dressed in white finery, she marveled: "Now who would b'lieve clo'es could do de like o'dat? Dog my cats if it ain't all *I* kin do to tell t'other fum which, let alone his pappy" (14). When babies are fledgling individuals, one as good as another in anticipation of each one's self-making, pappys can-not tell one from another, for indeed paternity is irrelevant. But when racial nature enters into identity, paternity becomes all-important.

Roxy announces Tom's blackness to him by saying "You ain't no more kin to old Marse Driscoll den I is!" With this she claims him—"you's my *son*" (41)—but the ground of this claim is a renunciation. Even as she demands that he recognize her maternal authority—"You can't call me *Roxy*, same as if you was my equal. Chillen don't speak to dey mammies like dat. You'll call me Ma or mammy, dat's what you'll call me . . ." (42)—she abdicates the tran-scendent authority that earlier enabled her to name *him* into an identity she had more than borne: created. Henceforth he may call her "Ma or mammy" and accede to her orders, but for both this will ratify subjection, in fact servitude. Even the reclamation of this maternal authority is limited, bounded by the surrounding patriarchy. "You'll call me Ma or mammy," Roxy storms, "leastways when dey ain't nobody aroun'." For him to recognize her as his mother in public, of course, would reveal his real identity as a slave, whereupon Roxy would lose him to the authority of his father, and to the paternal authority of the slave system. Roxy had been able on her own to make Tom white, when she was in charge and nature and race were in abeyance, but making him black requires her to invoke white patriarchal authority.

Through a master irony the revelation of his real white father seals Tom's status as a black son: a chastened Tom surrenders to his new status by asking timidly, "Ma, would you mind telling me who was my father?" (43). The final link connecting Tom to his mother—identifying him as a slave—is her knowledge, her ability to call on the name of a white man. And through the medium of Roxy's pride as she tells him that his father was "de highest quality in dis whole town—Ole Virginny stock, Fust Famblies" (43), the authority of Cunnel Cecil Burleigh Essex parodically but surely reaches forward from that past all-generating moment when he could command Roxy to bear his son, to declare that son now a black slave. "Dey ain't another nigger in dis town dat's as high-bawn as you is," she ends, proferring an identity that is the fatal opposite of the one she had conferred on him at the start of the story. "Jes' you hold yo' head up as high as you want to—you has de right, en dat I kin swah" (43).

One sign of Roxy's demotion to the status of just another fond mother is that she is wrong about this: Tom has neither the right nor the capacity to hold up his head. Despite his excellent white descent, he is simply not of cavalier mettle. And on the occasion when he runs away from a challenge to duel, Roxy herself sadly draws the inevitable conclusion: not even his superior white siring can redeem his fatal flaw: "It's de nigger in you, dat's what it is. Thirty-one parts o'you is white, en on'y one part nigger, en dat po' little one part is yo' *soul*. 'Tain't wuth savin'; 'tain't wuth totin' out on a shovel en tho'in in de gutter. You has disgraced yo' birth. What would yo' pa think o' you? It's enough to make him turn in his grave" (70).

Roxy's racism is comically undercut certainly, but in the service of what alternative view? We are the more at a loss for a proper liberal riposte in that Roxy's parting shot travels directly to the end of the novel and its definitive return of Tom to the now unproblematical status of "nigger." "Ain't nigger enough in him to show in his finger-nails," she mutters, "'en dat takes mightily little—yit dey's enough to paint his soul" (70). It was because of his white, thus raceless or race-transcendent fingernails that she had been able to raise him to the status of master. But now it turns out that his fingernails did not accurately represent the case. Rather, as all discover, his identity lies in his fingerprints, and no one transcends his fingerprints.

Wilson's resort to fingerprints to establish Tom's true identity solves more than the judge's murder. It provides a more encompassing resolution of the novel as a whole, for his astounding revelation restores both racial and sexual order. Indeed, since any satisfactory ending would require that the truth be revealed and, because only Roxy could reveal it, it is not easy to imagine how else Twain could have ended his story. For Roxy to solve the mystery would not constitute an ending, not so much because her confession would be dramatically unlikely as, on the contrary, because by identifying Tom and Chambers accurately she would reassert precisely the power to identify that has so badly compromised Dawson's Landing. For Roxy to name her son and his white counterpart a second time would confirm her authority, thus perpetuating the racial dilemma of *Pudd'nhead Wilson*. Reconstruction would continue.

In Pudd'nhead Wilson, however, Twain finds an alternative truth-teller. Male to a fault in his entire self-sufficiency, Wilson counters, then surpasses, Roxy's authority: to the babies' identical fingernails which enabled Roxy to declare them identical, Wilson opposes fingerprints representing the apotheosis of difference, uniqueness. Now, fingerprints are not racially but individually distributed. Therefore they cannot testify to Tom's racial nature but only to his personal character. Nonetheless, in the courtroom scene, Wilson invokes the telltale fingerprints categorically, to rule out categories of persons in order to identify the individual miscreant as himself the representative of a category.

Wilson, who represents the category of authoritative white men commanding both law and language, begins by announcing this authority to the community: "I will tell you." This is what he tells them: "For a purpose unknown to us, but probably a selfish one, somebody changed those children in the cradle" (112). So far is the story from casting doubt on any aspect of this emerging elucidation, its miraculous verity is reinforced when the narration turns briefly to Roxy portrayed thinking pathetically that "Pudd'nhead Wilson could do wonderful things, no doubt, but he couldn't do impossible ones," and that therefore her secret is safe. But what is impossible to her is as nothing to Wilson. Having named the exact time of the exchange (thus returning to the crime's origin to master it whole) and having identified the perpetrator, he continues in the irrefutable idiom of scientific formulas: "*A* was put into *B*'s cradle in the nursery; *B* was transferred to the kitchen, and became a negro and a slave . . . but within a quarter of an hour he will stand before you white and free!" He controls time and place. "From seven months onward until now, *A* has still been a usurper, and in my fingerrecords he bears *B*'s name." And now the coup de grâce: "The murderer of your friend and mine—York Driscoll, of the generous hand and the kindly spirit—sits among you. Valet de Chambre, negro and slave." Roxy's response is poignantly telling. Before the miracle of white masculine omniscience, she can only pray: "De Lord have mercy on me, po' miserable sinner dat I is!" (112–13)

Wilson's godlike authority has appropriated the story, raveling the order of the white community as he unravels the case. In the process the story has also been rewritten, however, with a new beginning that brushes Roxy's motive aside with the casual conclusion that whatever this motive was, it was selfish (in context a stunningly ironic term that the text leaves uninflected) and re-drawing its characters and issues in stark blacks and whites.

And what about Pudd'nhead himself? The instrument of resolution, what is his relation to the order he restores? First, although he wields the authority of the white patriarchy, he is not himself a father but a bachelor, a lone, even an outcast figure whose own authority the village has only this moment rec-ognized and then only because of his trick with the fingerprints. For himself, although he rescues the established order, he is acutely and at times bitterly aware that those who administer it are not often worthy of their power. The joke that earns him the nickname "Pudd'nhead" has turned out more serious than it seemed. On his first day in town, Wilson became a fool in the eyes of his neighbors when he declared that he wished he owned half a loudly bark-ing dog so he might kill his half. Now he has saved half a dog, while the other half dies. There is nothing joyous in restoring the status quo of Dawson's Landing. Twain may have been reluctant to see black men acquire the power of whites and may have viewed their bid for a share of power as outright usurpation. He did not vindicate white society. This is a familiar dilemma in his work generally which frequently ends, as does *Pudd'nhead Wilson,* in a stalemate between radical criticism and an implicit conservatism expressed in the refusal or the inability, when it comes to it, to imagine significant change. The stalemate here seems particularly frustrating: change must be defeated, yet nothing of the established way of life appears worth preserving.

The depth of *Pudd'nhead Wilson*'s concluding depression may gauge the sounding it takes of perhaps the most profoundly embedded images in the American mind, the images of race and sex. Separately but especially inter-acting, these images sometimes not only activate the imagination, but they also disable it, trapping it as Mark Twain seems to have been by the impossible adjuncts of racial equality and white authority, of maternal justice and patriarchal right. When in the end the rule of the white fathers is reestablished by the fiat of law, there is no rejoicing. Pudd'nhead Wilson himself is an outcast and a failure. Playing out his private charades alone in his study, he represents the writer as outcast and failure. If he also represents the writer as lawgiver and defends the system he hates, even against its victims who threaten it by trying to lift their oppression, this is not a productive paradox but a paralyzing contradiction. Pudd'nhead Wilson, expressing his author's own anguish, would really have liked to kill his half of the dog but was afraid finally of leaving the house unguarded.

While all criticism is of its time, the discussion below addresses its context very directly. But, since the problem it treats remains current and might be perennial, I have not attempted to translate either the essay's references or its terms, thinking in fact that their use may have its own historical interest.

I

Feminist thinking is really *re*thinking, an examination of the way certain assumptions about women and the female character enter into the fundamental assumptions that organize all our thinking. For instance, assumptions such as the one that makes intuition and reason opposite terms parallel to female and male may have axiomatic force in our culture, but they are precisely what feminists need to question—or be reduced to checking the arithmetic, when the issue lies in the calculus.

Such radical skepticism is an ideal intellectual stance that can generate genuinely new understandings; that is, reconsideration of the relation between female and male can be a way to reconsider that between intuition and reason and ultimately between the whole set of such associated dichotomies: heart and head, nature and history. But it also creates unusual difficulties. Somewhat like Archimedes, who to lift the earth with his lever required someplace else on which to locate himself and his fulcrum, feminists questioning the presumptive order of both nature and history—and thus proposing to remove the ground from under their own feet— would appear to need an alternative base. For as Archimedes had to stand somewhere, one has to assume something in order to reason at all. So if the very axioms of Western thought already incorporate the sexual teleology in question, it seems that, like the Greek philosopher, we have to find a standpoint off this world altogether.

Archimedes never did. However persuasively he established that the earth could be moved from its appointed place, he and the lever remained earthbound and the globe stayed where it was. His story may point another moral, however, just as it points to another science able to harness forces internally and apply energy from within. We could then conclude that what he really needed was a terrestrial fulcrum. My point here, similarly, will be that a terrestrial fulcrum, a standpoint from which we can see our conceptual universe whole but which nonetheless rests firmly on male ground, is what feminists really need. But perhaps because being at once on and off a world seems an improbable feat, the prevailing perspectives of feminist studies have located the scholar one place or the other.

Inside the world of orthodox and therefore male-oriented scholarship, a new category has appeared in the last decade, the category of women. Economics textbooks now draw us our own bell curves, histories of medieval Europe record the esoterica of convents and the stoning of adulterous wives, zoologists calibrate the orgasmic capacities of female chimpanzees. Indeed, whole books on "women in" and "women of" are fast filling in the erstwhile blanks of a questionnaire—one whose questions, however, remain unquestioned. They never asked before what the mother's occupation was, now they do. The meaning of "occupation," or for that matter of "mother," is generally not at issue.

It is precisely the issue, however, for the majority of feminist scholars who have taken what is essentially the opposite approach; rather than appending their findings to the existing literature, they generate a new one altogether in which women are not just another focus but the center of an investigation whose categories and terms are derived from the world of female experience. They respond to the Archimedean dilemma by creating an alternative context, a sort of female enclave apart from the universe of masculinist assumptions. Most "women's studies" have taken this approach and stressed the global, structural character of their separate issues. Women are no longer to be seen as floating in a man's world but as a coherent group, a context in themselves. The problem is that the issues and problems women define from the inside as global, men treat from the outside as insular. Thus, besides the exfoliation of reports on the state of women everywhere and a certain piety on the subject of pronouns, there is little indication of feminist impact on the universe of male discourse. The theoretical cores of the various disciplines remain essentially unchanged, their terms and methods are as always. As always, therefore, the intellectual arts bespeak a world dominated by men, a script that the occasional woman at a podium can hardly revise. Off in the enclaves of women's studies, our basic research lacks the contiguity to force a basic reconsideration of all research, and our encapsulated revisions appear inorganic (or can be made to appear inorganic) to the universal system they mean to address. Archimedes' problem was getting off the world, but ours might be getting back on.

For we have been, perhaps, too successful in constructing an alternative footing. Our world apart, our female intellectual community, becomes increasingly cut off even as it expands. If we have little control over being shunted aside, we may nonetheless render the isolation of women's scholarship more difficult. At least we ought not to accept it, as in a sense we do when we ourselves conflate feminist thought with thinking about women, when we remove ourselves and our lever off this man's world to study the history or the literature, the art or the anatomy of women alone. This essay is about devising a method for an alternative definition of women's studies as the investigation, from women's viewpoint, of everything, thereby finding a way to engage the dominant intellectual systems directly and organically: locating a feminist terrestrial fulcrum. Since feminist thinking is the thinking of an insurgent group that in the nature of things will never possess a world of its own, such engagement would appear a logical necessity.

Logical but also contradictory. To a degree, any analysis that rethinks the most basic assumptions of the thinking it examines is contradictory or at least contrary, for its aim is to question more than to explain and chart. From it we learn not so much the intricacies of how a particular mode of thinking works as the essential points to which it can be reduced. And nowhere is such an adversarial rather than appreciative stance more problematical than it is in literary criticism. This is my specific subject here, the perils and uses of a feminist literary criticism that confronts the fundamental axioms of its parent discipline.

What makes feminist literary criticism especially contradictory is the peculiar nature of literature as distinct from the objects of either physical or social scientific study. Unlike these, literature is itself already an interpretation that it is the critic's task to decipher. It is certainly not news that the literary work is biased; indeed that is its value. Critical objectivity enters in only at a second level to provide a reliable reading, though even here many have argued that reading too is an exercise in creative interpretation. On the other hand, while biologists and historians will concede that certain a priori postulates affect their gathering of data, they always maintain that they have tried to correct for bias, attempting, insofar as this is ever possible, to discover the factual, undistorted truth. Therefore expositions of subjectivity are always both relevant and revelatory about the work of biologists and historians. But as a way of judging the literary work per se, exposing its bias is essentially beside the point. Not that literature transcends subjectivity or politics. Paradoxically, it is just because the fictional universe is wholly subjective and therefore ideological that the value of its ideology is almost irrelevant to its literary value. The latter instead depends on what might be thought of as the quality of the apologia, how successfully the work transforms ideology into ideal, into a myth that works to the extent precisely that it obscures its provenance. Disliking that provenance implies no literary judgment, for a work may be, from my standpoint, quite wrong and even wrongheaded about life and politics and still an extremely successful rendering of its contrary vision. Bad ideas, even ideas so bad that most of humanity rejects them, have been known to make very good literature.

I am not speaking here of what makes a work attractive or meaningful to its audience. The politics of a play, poem, or story may render it quite unreadable or, in the opposite case, enhance its value for particular people and situations. But this poses no critical issue, for what we like, we like and can justify that way; the problem, if we as feminists want to address our whole culture, is to deal with what we do not like but recognize as nonetheless valuable, serious, good. This is a crucial problem at the heart of feminism's wider relevance. No wonder we have tried to avoid it.

One way is to point out that "good" changes its definition according to time and place. This is true, but not true enough. Perhaps only because we participate in this culture even while criticizing it, we do (most of us) finally subscribe to a tradition of the good in art and philosophy that must sometimes be a political embarrassment—and what else could it be, given the entire history of both Western and Eastern civilizations and their often outright dependence on misogyny? Nor is it true enough, I believe, to argue that the really good writers and thinkers unconsciously and sometimes consciously rejected such misogyny. As couched in the analogous interpretation of Shylock as hero because Shakespeare could not really have been anti-Semitic, this argument amounts to second-guessing writers and their works in terms of a provincialism that seems especially hard to maintain in these linguistically and anthropologically conscious times. For such provincialism not only assumes that our view of things is universal and has always been the substance of reality but also that all other and prior representations were insubstantial. So when Shakespeare depicted bastards as scheming subversives, Jews as merchants of flesh, and women as hysterics, he meant none of it but was only using the local idiom. What he meant, thereby demonstrating his universality, was what we mean.

I want to suggest that we gain no benefit from either disclaiming the continuing value of the "great tradition" or reclaiming it as after all an expression of our own viewpoint. On the contrary, we lose by both. In the first instance, we isolate ourselves into irrelevance. In the second—denying, for example, that Shakespeare shared in the conventional prejudices about women—we deny by implication that there is anything necessarily different about a feminist outlook. Thus, discovering that the character of Ophelia will support a feminist interpretation may appear to be a political reading of *Hamlet,* but, in fact, by its exegetical approach it reaffirms the notion that the great traditions are all-encompassing and all-normative, the notion that subsumes women under the heading "mankind."

It seems to me perfectly plausible, however, to see Shakespeare as working within his own ideology that defined bastards, Jews, and women as by nature deformed or inferior, and as understanding the contradictions of that ideology without rejecting its basic tenets—so that, from a feminist standpoint, he was a misogynist—and as being nonetheless a great poet. To be sure, greatness involves a critical penetration of conventions but not necessarily or even frequently a radical rejection of them. If, in his villains, Shakespeare revealed the human being beneath the type, his characterization may have been not a denial of the type but a recognition of the complexity of all identity. The kingly ambition of the bastard, the "white" conscience of the Moor, the father love of the Jew, the woman's manly heart: these complexities are expressed in the terms of the contemporary ideology, and in fact Shakespeare uses these terms the more tellingly for not challenging them at the root.

But the root is what feminists have to be concerned with: what it means not to be a good woman or a bad one but to be a woman at all. Moreover, if a great writer need not be radical, neither need a great radical writer be feminist—but so what? It was only recently that the great Romantic poets conned us into believing that to be a great poet was to tell *the* absolute truth, to be the One prophetic voice for all Mankind. As the philosophy of the other, feminism has had to reject the very conception of such authority—which, by extension, should permit feminist critics to distinguish between appreciative and political readings.

We should begin, therefore, by acknowledging the separate wholeness of the literary subject, its distinct vision that need not be ours—what the formalists have told us and told us about: its integrity. We need to acknowledge, also, that to respect that integrity by not asking questions of the text that it does not ask itself, to ask the text what questions to ask, will produce the fullest, richest reading. To do justice to Shelley, you do not approach him as you do Swift. But doing justice can be a contrary business, and there are aspects of the text that, as Kate Millett demonstrated,[1] a formalist explication actively obscures. If her intentionally tangential approach violated the terms of Henry Miller's work, for example, it also revealed aspects of the work that the terms had masked. But she would not claim, I think, that her excavation of Miller's underlying assumptions had not done damage to his architecture.

The contradiction between appreciation and political analysis is not peculiar to feminist readings, but those who encountered it in the past did not resolve it either. In fact, they too denied it, or tried to. Sartre, for instance, argued in *What Is Literature?* that a good novel could not propound fascism. But then he also recognized that "the appearance of the work of art is a new event which cannot *be explained* by anterior data."[2] The Marxist Pierre Macherey hung on the horns of the same dilemma by maintaining that the literary work is tied inextricably to the life that produces it, but, although not therefore "independent," it is nonetheless "autonomous" in being defined and structured by laws uniquely proper to it.[3] (I cite Sartre and Macherey more or less at random among more or less left-wing critics because theirs is a situation somewhat like that of feminists, though less difficult, many would argue, in that they already have a voice of their own. Perhaps for that reason, the position of black critics in a world dominated by whites would more closely resemble that of women. But at any rate, the large category to which all these belong is that of the literary critic who is also and importantly a critic of her/his society, its political system, and its culture.)

My point is simply that there is no reason to deny the limits of ideological criticism, its reduction of texts that, however, it also illuminates in unique ways. As feminists at odds with our culture, we are at odds also with its literary traditions and need often to talk about texts in terms that the author did not use, may not have been aware of, and might indeed abhor. The trouble is that this necessity goes counter not only to our personal and professional commitment to all serious literature but also to our training as gentlemen and scholars, let alone as Americans, taught to value, above all, value-free scholarship.

Doubtless the possibility of maintaining thereby a sympathetic appreciative critical posture is one of the attractions of dealing only or mainly with women's writings. With such material, ironically, it is possible to avoid political judgment altogether, so that the same approach that for some represents the integration into their work of a political commitment to women can serve Patricia Meyer Spacks to make the point that "criticism need not be political to be aware."[4] She means by this that she will be able to recognize and describe a distinct female culture without evaluating either it or its patriarchal context politically. Of course she understands that all vision is mediated, so that the very selection of texts in which to observe the female imagination is judgment of a kind. But it is not ideological or normative judgment; rather it is an "arbitrary decision" that "reflects the operations of [her] imagination," a personal point of view, a "particular sensibility" with no particular political outlook. The important thing is that her "perception of the problems in every case derived from her reading of the books; the books were not selected to depict preconceived problems."

Spacks seeks in this way to disavow any political bias; but even critics who have chosen a woman-centered approach precisely for its political implications reassure us about their analytical detachment. Ellen Moers stipulates in her preface to *Literary Women* that "the literary women themselves, their language, their concerns, have done the organizing of this book." At the same time she means the book to be "a celebration of the great women who have spoken for us all."[5] Her choice of subject has thus been inspired by feminist thinking, but her approach remains supposedly neutral for she has served only as an informed amanuensis. The uncharacteristic naiveté of this stance is enforced, I think, by Moers's critical ambivalence—her wish, on the one hand, to serve a feminist purpose, and her sense, on the other, that to do so will compromise the study as criticism. So she strikes a stance that should enable her to be, like Spacks, aware but not political. Since in posing a question one already circumscribes the answer, such analytical neutrality is a phantom, however; nor was it even Spacks's goal. Her method of dealing with women separately but traditionally, treating their work as she would the opus of any mainstream school, suits her purpose, which is to define a feminine aesthetic transcending sexual politics. She actively wants to exclude political answers. Moers, seeking to discover the feminist in the feminine, is not as well served by that method; and Elaine Showalter's explicitly feminist study, *A Literature of Their Own*,[6] suggests that a political criticism may require something like the methodological reverse.

Showalter wrote her book in the hope that it would inspire women to "take strength in their independence to act in the world" and begin to create an autonomous literary universe with a "female tradition" as its "center." Coming at the end of the book, these phrases provide a resonant conclusion, for she has shown women writing in search of a wholeness that the world denies them and creating an art whose own wholeness seems a sure ground for future autonomy. But if, in an effort to flesh out this vision, one turns back to earlier discussions, one finds that there she has depicted not actual indepen-

dence but action despite dependence—and not a self-defined female culture
either, but a subculture born out of oppression and either stunted or victorious only at often-fatal cost. Women, she writes at the beginning of the book,
form such a "subculture within the framework of a larger society," and "the
female literary tradition comes from the still-evolving relationships between
women writers and their society." In other words, the meaning of that tradition has been bound up in its dependence. Now, it seems to me that much of
what Showalter wants to examine in her study, indeed much of what she does
examine, resolves itself into the difference for writers between acting independently as men do and resisting dependence as women do. If her conclusion on the contrary conflates the two, it is because the approach she takes, essentially in common with Spacks and Moers, is not well suited to her more
analytical goals.

Like theirs, her book is defined territorially as a description of the circumscribed world of women writers. *A Literature of Their Own* is thus "an attempt to fill in the terrain between [the Austen peaks, the Brontë cliffs, the
Eliot range, and the Woolf hills] and to construct a more reliable map from
which to explore the achievements of English women novelists." The trouble
is that the map of an enclosed space describes only the territory inside the en-
closure. Without knowing the surrounding geography, how are we to evalu-
ate this woman's estate, whose bordering peaks we have measured anyway, not
by any internal dimensions, but according to those of Mount Saint Dickens
and craggy Hardy? Still less can one envision the circumscribed province as
becoming independently global—hence probably the visionary vagueness of
Showalter's ending. Instead of a territorial metaphor, her analysis of the world
of women as a subculture suggests to me a more fluid imagery of interacting
juxtapositions the point of which would be to represent not so much the territory as its defining borders. Indeed, the female territory might well be envisioned as one long border, and independence for women not as a separate
country but as open access to the sea.

Women (and perhaps some men not of the universal kind) must deal with
their situation as a *precondition* for writing about it. They have to confront
the assumptions that render them a kind of fiction in themselves in that they
are defined by others, as components of the language and thought of others.
It hardly matters at this prior stage what a woman wants to write; its political
nature is implicit in the fact that it is she (a "she") who will do it. All women's
writing would thus be congenitally defiant and universally characterized by
the blasphemous argument it makes in coming into being. And this would
mean that the autonomous individuality of a woman's story or poem is

framed by engagement, the engagement of its denial of dependence. We might think of the form this necessary denial takes (however it is individually interpreted, whether conciliatory or assertive) as analogous to genre, in being an issue, not of content, but of the structural formulation of the work's relationship to the inherently formally patriarchal language which is the only language we have.

Heretofore, we have tended to treat the anterior act by which women writers create their creativity as part of their lives as purely psychological, whereas it is also a conceptual and linguistic act: the construction of an enabling relationship with a language that of itself would deny them the ability to use it creatively. This act is part of their work as well and organic to the literature that results. Since men (on the contrary) can assume a natural capacity for creation, they begin there, giving individual shape to an energy with which they are universally gifted. If it is possible, then, to analyze the writings of certain men independently—not those of all men, but only of those members of a society's ruling group whose identity in fact sets the universal norm—this is because their writings come into existence independent of prior individual acts. Women's literature begins to take its individual shape before it is properly literature, which suggests that we should analyze it inclusive of its *ur*-dependence.

In fact, the criticism of women writers has of late more and more focused on the preconditions of their writing as the inspiration not only of its content but also of its form. The writer's self-creation is the primary concern of Sandra Gilbert and Susan Gubar's *Madwoman in the Attic,*[7] whose very title identifies global (therefore mad) denial as the hot core of women's art. This impressive culmination of what I have called the territorial approach to feminist criticism does with it virtually everything that can be done. In a way of culminations, it delivers us then before a set of problems that cannot be entirely resolved in its terms but that Gilbert and Gubar have uncovered. My earlier questioning can thus become a question: What do we understand about the world, about the whole culture, from our new understanding of the woman's sphere within it? This question looks forward to a development of the study of women in a universal context, but it also has retrospective implications for what we have learned in the female context.

Gilbert and Gubar locate the female territory in its larger context and examine the borders along which the woman writer defined herself. Coming into being—an unnatural being, she must give birth to herself—the female artist commits a double murder. She kills "Milton's bogey" and the specter Virginia Woolf called the "angel in the house," the patriarch and his wife, returning then to an empty universe she will people in her own image. Blasphemy was not until the woman artist was, and the world of women writers is created in sin and extends to a horizon of eternal damnation. For all women must destroy in order to create.

Gilbert and Gubar argue with erudition and passion, and their projection of the woman writer has a definitive ring. It also has a familiar and perhaps a contradictory ring. The artist as mad defiant blasphemer or claustrophobic deviant in a society that denies such a person soulroom is a Romantic image that not only applies also to men but does so in a way that is particularly invidious to women, even more stringently denying them their own identities than earlier ideologies did. That there be contradiction is only right, for when Blake hailed Satan as the hero of *Paradise Lost,* he cast heroism in a newly contradictory mold. Satan is archfiend and Promethean man, individualistic tyrant and revolutionary, architect and supreme wrecker of worlds. It should not be surprising that he is also at once the ultimate, the protoexploiter of women, and a feminist model. But it does complicate things, as Gilbert and Gubar recognize: Mary Shelley found, in Milton, cosmic misogyny to forbid her creation—and also the model for her rebellion. But then, was her situation not just another version of the general Romantic plight, shared with her friends and relatives, poet-blasphemers all?

No, because she confronted a contradiction that superseded and preceded theirs; she was additionally torn and divided, forbidden to be Satan by Satan as well as by God, ambivalent about being ambivalent. If Satan was both demon and hero to the male poets, he offered women a third possibility, that of Byronic lover and master, therefore a prior choice: feminist assertion or feminine abandon. Here again, women had to act before they could act, choose before they could choose.

But it is just the prior choosing and acting that shape the difference between women's writing and men's that no study of only women's writing can depict. So, for instance, Gilbert and Gubar suggest that the monster in Mary Shelley's *Frankenstein* embodies in his peculiar horror a peculiarly female conception of blasphemy. It may well be, but I do not think we can tell by looking only at *Frankenstein.* At the least we need to go back and look at Satan again, not as a gloss already tending toward *Frankenstein* but as an independent term, an example of what sinful creation is—for a man. Then we need to know what it was for Mary Shelley's fellow Romantics. We might then see the extra dimension of her travail, being able to recognize it because it was extra—outside the requirements of her work and modifying that work in a special way. To reverse the frame of reference, if male critics have consistently missed the woman's aspect of *Frankenstein,* it may be only in part because they are not interested. Another reason could be that in itself the work appears as just another individual treatment of a common Romantic theme. Put simply, then, the issue for a feminist reading of *Frankenstein* is to distinguish its female version of Romanticism: an issue of relatedness and historicity. Women cannot write monologues; there must be two in the world for one woman to exist, and one of them has to be a man.

So in *The Madwoman in the Attic,* building on *Literary Women* and *A Literature of Their Own,* feminist criticism has established the historical relativity of the gender definitions that organize this culture; the patriarchal universe that has always represented itself as absolute has been revealed to be man-tailored to a masculine purpose. It is not nature we are looking at in the sexual politics of literature, but history: we know that now because women have rejected the natural order of ying and yang and lived to tell a different tale. I have been arguing that, to read this tale, one needs ultimately to relate it to the myths of the culture it comments on. The converse is also true; in denying the normative universality of men's writing, feminist criticism historicizes it, rendering it precisely, as "men's writing." On the back cover of *The Madwoman in the Attic* Robert Scholes is quoted as having written that "in the future it will be embarrassing to teach Jane Austen, Mary Shelley, the Brontës, George Eliot, Emily Dickinson, and their sisters without consulting this book." Not so embarrassing, one would like to add, as it should be to teach Samuel Richardson, Percy Bysshe Shelley, Charles Dickens, William Makepeace Thackeray, Walt Whitman, and their brothers without consulting a feminist analysis.

Indeed, in suggesting here that women critics adopt a method of radical comparativism, I have in mind as one benefit the possibility of demonstrating thereby the contingency of the dominant male traditions as well. Comparison reverses the territorial image along with its contained methodology and projects instead, as the world of women, something like a long border. The confrontations along that border between, say, *Portrait of a Lady* and *House of Mirth,* two literary worlds created by two gods out of one thematic clay, can light up the outer and most encompassing parameters (perimeters) of both worlds, illuminating the philosophical grounds of the two cosmic models, "natures" that otherwise appear unimpeachably absolute. This border (this no-man's-land) might have provided Archimedes himself a standpoint. Through the disengagements, the distancings of comparative analyses, of focusing on the relations between situations rather than on the situations themselves, one might be able to generate the conceptual equivalent of getting off this world and seeing it from the outside. At the same time, comparison also involves engagement by requiring one to identify the specific qualities of each term. The overabstraction of future visions has often been the flip side of nonanalytical descriptions of the present viewed only in its own internal terms. To talk about then and now as focuses of relations may be a way of tempering both misty fantasies and myopic documentations.

Thus the work of a woman—whose proposal to be a writer in itself reveals that female identity is not naturally what it has been assumed to be—may be used comparatively as an external ground for seeing the dominant literature whole. Hers is so fundamental a denial that its outline outlines as well the assumption it confronts. And such comparison works in reverse, too, for juxtaposed with the masculinist assumption we can also see whole the feminist denial and trace its limits. Denial always runs the risk of merely shaping itself in the negative image of what it rejects. If there is any danger that feminism may become trapped, either in winning for women the right to be men or in taking the opposite sentimental tack and celebrating the feminine identity of an oppressed past as ideal womanhood, these extremes can be better avoided when women's assumptions too can be seen down to their structural roots—from the other ground provided by men's writing.

Lest it appear that I am advocating a sort of comparison mongering, let me cite as a model, early blazing a path we have not followed very far, a study that on the surface is not at all comparative. Millett's *Sexual Politics* was all about comparison, however, about the abysses between standpoints, between where men stood to look at women and where women stood to be looked at. Facing these two at the book's starting point was Millett's construction of yet another lookout where a feminist might stand. As criticism per se, *Sexual Politics* may be flawed by its simplifying insistence on a single issue. But as ideological analysis, as model illuminator and "deconstructor," it remains our most powerful work. It is somewhat puzzling that, since then, so little has been written about the dominant literary culture whose ideas and methods of dominance were Millett's major concerns.[8] It may be that the critical shortcomings of so tangential an approach have been too worrisome. Certainly it is in reading the dominant "universal" literature that the contradictions of an ideological criticism become most acute. There are many ways of dealing with contradictions, however, of which only one is to try to resolve them. Another way amounts to joining a contradiction—engaging it not so much for the purpose of overcoming it as to tap its energy. To return one last time to the fulcrum image, a fulcrum is a point at which force is transmitted—the feminist fulcrum is not just any point in the culture where misogyny is manifested but one where misogyny is pivotal or crucial to the whole. The thing to

look for in our studies, I believe, is the connection, the meshing of a definition of women and a definition of the world. And insofar as the former is
deleterious, the connection will be contradictory; indeed, as the literary examples that follow suggest, one may recognize a point of connection by its
contradictions. It will turn out, or I will try to show, that contradictions just
such as that between ethical and aesthetic that we have tried to resolve away
lest they belie our argument frequently are our firmest and most fruitful
grounds. The second part of this essay will attempt to illustrate this use of
contradiction through the example of the American sentimental novel, a
kind of women's writing in which the contradiction between ideology and
criticism would appear well-nigh overwhelming.

II

The problem is all too easily stated: the sentimental novels that were best sell-
ers in America from the 1820s to the 1860s were written and read mostly
by women, constituting an oasis of women's writing in an American tradition that was otherwise exceptionally (by comparison to European traditions)
dominated by men. But this oasis holds scant refreshment; most of the
women's writing is awful. So there it is, the *one* area of American writing that
women have defined ostensibly in their own image, and it turned out just as
the fellows might have predicted. Henry Nash Smith guessed that Susan
Warner's *Wide Wide World* set "an all-time record for frequency of references
to tears and weeping."[9] Hawthorne, whose cri de coeur against the "damned
mob of scribbling women" resonated down the century, did not invent the association between sentimentality and women. The scribbling women themselves did, ascribing their powers to draw readers deep into murky plots and
uplift them to heavenly visions to the special gifts of a feminine sensibility. If
there is no question of celebrating in the sentimentalists "great women who
have spoken for us all," it seems just as clear that they spoke as women to
women, and that, if we are to criticize the place of women in this culture, we
need to account for the very large place they occupied—and still do; the sentimental mode remains a major aspect of literary commerce, still mostly written and read by women.

Although at bottom either way presents the same contradiction between
politics and criticism, the sentimental novel would seem, therefore, to flip the
problems encountered in *A Literature of Their Own, Literary Women,* and *The
Madwoman in the Attic.* The issue there was to uncover new aspects of works
and writers that had more or less transcended the limitations of the patriarchal
culture—or failed and found tragedy. Inspired by their example, one had

nonetheless to temper admiration with critical distance. Here the difficulty lies instead in tempering rejection with a recognition of kinship, kinship one is somewhat hesitant to acknowledge in that it rests on a shared subordination in which the sentimental novel appears altogether complicitous. For the sentimentalists were prophets of compliance, to God the patriarch as to his viceroys on earth. Their stories are morality dramas featuring heroines prone at the start to react to unjust treatment by stamping their feet and weeping rebellious tears, but who learn better and in the end find happiness in "unquestioning submission to authority, whether of God or an earthly father figure or society in general." They also find some more substantial rewards, Mammon rising like a fairy godmother to bestow rich husbands and fine houses. Conformity is powerful, and Henry Nash Smith's explication of it all has a definitive clarity: "The surrender of inner freedom, the discipline of deviant impulses into rapturous conformity, and the consequent achievement of both worldly success and divine grace merge into a single mythical process, a cosmic success story."[10] If that success is ill-gotten by Smith's lights, it can only appear still more tainted to a feminist critic whose focus makes her acutely aware that the sweet sellout is a woman and the inner freedom of women her first sale. With overgrown conscience and shrunken libido, the sentimental heroine enumerating her blessings in the many rooms of her husband's mansion is the prototype of that deformed angel Virginia Woolf urged us to kill.

To kill within ourselves, that is. Thus we return to the recognition of kinship that makes it necessary to understand the sentimentalists not only the way critics generally have explained them but also as writers expressing a specifically female response to the patriarchal culture. This is a controversial venture that has resulted thus far in (roughly defined) two schools of thought. One of these starts from Hawthorne's charge that the popular novels usurped the place of serious literature. The title of Ann Douglas's *Feminization of American Culture*[11] announces her thesis that the sentimentalists exploited a literary Gresham's law to debase the cultural currency with their feminine coin. This bad money devalued outright Hawthorne's and Melville's good. A tough, iconoclastic, and individualistic masculine high culture, the potential worthy successor of the tough Puritan ethos, was thus routed from the national arena by a conservative femininity that chained the arts to the corners of hearths and to church pews. Henceforth, and still today, a stultifying mass culture has emasculated the American imagination. Douglas does not blame women for this, for she sees them as themselves defined by their society. Even in the exploitation of their destructive power, she thinks, they meant well; nor would she wish for an equivalently simpleminded macho replacement to the feminized culture. But the implied alternative is nonetheless definitely masculine—in a good way, of course: strong, serious, and generously accepting of women who have abjured their feminine sensibilities. Not a hard thing to do, for if the choice is between Susan Warner and Melville, why were we not all born men?

That choice, however, is just the problem, its traditional limits generated by the Archimedean bind of trying to think about new issues in the old terms, when those terms do not merely ignore the new issues but deny them actively and thus force one instead into the old ways, offering choices only among them. The terms here are masculine and feminine as they participate in clusters of value that interpret American history and culture. It has been generally understood among cultural and social historians that the creative force in America is individualistic, active . . . masculine. Perhaps to a fault: Quentin Anderson would have liked the American self less imperially antisocial,[12] and before him Leslie Fiedler worried that its exclusive masculinity excluded heterosexual erotic love.[13] These analysts of American individualism do not necessarily come to judge it the same way, but they define it alike and alike therefore project as its logical opposition conformity, passive compliance, familialism . . . femininity. Huck Finn and Aunt Polly. The critical literature has until now mostly concentrated on Huck Finn, and *The Feminization of American Culture* completes the picture by focusing on Aunt Polly.

In the sense that its features are composed from real models, "Aunt Polly" may well be a true picture. But her position in the composite American portrait, opposed in her trite conventionality to "his" rugged individualism, is not a function of models alone but also of an interpretive scheme secured by a set of parallel dichotomies that vouch for one another: Aunt Polly is to Huck as feminine is to masculine; feminine is to masculine as Aunt Polly is to Huck. Only if we pull these apart will we be able to question the separate validity of either.

Potentially even more radically, Nina Baym[14] sets out to reconsider the component terms of the generally accepted dichotomy in the nineteenth century between female conformity and manly individualism, between female social conservatism and masculine rebellion. Representing the other school of thought about sentimentalism, this one in line with recent historical reconsideration of such ridiculed women's movements as temperance and revivalism, she argues that the women novelists too had their reasons. She answers Smith's accusation that the novels' "cosmic success story" pointed an archconservative moral by suggesting that for disenfranchised and property-deprived women to acquire wealth, social status, and some measure of control over their domestic environment could be considered a radical achievement, as ruling a husband by virtue of virtue might amount to subversion. The heroines of the novels Baym treats do not run their society and never hope to, so, short of revolution, no direct action can be taken. Even from their state of total dependence, however, these women can rise to take practical charge of their lives and acquire a significant measure of power by implementing the conservative roles to which the patriarchal society has relegated them. In this light, what Smith terms their "ethos of conformity" takes on another aspect and almost becomes a force for change, all depending on how you look at it.

Which is precisely the problem of this essay, emerging here with unusual clarity because both Smith and Baym approach the material ideologically. Even their descriptions, let alone their interpretations, show the effects of divergent standpoints. Consider how each summarizes the typical sentimental plot. Smith reports that *Wide Wide World* is the tale of "an orphan exposed to poverty and psychological hardships who finally attains economic security and high social status through marriage."[15] Baym reads the same novel as "the story of a young girl who is deprived of the supports she had rightly or wrongly depended on to sustain her throughout life and is faced with the necessity of winning her own way in the world" (11). The second account stresses the role of the girl herself in defining her situation, so that the crux of her story becomes her passage from passivity to active engagement. On the contrary, with an eye to her environment and its use of her, Smith posits her as passive throughout, "exposed" at first, in the end married. Clearly this is not a matter of right or wrong readings but of a politics of vision.

It is as a discussion of the politics of vision that *Woman's Fiction* is perhaps most valuable. Baym has set out to see the novels from a different perspective, and indeed they look different. The impossible piety of the heroine, for instance, Baym views as an assertion of her moral strength against those who consider her an empty vessel, lacking ego and understanding and in need of constant supervision. Typically the heroine starts out sharing this view, taking herself very lightly and looking to the world to coddle and protect her. With each pious stand she takes over the course of the novel, she becomes more self-reliant, until by the end she has "developed a strong conviction of her own worth" (19) and becomes a model for female self-respect. Thus, the heroine's culminating righteousness and its concomitant rewards, that from one viewpoint prove the opportunistic virtues of submission, indicate to Baym a new and quite rare emergence of female power manifested in the avalanche of good things with which the story ends. To Smith those cornucopia endings are the payoff for mindless acquiescence, sweets for the sweet ruining the nation's palate for stronger meat. For Douglas they are a banquet celebrating the women's takeover; a starving Melville is locked out. But for Baym the comfort in which the heroine rests at last is her hard-earned just reward, the sentimental cult of domesticity representing a pragmatic feminism aimed primarily at establishing a place for women under their own rule.

In that spirit, she sees a more grown-up kind of sense than do most critics in the novels' prudishness, pointing out that, when they were written, the Richardsonian model they otherwise followed had become a tale of seduction. The women novelists, she suggests, were "unwilling to accept . . . a concept of woman as inevitable sexual prey" (26); in a world where sexual politics hardly offered women a democratic choice, they preferred to eschew sex altogether rather than be raped. Here again, point of view is all. One recalls that Fiedler had a more ominous reading. According to him, the middle-class ladies who wrote the sentimental fiction had "grown too genteel for sex" but, being female, they still yearned "to see women portrayed as abused and suffering, and the male as crushed and submissive in the end";[16] so they desexed their heroes by causing them to love exceptionally good girls with whom sex was unthinkable.

Without sharing Fiedler's alarm over the state of American manhood, one has to concede that the sentimental novel, with its ethereal heroines and staunchly buttoned heroes, was indeed of a rarefied spirituality. That its typical plot traced, instead of physical seduction, the moral regeneration and all-around strengthening of erstwhile helpless women would appear all to the good; it is surely an improvement for women to cease being portrayed as inevitable victims. But the fact is that the sentimental heroines, perhaps rich as models, are rather poor as characters. Those inner possibilities they discover in becoming self-sufficient seem paradoxically to quench any interior life, so that we nod in both senses of the word when such a heroine "looks to marry a man who is strong, stable and safe." For, "she is canny in her judgment of men, and generally immune to the appeal of a dissolute suitor. When she feels such attraction, she resists it" (41). Quite right, except we actually wish she would not: do we then regret the fragile fair who fell instantly and irrevocably in an earlier literature, or the "graceful deaths that created remorse in all one's tormentors" (25) and in the story some sparks of life?

Baym is well aware of the problem and offers two possible analyses. In the first place, she says, the women novelists never claimed to be writing great literature. They thought of "authorship as a profession rather than a calling, as work and not art. Often the women deliberately and even proudly disavowed membership in an artistic fraternity." So they intentionally traded art for ideology, a matter of political rather than critical significance. "Yet," she adds (and here she is worth quoting at length because she has articulated clearly and forcefully a view that is important in feminist criticism),

> I cannot avoid the belief that "purely" literary criteria, as they have been employed to identify the best American works, have inevitably had a bias in favor of things male—in favor, say of whaling ships rather than the sewing circle as a symbol of the human community; in favor of satires on domineering mothers, shrewish wives, or betraying mistresses rather than tyrannical fathers, abusive husbands, or philandering suitors; displaying an exquisite compassion for the crises of the adolescent male, but altogether impatient with the parallel crises of the female. While not claiming literary greatness for any of the novels introduced in this study, I would like at least to begin to correct such a bias by taking their content seriously. And it is time, perhaps—though this task lies outside my scope here—to reexamine the grounds upon which certain hallowed American classics have been called great. (14–15)

On the surface this is an attractive position, and, indeed, much of it is unquestionably valid; but it will not bear a close analysis. She is having it both ways, admitting the artistic limitations of the women's fiction ("I have not unearthed a forgotten Jane Austen or George Eliot, or hit upon even one novel that I would propose to set alongside *The Scarlet Letter*" [14]) and at the same time denying the validity of the criteria that measure those limitations; disclaiming any ambition to reorder the literary canon, and, on second thought, challenging the canon after all—or rather challenging not the canon itself but the grounds for its selection.

There is much reason to reconsider these grounds, and such reconsideration should be one aim of an aggressive feminist criticism. But it has little to do with the problem at hand—the low quality of the women's fiction—that no reconsideration will raise. True, whaling voyages are generally taken more seriously than sewing circles, but it is also true that Melville's treatment of the whale hunt is a more serious affair than the sentimentalists' treatment of sewing circles. And the latter, when treated in the larger terms of the former, do get recognized—for example, Penelope weaving the shroud for Ulysses surrounded by her suitors, or, for that matter, the opening scene of *Middlemarch* in which two young girls quibble over baubles, situations whose resonance not even the most misogynist reader misses.

The first part of the explanation, that the women did not take *themselves* seriously, seems more promising. Baym tells us that they "were expected to write specifically for their own sex and within the tradition of their woman's culture rather than within the Great Tradition"; certainly, "they never presented themselves as followers in the footsteps of Milton or Spenser, seekers after literary immortality, or competitors with the male authors of their own time who were aiming at greatness" (178). With this we come closer to the writing itself and therefore to the sources of its intrinsic success or failure. I want to stress intrinsic here as a way of recalling the distinction between a work as politics—its external significance—and as art. So when seeking to explain the intrinsic failures of the sentimentalists, one needs to look beyond their politics, beyond their relationships with publishers, critics, or audiences, to their relationship to writing as such. Melville wrote without the support of publishers, critics, and audiences—indeed, despite their active discouragement—so those cannot be the crucial elements. He did, however, have himself, he took himself seriously; as Whitman might have said, he *assumed* himself.

Now, no woman can assume herself because she has yet to create herself, and this the sentimentalists, acceding to their society's definition, did not do. To the extent that they began by taking the basic order of things as given, they forswore any claim on the primary vision of art[17] and saw themselves instead as interpreters of the established ethos, its guardians, or even, where needed, its restorers. My point is that, for all their virtual monopoly of the literary marketplace, the women novelists, being themselves conceived by others, were conceptually totally dependent. This means dependent on Melville himself and on the dominant culture of which he, but not they, was a full, albeit an alienated or even a reviled, member. His novel in the sentimental mode could take on sentimentalism because he had an alternative world on which to stand: himself. And although no one would wish on a friendly author the travail that brought forth *Pierre,* there it is nonetheless, the perfect example of what no woman novelist conceiving of herself not as an artist or maker but as a "professional"—read practitioner, implementor, transmitter, follower of a craft—could ever have written. *Pierre* does not know how to be acquiescently sentimental, it can only be *about* sentimentalism. The issue is self-consciousness, and in self-consciousness, it is self. With the example of Melville, we might then reconsider the relationship of the rebel to conventions. The rebel has his conventional definition too—that is, his is one possible interpretation of the conventions—so that he stands fully formed within the culture, at a leading edge. On the other hand, in this society women stand outside any of the definitions of complete being; hence perhaps the appeal to them of a literature of conformity and inclusion—and the extraordinary difficulty, but for the extraordinary few, of serious writing.

Indeed, Baym's defense of the women novelists, like that generally of the lesser achievement of women in any art, seems to me finally unnecessary. If history has treated women badly, it is entirely to be expected that a reduced or distorted female culture, one that is variously discouraged, embittered, obsessively parochial, or self-abnegating, will show it. There is little point then in claiming more than exists or in looking to past achievement as evidence of future promise: at this stage of history, we have the right, I think, simply to assert the promise.

If there is no cause for defensiveness, moreover, it does have its cost. In the case of the sentimental novel, for instance, too much apologia can obscure the hard question Baym implies but does not quite articulate, to wit, why are the ways in which the sentimental novel asserts that women can succeed precisely the ways that it fails as literature? *Is its ideological success tied to its artistic failure?* Is its lack of persuasiveness as art in some way the result of the strong ideological argument it makes for female independence? The issue, it seems, is not merely neglecting art for the sake of politics but actively sacrificing it. Which brings the discussion back to the Douglas thesis that since the sentimentalists universalized (Americanized) a debased feminine culture, the more powerful the women (authors and heroines both), the worse the literature and thereby the consequences for the whole culture. The great appeal of this argument is that it confronts squarely the painful contradiction of women becoming powerful not by overcoming but by exploiting their impotence.

I would like to suggest another possible explanation. The contradiction between the art and the politics of the sentimental novel arises, not surprisingly, at the point where the novelists confronted the tradition in which they were working and, for political reasons, rejected it formally: when they refused to perpetuate the image of the seduced and abandoned heroine and substituted in her stead the good girl who holds out to the happy (bitter or boring) end. The parent tradition is that of the novel of sensibility as it was defined in *Clarissa*. But before *Clarissa,* Richardson wrote *Pamela,* probably the prototype of the female "cosmic success story." Pamela begins powerless and ends up in charge, rewarded for her tenacious virtue (or her virtuous tenacity) by a commodious house, a husband, and all those same comforts of upper middle-class life that crowned the goodness of America's sentimental heroines. Indeed, *Pamela* had helped set up their new world, being the first novel actually printed here—by Benjamin Franklin, who understood both romance and commerce and knew how well they could work together. So did

Pamela, of course, a superb pragmatist who not only foils a seducer but also turns him into a very nice husband. She is perhaps not so finely tuned or morally nice as her sentimental descendants, but she is quite as careful and controlled, as certain of her values, as unwilling to be victimized—and ultimately as triumphant. In contrast, Clarissa is helplessly enamored, seduced, destroyed. She is also the more interesting character and *Clarissa* the more complex story—can it be that weak victimized women make for better novels?

In the first part of this discussion, I made the point that the madness into which women artists are characterized as driven by social constraints needs to be compared with the similar state often attributed to male artists. The same need arises here, for male protagonists too are generally defeated, and, of course, Clarissa's seducer Lovelace dies along with her. But he is neither weak (in the helpless sense that she is) nor victimized; nor (to name doomed heroes at random) is Stendhal's Julien Sorel or Melville's Pierre. There is certainly no surprise in the contrast as such; we expect male characters to be stronger than female. The juxtaposition, however, may be suggesting something not already so evident: that as the distinctive individual identity of a male character typically is generated by his defiance, so that of a female character seems to come from her vulnerability, which thus would be organic to the heroine as a novelistic construct.

It seems reasonable to suppose that the novel, envisioning the encounter of the individual with his world in the modern idiom, posits as one of its structuring assumptions (an assumption that transcends the merely thematic, to function formally) the special form that sexual hierarchy has taken in modern times. The novel, we know, is organically individualistic: even when it deals with several equally important individuals, or attacks individualism itself, it is always about the unitary self versus the others. Moreover, it is about the generation, the becoming, of that self. I want to suggest that this process may be so defined as to require a definition of female characters that effectively precludes their becoming autonomous, so that indeed they would do so at the risk of the novel's artistic life.

Pamela represents the advent of a new form to deal with such new problems of the modern era as the transformation of the family and the newly dynamic mode of social mobility. *Pamela* works these out very well for its heroine, but there is something wrong in the resolution. Pamela's triumph means the defeat of Mr. B., who in his chastened state can hardly be the enterprising, potent entrepreneur that the rising middle class needs him to be. Her individualism has evolved at the cost of his; later Freud would develop a special term for such misadventures, but Richardson must already have known that this was not the way it should be.

At any rate, he resolved this difficulty in his next work simply by raising the social status of his heroine. Since she was a servant, Pamela's quest for independent selfhood necessarily took a public form. To affirm her value and remain in possession of her self, Pamela had to assert her equality publicly; to claim herself, she had, in effect, to claim power. But as an established member of the powerful class, Clarissa is in full possession of its perquisites, notably that of being taken as honorably marriageable by the lords of her world. Though it is true that her family's greed for yet more wealth and status precipitates her crisis, the problems she faces are really not those of upward mobility. Standing at the other end of that process, she is profoundly unhappy with its results and with the internal workings of her society. Her story is about the conflict within, the problems that arise inside the middle-class world; and its marvelously suited theater for exploring these is the self within.

In thus locating itself inside the life of its dominant class, the novel only followed suit after older genres. But what is peculiar to this genre is that it locates the internal problems of its society still deeper inside, inside the self. Richardson's earlier novel had retained an older conception more like that of Defoe, identifying the self externally—hence *Pamela*'s interpretation of romance as commerce. *Clarissa,* on the contrary, now treats commerce in the terms of romance. Pamela had projected her inner world outward and identified her growth as a character with the extension of her power. But this approach tends to vitiate the distinction between the private self and the world out there that is the powerful crux of middle-class identity. *Clarissa* takes that distinction as its theme, and the locale of the novel henceforth is the interior life. I want to propose the thesis that this interior life, *whether lived by man or woman, is female,* so that women characters define themselves and have power only in this realm. Androgyny, in the novel, is a male trait enabling men to act from their male side and feel from their female side.

One common feminist notion is that the patriarchal society suppresses the interior lives of women. In literature, at least, this does not seem altogether true, for indeed the interior lives of female characters are the novel's mainstay. Instead, it is women's ability to act in the public domain that novels suppress, and again Richardson may have shown the way. *Pamela* developed its heroine by reducing its hero (in conventional terms). This compensation was, in fact, inevitable as long as the characters defined themselves the same way, by using and expanding the individualistic potency of the self. Since by this scheme Pamela would be less of a person and a character if she were less active, she had to compete with Mr. B. to the detriment of one of them—to the detriment also of conjugal hierarchy and beyond that, of their society, whose resulting universal competitiveness must become dangerously atomizing and possibly centrifugal. In a middle-class society, however, the family unit is meant to generate coherence, in that the home provides both a base and a terminus for the competitive activity of the marketplace. The self-reliant man necessarily subsumes his family, chief among them his wife, to his own identity; it is in the middle-class society above all that a man's home is his castle. But how can this subsuming be accomplished without denying identity to women altogether and thus seriously undermining their potency as helpmates as well? The problem lies in retaining this potency, that can come only from individualism, without suffering the consequences of its realization in individualistic competition. Tocqueville particularly admired the way this problem had been resolved in America. Women in the New World were free, strong, and independent, but they *voluntarily* stayed home. In other words, their autonomy was realized by being freely abandoned, after which, of course, they ceased to exist as characters—witness their virtual absence from the American novel.

The European novelist, at least the English and the French, either less sanguine about the natural goodness of middle-class values or more embattled with older norms, saw that this voluntary subjugation could be problematical. If women too are people, and people are individualists, might they not rebel? If they succeeded in this, social order would crumble; indeed, they could not succeed because they did not have the power. But the possibility, arising from the most basic terms of middle-class thought and also doomed by the very prevalence of that thought, emerged as the central drama of the modern imagination. It is precisely the drama of the suppressed self, the self who assumes the universal duty of self-realization but finds its individual model in absolute conflict with society. Then as it becomes the more heroically individualistic, the more self-realized, the more it pushes toward inevitable doom. If there is a tragic dimension to the novel, it is here in the doomed encounter between the female self and the middle-class world. This is the encounter Gilbert and Gubar have observed and attributed, too exclusively I think, to women. The lack of a comparative dimension can tend to obscure the distinction between representation and reality, to fuse them so that the female self simply is woman, if woman maligned. But, as Flaubert might have pointed out, many a male novelist has represented at least part of himself as female.

Which is not to suggest that European novelists were champions of women's rights. Their interest lay rather in the metaphorical potential of the female situation to represent the great Problem of modern society, the reconciliation of the private and the public realms, once the cornerstone of the new social and economic order has been laid in their alienation. Such reconciliation is problematical in that the self, granted its freedom, may not willingly accept social control; it may insist on its separate and other privacy, on the integrity of its interior vision. Clarissa wants to be and do otherwise than her world permits, and with that impulse, her inner self comes into view. It grows as she becomes less and less able to project her will, or rather as the incursions against her private self become more ferocious. Who, and what, Clarissa is finally *is* that private world.

I want to stress that in championing her alienated private self, the novel is not taking the side of real women, or even of female characters as female. Recent praise of *Clarissa* as a feminist document, or vindications of its heroine's behavior against her patriarchal oppressors, have not dealt clearly enough with the fact that her creator was a patriarch. If nonetheless he envisioned his heroine in terms with which feminists may sympathize, it is, I believe, because he viewed her as representing not really woman but the interior self, the female interior self in all men—in all men, but especially developed perhaps in writers, whose external role in this society is particularly incommensurate with their vision, who create new worlds but earn sparse recognition or often outright scorn in this one.

It is in this sense, I think, that Emma Bovary was Flaubert, or Anna Karenina, Tolstoy, or Isabel Archer, James. But the way Dorothea Brooke was George Eliot reveals the edge of this common identification between author and heroine, for Eliot, though herself a successful woman, cannot envision Dorothea as equally so.[18] One might suppose that she at least could have imagined her heroine, if not triumphant like Julien Sorel, acting out her doom rather than accepting it. It is one thing for male novelists to assume that women are incapable of effective action, but that women do so as well is more disturbing. I am suggesting that George Eliot was compelled by the form of her story to tell it as she did, that the novel as a genre precludes androgynously heroic women while and indeed *because* it demands androgynous heroes. In other words, the novel demands that the hero have an interior life and that this interior life be metaphorically female. The exterior life, on the other hand, is just as ineluctably male (and the novel has its share of active, manly women). These identifications are not consciously made as being convenient or realistic, in which case they would be vulnerable to conscious change. They are assumed, built into the genre as organic and natural; for, if action were either male or female, we would be back with the potentially castrating Pamela. She, however, bent her considerable force to enter the middle class, endorsing its values wholeheartedly. A similarly active Clarissa, an effective and militant Dorothea, must threaten the entire order of things.

The novel is critical, it examines and even approves the rebellions of Clarissa and Dorothea, but only after signaling its more basic acceptance of an order it locates, beyond political attack, in nature itself. Julien Sorel's alienation, however Napoleonic his aspirations, is associated throughout with the female part of his character; his sensitivity, his inability to accept the life and values his father offers him, these are repeatedly described as feminine traits, and the final act that destroys him bespeaks his feminine nature, much to the dismay of his male friends. In the mirror world of this and other novels, femaleness is not conservative but potentially revolutionary. At the same time, it is by cultural definition incapable of active fulfillment. In taking woman as metaphor for the interior life, then, and—far from suppressing her—expanding hers almost to the exclusion of any other life, the novel both claimed its interior, individualistic, alienated territory and placed the limits of that territory within the structures of the middle-class world it serves. George Eliot could have made Dorothea strong only by challenging these structures or by accepting them and depicting her as manly, thereby telling another story, perhaps *The Bostonians.* And no more than this latter would that story have challenged the conventional notions of feminine and masculine.

There is a third possibility for the novel, which is to return to *Pamela* and close down the alienated interior realm by having Dorothea act not out of internal impulses but in response to social dictates. This is what the sentimental novel does, its heroines realizing themselves in society actively but in full accord with its values and imperatives. This solution to the subversive threat posed by female individualism amounts to reversing the Richardsonian development from *Pamela* to *Clarissa.* We have a precise representation of that reversal—wrought, one is tempted to think, in deference to the greater solidity of the middle-class ethic in this country—in the first American novel, *Charlotte Temple* (1791). Its author, Susanna Rowson, copies the contemporary fashion of *Clarissa*-like stories but then, apparently thinking the better of such downbeat endings, tacks on a *Pamela* conclusion. Charlotte Temple, the disastrously fragile English heroine of the story, is carried off by a soldier en route to America; no sooner carried off than pregnant, no sooner pregnant than abandoned, no sooner abandoned than wandering the icy roads in winter in slippers and a thin shawl. She is charitably taken in to a hospitable fireside only to pass away, leaving an innocent babe and much remorse all around. At this point, however, with one perfectly satisfactory ending in place, Susanna Rowson adds a second.

While neglecting Charlotte, her faithless lover Montraville has fallen in love with New York's most desirable belle, Julia Franklin, an orphaned heiress who is "the very reverse of Charlotte Temple." Julia is strong, healthy, and of independent means and spirit. Her guardian entertains "too high an opinion of her prudence to scrutinize her actions so much as would have been necessary with many young ladies who were not blest with her discretion." Though Montraville has behaved badly toward the hapless Charlotte, he seems to be capable of a New World redemption. Overcome by guilt at Charlotte's death, he fights a duel to avenge her honor and is dangerously wounded but, more fortunate than Lovelace, is nursed back to health by the discreet Julia. A representative of the new American womanhood, far too sensible to be tempted by rakes, far too clear about the uses of romantic love ever to separate it from marriage, Julia has accomplished the "Pamela" reform. She marries Montraville, and he becomes one of New York's most upright (and affluent) citizens, the fallen seducer risen a husband through the ministrations of a woman who is not merely good but also strong—strong, of course, in being all that she should be. Thus in Julia Franklin the private and the public selves are one, and the novel, with no relation between them to explore and therefore no way or need to envision the private, comes to a speedy end. About Charlotte a far better novel could have and has been written, but about Julia really nothing but exemplary tales for young girls and their spinster aunts. Pioneer mother of sentimental heroines, she deeds them an ability to take care of themselves (by taking care) that Baym rightly applauds from a feminist viewpoint but that effectively does them in as literature. This implies a possibility no less drastic than that the novel, evolved to deal with the psychological and emotional issues of a patriarchal society, may not permit a feminist interpretation.

The possibility that an impotent feminine sensibility is a basic structure of the novel, representing one of the important ways that the novel embodies the basic structures of this society, would suggest more generally that the achievement of female autonomy must have radical implications not only politically but also for the very forms and categories of all our thinking. Yet as students of this thinking, we are not only implicated in it but many of us committed to much of it. Literary criticism especially, because it addresses the best this thinking has produced, exposes this paradox in all its painful complexity—while also revealing the extraordinary possibility of our seeing the old world from a genuinely new perspective.

This analysis of novelistic form has been speculative, of course, a way of setting the issues of women's writing in the context of the whole literature in order to illustrate the uses of a comparative viewpoint as an alternative footing at the critical distance needed for re-vision. It has also been an exercise in joining rather than avoiding the contradiction between ideological and appreciative criticism on the supposition that the crucial issues manifest themselves precisely at the points of contradiction. As a method this has further implications I cannot pursue here. Let me suggest only that to focus on points of contradiction as the places where we can see the whole structure of our world most clearly implies the immanent relativity of all perception and knowledge. Thus, what appears first as a methodological contradiction, then becomes a subject in itself, seems finally to be shaping something like a new epistemology. But then, it is only right that feminism, as rethinking, rethink thinking itself.

Flaubert's *Dictionary of Received Ideas* offers, for the entry "Colonies (our)," a cautionary definition: "Register sadness in speaking of them." With this recommendation, the author, as is his wont, mocks his compatriots of good conscience, ridiculing hypocrisies that mask horrors. The empire here joins romance, bourgeois marriage, and the excellence of provincial virtue in Flaubert's catalog of foundational falsehoods of the nineteenth century. In his time, the creed of empire was as basic to French and European right-thinking as that of domesticity, was indeed the complement of domesticity since the common wisdom held until well into the twentieth century that an imperial impulse was the very pulse of Western man and colonies the natural fruit of his overflowing virility. Though the West's civilizing mission might occasionally lapse and was often disappointed (inducing sadness), colonizing lay in the order of things and those who questioned that order were alienated souls who probably also had doubts about conjugal love.

Now however, at the beginning of a new millennium and concurrently nightfall in the empire whose day began five centuries ago, most Westerners living through the end of this era have taken skepticism for their familiar. If the empire seemed to rest on a natural foundation when it encircled the globe, for us who mainly fear having made the whole world unnatural, history is too clearly of human provenance. Even the annexation of the American continents, where Europeans made themselves so thoroughly at home they considered removing the former inhabitants just housekeeping, no longer seems so self-evident. It is not obvious any more that the Spanish, the French, and the English would naturally impose their civilizations upon two continents on the other side of the world. The conquest of America suddenly needs explaining.

At the same time, out of the empire's penumbra, the civilizations it long shadowed are emerging with renewed clarity. Indeed these formerly eclipsed civilizations themselves, particularly through the narrative of their colonization, seem to be coining the dominant idiom—as one would have said, the King's English—of the current international conversation. Postcolonial recuperations and reconstructions are providing the organizing terms of an increasingly influential revisionary history that attempts to turn the analytical tables on Europe itself (and as well on Europe-in-America). Such a refraction of Europe through the colonies is perfectly in line, of course, since European civilization is inconceivable without its empire. Equally, the experience of colonization fundamentally reshaped the colonized; so we ought not to be surprised if, even as it dissolves, the empire proves as adhesive as ever, conquest and colonization remaining central issues of national self-definition for former imperialists and imperialized alike. But though unsurprising, this adhesiveness needs noting, both in itself as a political and cultural phenomenon and because it glosses one of the key words of the current analytical discourse, the word "difference."

In turn, "difference" glosses another key word, "other," glosses it by attempting to replace it as oppressive to those so designated.[1] Naming them "other" seems to cast the speaker's cultural interlocutors in an inferior position by rendering them mere negative quantities defined by an opposition to which they do not contribute. The term "different" proposes to right this imbalance by granting others identities of their own. With the substitution of "difference" for "otherness," it is hoped that the imperial monologue becomes a two-sided exchange. Describing oneself or one's kind as "other," one would not only represent the very meaning of alienation but be incapable of further self-definition and even speech; while to declare oneself "different" leads logically to self-description, even to monologue. Let's just say "Rousseau" and move on.

Derridean deconstruction lends a certain formulaic rigor to the notion of difference as part of the neologism "différance." Différance, gerundial and antinomian, combines two verbs, to differ and to defer, to explain how (also why) no definition can ever attain a definitive authority. In time, difference is the stuff of Zeno's paradox, preventing any account from reaching a final truth. The race that never ends cannot go to the swift. In space, difference denies the centrality of any point of view and the all-encompassingness of any horizon. All this amounts to denying the ground for the transcending self-sufficiency that authorizes designating the Emersonian "Not-Me" as "the other." To return to our original vocabulary, difference is the anticolonial response to the imperial history of otherness.

Students of difference might be said to be the reluctant heirs of Europe's late empire, dismantling its house and marking for return piles of looted goods. Edward Said's analysis of "orientalism" suggests why the metaphysical goods have been especially difficult to catalog. In the American colonies, a mass of European presumption overwhelmed Amerindian cultures, perhaps beyond extricating. The arriving Europeans were so intent on taking over that few even registered the indigenous cultures. The discoverer himself began his first letter home not with what he found but what he did to it. "I reached the Indian sea," Columbus reported, "where I discovered many islands, thickly peopled, of which I took possession without resistance in the name of our most illustrious Monarch, by public proclamation and with unfurled banners."[2] (Proving, in this invocation of sonorous Spanish and snappy standards deployed on an innocent beach, that when you have the upper hand you can afford to look ridiculous.) Columbus's admirably succinct account of his landfall would do as the first example in a primer of imperial prose. "I reached . . . I discovered . . . I took," he writes; the objects of my actions were both abundant and anonymous, "many islands, thickly peopled," an indefinite, possibly infinite plenitude lacking only the agency to resist. Therefore imposing my will, which is the will of white civilization, was only natural and right. "I took possession" of this latent world and named it: in making it mine I made *it,* imparting to it political capability, bringing it into the Law. I baptized it in the name of "our most illustrious Monarch" with the ceremonies and symbols in which civilization inheres, with rhetoric and flags. I acted as a prime mover, creating order and meaning, making objects into subjects; or rather subjects into objects and thus subjects of the Spanish Crown.

An accounting follows: "The inhabitants of both sexes in this island," Columbus notes, ". . . go always naked as when they were born, with the exception of some of the women. . . . None of them . . . are possessed of any iron, neither have they weapons, being unacquainted with, and indeed incompetent to use them, not from any deformity of body (for they are well-formed), but because they are timid and full of fear." The lineaments of the benign savage emerge, his simplicity, honesty, and rather foolish generosity. Withal he is not stupid "but of very clear understanding" demonstrated in one or two "ad-

mirable descriptions" local informants have contributed to Columbus's report. So far so good; the expropriation of the New World—which Columbus will never quite recognize as such—is progressing unproblematically
through the arrogation not only of the Indians' land but of their intellectual
resources which, in these first passages describing their cooperative quies-
cence, is simply another piece of the local treasure. Thus far too the difference
between Indians and Spanish is both absolute and inert, that is, without implications beyond those that pertain to the New World generally as a place of
yet untapped resources. At this point the relations between conqueror and
conquered are still not political. One does not have political relations with a
beach or a tree; in Columbus's first *Letter,* the inhabitants of San Salvador are
not even properly other, do not yet comprise a negative term.

But when subsequent explorations discover a second and much different group of islanders, the bloodthirsty Caribs who will shortly lend their
name to coin the appalling "cannibal," the process of mastering foreign peoples reveals itself more complicated than just taking over their land. The
Arawaks are morally uninflected, benign like the local climate but not actually
"good," until they come to contrast with the "bad" Caribs. This moral differ-
entiation entails more than a refinement, a transformation of categories: the
bad Caribs reveal the Indians as human beings not fruit trees. The rhetoric of
oppression often characterizes victims as in- or subhuman but the meaning of
that accusation is worth investigating further. "Inhuman" may not be meant
literally but, like "unthinkable," as judgment rather than fact. Were inhumanity a fact it would preclude a self-justifying condemnation. The enemy on the
battlefield arouses not only repugnance but anger, resentment, indignation,
rage. These emotions directed at inanimate objects or animals involve an ancillary anthropomorphism. In the same way the Caribs/cannibals need to be
granted a portion of humanity before they can be seen worthy of annihilation
for their inhumanity.[3] Thus it is their categorical humanity that places them
beyond the pale; savagery has its ethics just like civilization. Discovering the
humanity of the New World savages when he finds that some are actively evil,
Columbus tells a story ironically paralleling that of the Fall in which being
bad similarly achieves a distinct human status defined basically as the capacity
to choose between good and evil. The irony, of course, lies in acknowledging
that the Indians are categorically people as a step toward enslaving them;
down that road, the vision of the New World as potentially a second Eden
will inspire the genocide of its first inhabitants whose difference from the Europeans is now qualified (limited), in that they *are* human, but insuperable and
fraught with implications for their violent suppression. To kill Indians with

conviction, Columbus had to attribute to them a mode of life whose very evil made it basically commensurate with his own.

That is a sword that cuts both ways. With the edge sharpened by a view of the savages as unworthy of humane treatment, it kills them with moral impunity. But Flaubert's ancestor, Montaigne, honed its other edge in an essay entitled "Of Cannibals" (1578–80) which argues that bad as New World anthropophagites may be, we (sixteenth-century Frenchmen) are worse, more deeply fallen and further alienated from our common human nature. Like us but unlike us, the cannibals deserve freedom for their—not otherness (since they are comparable) but difference. Human like us and therefore deserving humane treatment, they have an entirely different civilization which, to behave humanely, we ought to respect.

The concept of cultural difference as an autonomous, self-generated mode appears new to us, even post-new, but it dates back at least to Montaigne's response to what he too saw as a lethal notion of otherness. The response was not entirely successful, however, for a closer look will reveal that Montaigne's anticolonial notion of difference remains tied to an irresistibly emerging sense of European centrality; that indeed, for all he resists, "difference" tends perhaps irresistibly to slide toward "otherness."

Yet, in "Of Cannibals" Montaigne sets out precisely to separate difference and otherness, explicitly rejecting the attitude that makes one's kind the universal standard. A returning colonizer's tales of the wild men of Brazil have had a contrary effect on Montaigne. "I think," he muses, "there is nothing barbarous and savage in that nation, from what I have been told, except that each man calls barbarism whatever is not his own practice; for indeed it seems we have no other test of truth and reason than the example and pattern of the opinions and customs of the country we live in." Hopelessly provincial, we are convinced that where we are is the epitome of all good things. "*There* is always the perfect religion, the perfect government, the perfect and accomplished manners in all things."[4]

Recent discoveries of alien peoples leading vastly different lives ought to be teaching us that other ways can also make sense, even better sense. A Brazilian tribe of cannibals surely represents the epitome of difference,[5] yet these proverbial pariahs of civilized society nonetheless have their virtues. Montaigne finds much about them to admire, like their honesty and generosity, their innocence of any lust for riches. Comparison does not flatter Europe, for doing their worst, the cannibals still appear better people than the French. "I think there is more of barbarity," Montaigne observes referring to certain contemporary practices, "in eating a man alive than in eating him dead; and in tearing by tortures and the rack a body still full of feeling, in roasting a man bit by bit, in having him bitten and mangled by dogs and swine . . . than roasting and eating him after he is dead" (155). "We surpass them in every kind of barbarity" (156). Instead of their masters, we ought to be the cannibals' pupils. But we are too parochial to learn from others; all that Montaigne's compatriots seem capable of recognizing in the cannibal culture is that "they don't wear breeches" (159).

Five years later, when Montaigne again took up the theme of cultural difference, it was not to mock but to mourn. "Of Coaches" (1585–88) denounces the Spanish slaughter of the Incas in terms at first familiar from the cannibals essay. Children in an infant world, the Incas differ from us by their proximity to nature. They are innocent of our civilized perversions, simple and direct where we lie and cheat, loyal and true where we will resort to any guile to satisfy our bloated greed. Beyond this precocious projection of the concept of the noble savage—it will be another century before Rousseau codifies him—Montaigne moves in this essay toward a still more precocious anticolonialism. True, he does not formulate this opposition to the conquest of America as an absolute principle, since he can imagine a worthy and even improving colonization by the ancient Greeks and Romans (694–95). But these benign tutors, far from scorning the Incas as other, would have actually helped difference unfold, "strengthened and fostered the good seeds that nature had produced in them" (694).

The Spanish, on the other hand, are nowhere more vile than in their insistence that the humiliated Incas abandon their gods along with their goods and lands. Having used every form of treachery to defeat the Peruvian king, his ignoble captors "permitted [him] to buy his way out of the torment of being burned alive by submitting to baptism at the moment of execution" (696). Montaigne opposed conversion at a time when it was the empire's major ethical justification. Even Bartolome de Las Casas did not abandon the missionary pursuit when he saw where it could lead; but Las Casas, for all his outrage at the brutality of Spanish exploitation, disputed the administration of the empire, not its existence. More radically, for Montaigne the Incas' "indomitable ardor" in "the defense of their gods" represents an equal capacity for autonomy.

In fact the Incas are generally not at all inferior to their invaders, even on the battlefield where, Montaigne speculates, "if anyone had attacked them on equal terms, with equal arms, experience and numbers, it would have been just as dangerous for him as in any other war we know of, and more so." Unequal odds decided the outcome of the battle not unequal opponents. "Eliminate [the] disparity, I say, and you take from the conquerors the whole basis of many victories" (694). Military disparity is not to be taken as a sign of the sort of cultural/racial inferiority that Europeans invoked to justify colonization; disparity does not imply a disparaging difference. The problem, however, lies in the converse, that difference does seem to engender a disparaging disparity. Over the course of the narrative of the Indian defeat, the notion of difference as the ground for arguing against colonization develops complications that were not evident in the mere statement of the principle. Never a justification for the subjection of the Incas, difference in "Of Coaches" does tend to become an *explanation*.

Montaigne essays are typically labyrinthine and "Of Coaches" especially so. Tracing the singular path of the idea of Indian difference requires a plan of the whole. The essay, then, starts with the observation that the classics are not always reliable; even Aristotle and Plutarch were capable of reporting legend as truth. This bringing to mind that not only the figurative but the actual ground under one's feet is not always entirely firm reminds Montaigne that he is phobically afraid of falling which can make his travels unpleasant, particularly in swaying vehicles like boats and coaches. We have arrived at our coaches. These come in many varieties including war coaches drawn in ancient times by all sorts of odd beasts—stags, dogs, naked women, ostriches. To be sure, it was the plebes who paid for such princely displays but still, they were magnificent in those days and Montaigne doubts we will see their like again.

On the other hand history can take unexpected turns. Here, for example, it has just revealed a whole new world. With this Montaigne enters on the account of the Incas as above and the essay ends with an anecdote proving the Incas' moral excellence in their devotion to their king. As Montaigne tells it, the Inca monarch rode to his last battle on a golden litter borne by trusted warriors. As fast as the Spaniards killed these bearers others took their places so that the king would never have fallen had not a Spanish soldier, raised astride his horse to the height of the litter, seized the king bodily and dashed him to the ground. Montaigne's fear of falling makes this episode especially dramatic and, recalling his earlier discussion of various means of conveyance, not an absolutely incoherent conclusion to an essay about coaches.

One may ask what coaches have to do with Peru in the first place? A Montaigne scholar, Marcel Gutwirth, has proposed a link whereby coaches represent a crucial difference between Spaniard and Inca: coaches, that is, wheels. The Spanish have wheels and the Incas don't.[6] To be sure, Montaigne hastens to acknowledge, the Incas have accomplished amazing things without the wheel, notably a magnificent road from Quito to Cuzco that is easily the match of any in Europe. Roads being the trademark of the Roman empire, this is a most telling example of Inca achievement. Wheel-less, therefore, the Incas are different but not lesser. Indeed in another sense, they are different and therefore greater, since it takes a greater effort to build roads without pulleys or carts.

Exactly here, however, even as Montaigne directly affirms the equal worth of Inca civilization, the ambiguity of that affirmation begins to emerge. This ambiguity lies in the blurred status of wheellessness—an *occasion* for Inca virtue that is sliding toward becoming its *condition*. Does the lack of wheels merely provide an occasion for demonstrating Inca virtue (which exists independently of such occasions)? or does the need to overcome their wheellessness generate a special virtue not extant among those possessed of wheels? The problem with that question, of course, lies in the very asking, for the Incas, lacking the concept of the wheel, cannot query that lack themselves. Only Montaigne can pose that question and, to make things worse, by posing it, he demonstrates not only the epistemological ascendancy of having wheels but the additional power that accrues to those who know that others don't.

In other words, while Montaigne insists on the fundamental equality of all human beings (and proves that conviction when he shudders in identification with the Inca king's fall), this equality turns out to be limited to the fundamentally human. The Incas are only *fundamentally* human: the technology of the litter only extends the body. But the Spanish control, in addition to their fundamental humanity, a technology that transforms their bodily energy into something of which bodies on their own are incapable. Montaigne may be terrified when he imagines himself falling from a litter but, thank Heaven, litters are not his problem which is, fearsome enough but not fatal, coaches: witness the title of his essay. The Indian litter-bearers are exceedingly brave as the workers who build the Mexican road are surpassingly skilled, but all in vain. From being the *occasion* for virtue, then its *condition,* lacking the wheel has become the sign of its *futility.* Tragically and to its shame, the modern world has rendered certain virtues futile. But inasmuch as these virtues are associated with the technology of litters, it is difficult to regret them in the sense of wanting them back for ourselves.

While coaches embody the corruption of Europe, they also carry the weight of a history that has traded innocence for knowledge. Cowering in his coach, Montaigne dreads the wheels that the Incas lack; dreads as well the technology that will destroy the Incas. But since fear is here the measure of knowledge, he can hardly wish himself ignorantly fearless, however brave. As

"Of Coaches" develops the concept of difference beyond "Of Cannibals," it now figures as the remainder in a subtraction problem, so that the difference between the Spanish and the Incas equals the reason for the latters' defeat, a difference that, as the ground for anticolonialism, is as shaky as a coach.

• • •

In the twenty-first century, Europe's former colonies being at least nominally independent, anticolonialism means cultural liberation. And since this new definition makes the recognition of difference central, what we might call the problem of the wheel becomes commensurately greater. Almost four hundred years after Montaigne, Tzvetan Todorov wrote his book *The Conquest of America: The Question of the Other* and defined its subject as "the discovery *self* makes of the *other*."[7] Todorov's purpose is the same as Montaigne's, to denounce the concept of the other as a chief weapon of colonial outrage, and, revisiting essentially the same site, he writes about the fall of the Aztec empire a decade before the Inca. But to explain the defeat of a civilization in many respects easily Europe's match, the late twentieth-century Todorov is unimpressed by technology and seeks the determining force of history rather in culture, specifically in a profound difference (as he sees it) in the Aztec and Spanish conceptions of language and communication.

In brief, his thesis is that the Aztecs could not counter the alien assault for lack of a concept of the other; while the Spanish in their encounter with the New World discovered otherness and how to manipulate it. Unlike the Spanish who, for all their religiosity, saw themselves first as men among men, the Aztecs located themselves first in relation to a sacred plan whose laws they were to implement. This precedence of universal over human order was expressed with special force in their conception of language as the articulation of a world order. For the Spanish, language functioned instead as an instrument of human relations and a means of reordering things to their liking. In a word, the Spanish knew how to lie. Lying is language taking power by overthrowing rightful meanings, and lying won the Spanish their empire. In control of communication, Cortes plunged his prey into fatal confusion. Control of communication, in Todorov's account, is a second Spanish wheel.

As appalled as Montaigne by the ravages of colonization and more knowing, Todorov regrets the epistemological imbalance that gave the conquistadors their bloody victory. But to understand this unhappy event, he has had himself to know something of which the vanquished were ignorant, and this imbalance he can hardly regret. For while knowing is associated with the guilt of the conquest, ignorance was and remains annihilative. Remains so because

Todorov could not write his book nor we read it without knowing (indeed taking as fact) what the Spanish knew.

Is Todorov then doing what he denounces, rendering the Aztecs as Europe's negatives? This is certainly not what he intends. Indeed, some time after *The Conquest of America,* he took up the issue explicitly arguing in response to an essay by Abdul R. JanMohamed that we should be careful not to exaggerate differences.[8] Todorov finds JanMohamed's stipulation that understanding the other requires "negating one's very being" "excessively pessimistic." Even if "'one's culture is what formed that being,' . . . human beings are not trees, and they can be uprooted without provoking such dramatic consequences," he insists. For "We are not only separated by cultural differences; we are also united by a common human identity, and it is this which renders possible communication, dialogue, and, in the final analysis, the comprehension of Otherness—it is possible precisely because Otherness is never radical" (374).

In this concern that difference when it is cast as absolute precludes precisely the interactions it is intended to engender, Todorov joins a growing number of scholars, many themselves descended from or representing the peoples Europe designated "other," who are dissatisfied with studies that discover only divergence and distinctiveness.[9] Though these scholars are presumably the beneficiaries of a concept of difference that returns to them the agency of their own interpretation, they have been finding that what is represented as autonomy often turns out to be exclusion: that difference too easily reverses into otherness. The Native American writer Michael Dorris has complained that "the paradigm of European confusion" which renders Indians "objects of mystery and speculation, not people" still organizes a current scholarship willy-nilly producing images that are the complementary opposites of the old myths.[10] We need to "stipulate only a few givens," he writes with some impatience. "That human beings *qua* human beings, where and whenever they may live, share some traits; that Indians were and are human beings—then we have at least a start." And Dorris concludes his essay by urging that we "begin the hard, terribly difficult and unpredictable quest of regarding [Indians] as human beings" (104–5).

It is hard to disagree with such a program, but even harder to carry it out. The principle that one should explicate people's differences (in Dorris's words) "within the configurations of their own cultures," while at the same time "regarding [others] as human beings," seems clear enough stated abstractly, but its practice is another matter. Unfortunately, Todorov does not reflect upon his *Conquest of America* in relation to his later postulate that "Otherness is never radical." But the otherness of the Aztecs, defined as their inability to comprehend otherness, constitutes the very definition of "radical." At the same time, what content can one imagine imparting to the universal term "human being" that would render its universality genuinely multiform? If in the past the notion of the universal human being served the colonizing enterprise, as the anticolonial scholarship has been arguing for the last two decades, what is now going to make universality useful on the other side? What is a "human being" when he's at home? How do we keep him civil when he goes visiting?

In short, the universalities upon which Todorov falls back in order to temper radical otherness and transform it into relative difference are both vague with regard to future incarnations and discouraging in their past. Moreover, the logic that invokes universality as the counter to difference is the logic of otherness which reduces differences to an abstract negativity; and it is difficult to see how the same logic can organize an account of others that makes them *more* autonomously substantial. In that difference *is* substance or it collapses into otherness, resorting to universalities in order to correct extreme difference seems inauspicious, methodologically as well as politically. To qualify difference we need to know more about its content, not less. More content, in other words more history. Let us go back then and look more substantively at the history of the Aztecs.

As it happens, it is possible to reconstruct the Aztecs' own sense of their place in the history of American colonization with relative conviction in that, exceptionally among New World cultures at the time of the discovery, they had a written language in which they produced a conquest literature of their own.[11] The earliest of these Nahuatl writings by Aztec priests and wise men date from only seven years after the fall of Mexico. Their complicated account of the two-year war preceding the fall offers some unexpected perspectives.

For one thing, it comes as a surprise to find that, contrary to the European tradition of the first encounters, the Aztecs are not unambiguously impressed. Though amazed, as who would not have been, by their first sightings of the bedecked and bemetaled Spanish, they retain some critical distance from which they find the response to their welcoming gifts of gold and precious feathers less than inspiring. "They picked up the gold and fingered it like monkeys," recalls an Aztec observer. "Their bodies swelled with greed, and their hunger was ravenous; they hungered like pigs for that gold. They snatched at the golden ensigns, waved them from side to side and examined every inch of them." In this depiction the Spanish are flatly bestial, not super- but subhuman. Repugnantly different, others outside the pale: "They were like one who speaks a barbarous tongue," the writer continues: "everything they said was in a barbarous tongue" (51–52). In other words, they were of the category of person with whom by definition it is impossible to communicate. From the Aztec point of view, not surprisingly, it is the Spanish who cannot communicate.

At other times recounted in other passages, it seems true as tradition has it, that the Aztecs greeted the Spanish like gods, and overall the Mexicans perhaps understood their enemy less well than the reverse. But passages like the one just cited suggest that the Aztecs' perceptions were not entirely clouded, indicating that we might usefully look for other explanations besides cultural incapacity even for their misunderstandings. Explanations, for instance, like the fact that the invaders knew whence they came and to what end; while for the invaded the sudden irruption of strange peoples from unknown lands was an impenetrable mystery. The Aztecs' epistemological passivity seems a not unlikely response to impenetrable mysteries. Beyond this, granting that control of communication was a decisive factor in the Spanish victory, it seems well to note that Cortes controlled communication in large part through his control of a translator/interpreter, a slave woman whom he acquired upon landing on the Mexican coast and who then accompanied him on his progress to the capital city. Montezuma not only did not have a translator of his own, he depended on Cortes's: by this alone the Mexicans lost linguistic control to the point that they heard their own language speaking an enemy meaning. In the process of making available the world of the Mexicans along with their language, La Malinche, who is still referred to in Mexico as "the traitor" (and more ambiguously the "fucked one"), at several critical junctures in the campaign took the lead in manipulating the Indians, if not into submission, certainly into confusion. Alterity was not a mystery at least for her.[12]

Politics and biology can provide two other reasons for the Mexican defeat. The Aztecs were nomadic intruders who arrived in the region and established their city only around 1325. Thus the Aztec empire which at its height ruled several million people was rising, ironically, at the same time as the European. The opponents at the siege of Mexico City were politically more alike than either realized; and their resemblance may have worked as much as their difference to the advantage of the Spanish who were able to forge alliances with those the Aztecs had recently vanquished. By the end of the war the situation looked little like the puzzling story of a few hundred Spaniards in alien territory conquering hundreds of thousands of Indians on their home ground. The sides were probably roughly balanced. Cortes commanding, against no more than 300,000 Aztecs, at least 200,000 (some suggest 225,000) Indians in addition to his own men with their far more destructive arms.[13]

Finally, Alfred Crosby has argued that biology was the decisive factor, devastating the Mexican society so quickly that the role of technology and politics was essentially moot.[14] The Aztecs repelled the first Spanish assault on the city causing such losses among the attackers that their defeat became legend as "la triste noche." Upon his return, Cortes was reinforced not only by new Indian recruits but, within the walls, by the plague which, according to accounts on both sides, had heaped rotting corpses in all the streets of the city and left virtually none to defend it.

The factors suggested by Aztec documents as equally important in the conquest of Mexico as cultural difference are not inconsiderable: the possession of specific knowledge of the origins, the purposes, and the motives of the enemy; the balance of military force measured both in arms and men; the natural imbalance derived from the Aztecs' lack of biological immunity. Todorov stipulates all these, but seems not to consider them decisive in that they do not figure in his explanation of the final outcome. On the other hand, figuring them in profoundly changes the entire picture; though the Aztec defeat seems no less historically likely, it no longer appears inherently inevitable. Neither passive nor helpless, the Aztecs represent themselves in their own writings by acting, in relation to overwhelming odds, with reason (their own reasons) and will.

In traditional accounts of the Aztecs as helpless before the Spanish, one of the pieces of evidence is an account to be found in their conquest literature of omens said ten years before to have predicted the coming apocalypse. Of course the omens could be just that, in which case fate rules the world and there's nothing further to say about it. If however the omens are the creature of the conquest, there is another way to read them than as evidence of helplessness. For while they prophesy doom, they also hold out a certain hope. George Orwell wrote that who controls the past controls the future.[15] The catastrophic future predicted in the Aztec omens takes place, in relation to the invention of the omens themselves, in the present. The effect is to release the future— even if only for oppression—by restoring purposeful direction to a present that would otherwise appear to be the end of the world. If the present has grown out of the past, the future can be expected to grow out of the present, to *have* a future. In the omens, therefore, the Aztecs can be seen demonstrating instead of epistemological passivity, something like an opposite historical capability, one that is more congruent with the picture of interactions that emerges from their own accounts than with the view that they were culturally paralyzed.[16]

All these ways in which Aztecs and Spanish were not only unlike but also like (both relations, moreover, evolving over the course of their conflict)[17] seriously complicate notions of both difference and universality. Colonizer and colonized emerge as similar as they are different in that they profit and lose in the same ways from common situations: the imperialist Aztecs, for instance, lose out when their history in the region makes willing allies for Cortes who, when he wins, will kill and exploit like the Aztecs before him. On the other hand, it is difficult to talk of the Aztecs and the Spanish as simply universally "human" and let it go at that in the presence of their fundamentally different visions of the universe and of humanity's place in it. In that context, the term "universally human" just does not seem very useful.

This said, however, a solution or more modestly a strategy may be emerging out of these very difficulties. Dubbing them different, one reflects that they came together in related ways; dubbing them all human beings, one contrarily wants to point to the basic issues on which they oppose one another. In both cases, however, there is a common denominator which is precisely the commonality of their encounter, the common ground they construct, new to both, and on which they are neither the same nor different but only inextricably related; indeed neither the same nor different *through* their relation.

I would suggest that the encounter of Aztecs and Spanish offers the terms for avoiding, as the orientalist, exoticist tendencies of the concept of the other (the different) emerge, falling back into an equally worrisome universalism. From focusing on the history of the conquest—from locating oneself on the site of the encounter rather than attempting to project oneself simultaneously on both sides of it—a concept of commonality or common ground emerges that is not a compromise between the universal and the different, but a distinct third term.[18] This third term indeed stands opposed to both "human being" and "other/different." The shortcomings of "other" even when it is chastened into "different" we have already examined. As for "human being" shorn of its covert content—when it really means white man, prince of Denmark or president of the United States—one is hard put to say what it is. Besides mortality, the urge to satisfy three or four physical needs, a proneness to foregather, which human traits can be considered universal? On the contrary, commonalities abound being continuously generated by precisely the historical process that works to limit the realm of the universal.

One term that recurs in histories of difference is "contested zone," meaning cultural areas and social regions that different groups seek to define each its own way. The notion of "commonality" or common ground implies a reversal of that term, thus "zone of contest": a territory whose contours are sketched as overlappings rather than boundaries, a terrain of mediations and equally of confrontations. The history of the European empire seems exactly such a terrain upon which peoples define themselves as modalities of shared experience. The moment Columbus landed in San Salvador, as soon as the home of the Arawaks became San Salvador, the reason the European crossed the ocean became inextricable from what he found when he got to the other side. A passionate traveler, Montaigne sought, in difficult journeys he made more difficult by refusing an orderly itinerary, the same process of becoming he recorded in his essays. He understood that what he found upon his travels was inextricable from the finding, and that he himself would be transformed by both.

Put another way, all this has been to suggest that a difference so distinct as to constitute the opposite of universality cannot be. As vehicles of meaning, the ships that discovered America exploded on impact. After the landfall, all there was on the beach was a confusion of European timber and American sand. Difference being an analytical concept, its objective reality lies only in its construction of subjective realities. Thus while the Aztecs and the Spanish certainly existed before their encounter, the difference between them did not. *That* was the creature of the conquest. The children of difference as well as its students, we find ourselves, therefore, fulfilling the eighth and last Aztec omen, the appearance of "monstrous beings . . . ; deformed men with two heads but only one body." Monstrous, deformed, two- and many-headed, "human beings" and "others" in postcolonial America have one body divisible only by its own parts.

I myself had Indian blood in me. My grandmother is a Carib Indian. That makes
me one-quarter Carib Indian. But I don't go around saying that I have some
Indian blood in me. . . .

    Mariah says, "I have Indian blood in me," and underneath everything I
could swear she says it as if she were announcing her possession of a trophy.
How do you get to be the sort of victor who can claim to be the vanquished
also?   —Jamaica Kincaid, *Lucy*

The description of one's current writing as "work in progress" can be a little depressing. One reason lies in the evoca-
tion of the mountain still to climb, of course, but another,
more subversive reason is that the notion of progress seems
mockingly inaccurate to describe the experience of writing,
which is seldom so anticipatory. Typically, one proceeds by
retreating, first from the ignorant certainty that generates a
hypothesis, then to a better informed agnosticism until, if all
goes well, in an ecstasy of interrogation, one achieves full-
blown skepticism. Paranoia is an occupational disease in this
profession: there is always a prior plot, some yet-unexposed
premise structuring a deceptively self-evident meaning. One
advances backward into irony, the goal being finally to pose a
basic question that turns over the ground of previous convictions.

    This unsettling dynamic is nowhere more active than in
the study of the literature of American colonization, whose
subject is origins and the representation of origins. And
foundational accounts are the most suspect of all. Accordingly, historians of the year 1492 and all that have been ap-

proaching the representations of the origins of the New World as utterly unreliable narratives, antiscriptures to be read against. This would appear definitively skeptical, but in dealing only with the content of the imperial narratives, this skepticism leaves their form unquestioned. While suggesting,
therefore, that it is possible to disbelieve in ways that formally resemble believing it all, I want to propose one more step back from the conventional cer-
tainties of colonial history beyond a different account to a different *kind* of
account.

I

The early works of revisionary colonial history were often revelatory. Their
drama depended in part on the complacency of the historical vision they
challenged, which may be represented, only a little simplistically, by the writings of Samuel Eliot Morison, for whom Columbus was an epic hero and the
annexation of the American continents a romance in which "the New World
gracefully yielded her virginity to the conquering Castilians."[1] For Morison
and his colleagues, the discovery of America was an epiphany and its colonization at once inevitable and glorious. They saw the Europeanization of
America enacting the natural historical progress of civilization.

The very title of Edmundo O'Gorman's 1961 *Invention of America* repudi-
ated all that, and not just the established interpretation of the discovery but
the very fact. O'Gorman argued that there had been no "discovery"—certainly not by the Italian sea captain who himself denied to his death that
he had found a new world, but not even by those who did recognize that
America was not Asia. Amerigo Vespucci carried off the prize of making the
New World his namesake not by claiming the discovery but by inventing it,
retroactively.[2]

When everyone agrees that in 1492 Columbus crossed the ocean and
came upon a land hitherto unknown to Europe (or once known but at the
time forgotten), the difference between "discovery" and "invention" may not
appear very significant. But it is nothing less than the difference between destiny and history. Calling the New World landfall a discovery or an invention
means that the historian will either unfold a providential narrative or develop
an interpretation. With O'Gorman's book, the original moment of American
history ceased to be an epiphany and became an event whose significance
would lie in its interpretation. The new scholarship was thus revelatory in revealing a myth; since this was a myth about a revelation, the process of its exposure was especially ironic, suggesting that the historians were approaching
intellectual bedrock.

I do not want to exaggerate the darkness before this light. There is certainly a long and powerful tradition of examining basic terms in the discipline of American studies; Henry Nash Smith's *Virgin Land* in 1950, for instance, and R. W. B. Lewis's *The American Adam* in 1955 were precisely about uncovering foundational assumptions. But even as *Virgin Land* and *The American Adam* demystified the national myths of origin, they tacitly accepted the very first myth, the story of a discovery in which Europeans were the sole agents at a transcendent moment of human progress. Perry Miller's definition of his life's work as unfolding "the massive narrative of the movement of European culture into the vacant wilderness of America" has appropriately become the set piece of his generation.[3]

His successors' set piece, on the other hand, could be the epigraph with which Peter Hulme began his highly influential *Colonial Encounters*.[4] The epigraph quotes the Bishop of Avila telling Queen Isabella of Castile in 1492 that "language is the perfect instrument of empire."[5] The bishop's dictum encompasses the book's two-part thesis: first, that empire building was the center of Europe's interest in the New World (Morison, among others, listed empire as only one of a long list of inspirations, along with adventure, curiosity, and the quest for knowledge); and, second, that the narratives of colonization were essential to its progress. *Colonial Encounters* derives its historical evidence from a collection of colonial texts read closely and comparatively. "Language is the perfect instrument [for constructing an] empire"—and therefore for its dismantling.

The epigraph thus signals not only the thesis of the study but also its logic. It is to this logic that the rest of my discussion is addressed. I take *Colonial Encounters* as an exemplary work in discursive history, a masterly demonstration of this mode, all the more compelling for its author's stipulation that there is more to history than discourse and that historical narratives have in view a reality that is in part material. Yet, beginning with his epigraph, Hulme casts language as so powerfully instrumental that the deconstruction of narratives tends to co-opt his universe of explanation. My concern with this tendency lies in its corollary effects, with how, when critical readings co-opt the universe of explanation, explanations become either utterly impossible—because texts are utterly unreliable—or entirely certain, because texts are also entirely accessible.

Carlo Ginzburg described the first of these effects: the way the analysis of narrative evidence taken to be by definition unreliable becomes incapable of arriving at explanations. While positivist historians dealt with evidence "as an open window," he writes, "contemporary skeptics regard it as a wall, which by definition precludes any access to reality."[6] As I read them, some discursive histories of colonization do the reverse: they break down the "wall" and render the narrative once again an open window. Unreliability, if one thinks one understands its principle, can be decoded to reveal a narrative that now appears entirely reliable. The principle of unreliability in colonial narratives seems clear to many anticolonial historians today who, indeed, consider their work to be participating in a project of decolonization. Some of the resulting histories demonstrate the possibility for a radical uncertainty unanchored by material evidence to transmute, sometimes within the same essay, into an equal and opposite radical certainty. For instance, the proposition that "language is the perfect instrument of empire" does not lead in *Colonial Encounters* to uncertainty. I want first to describe this process and then, in the second part of this essay, to suggest how its determinism may be somewhat tempered.

The first indication that the bishop's proposition has inspired an excessive certainty is that Peter Hulme seems to take it at face value. Yet it is reasonable to ask whether the bishop was right; and even before that, what he meant, since it would appear unlikely that the words he used—*language, perfect, instrument, empire*—had exactly the same meaning in the fifteenth century as they have now. The occasion being the presentation to the Spanish queen of the first grammar of a modern European language—prompting her to ask, "What is it for?"— could the bishop have been just boasting in order to inflate the importance of his learned class?

Hulme does not pose this question but instead treats the statement "language is the perfect instrument of empire" as a truth to be elaborated. At the same time, by not questioning the bishop's motive, Hulme implies the prelate is a clear-eyed exploiter of linguistic power. There is a certain circularity verging on the tautological in the way the bishop and his statement testify to one another's villainy. The accuracy of the boast means that the bishop is not just boasting but is genuinely corrupt, that he is a man of letters and ideals willing to prostitute his learning to political and commercial greed. At the same time, one of the reasons to believe the statement is that it is spoken by a bishop implicated in the imperialist cause and in a setting of political and commercial greed; thus the bishop and his statement establish both one another's historical truth and moral duplicity. The bishop is as false as his dictum is true; the space between man and statement is not a stage for interactions that might qualify our understanding of both but only the site of his self-exposure.

In the construction of a history, tautology expresses itself as teleology, depicting the past such that it leads to what we already know to be its future.

And the same condition obtains in both linguistic tautology and historical teleology, that is, a determinism that appropriates agency for its own vision. Against all odds, *Colonial Encounters* projects a vision of the bishop hardly less prophetic than Morison's discoverer; of course, Hulme's bishop foresees the opposite prophecy: not life but death.

Yet Hulme is himself entirely clear about the need to avoid such reversals. Explaining that the Spanish account of a divided Caribbean inhabited by both gentle and violent peoples was an invention intended to rationalize colonial policy, he notes that "the temptation at this point . . . is simply to reverse the colonialist terms and to replace the traditional story with its negative image." He rejects such a move, which "would be merely another way off falling victim to those colonialist categories, and taking the native Caribbean out of history altogether." Instead, he offers "a hypothetical sketch . . . of . . . an alternative reading of some of the historical and ethnographic material" (73, 78). This sketch, which focuses on the institution of the chiefdom, replaces the binary arrangement of radically different cultures (justifying both the expectation of easy conquest and the necessity of violent suppression) with the picture of a unified Caribbean culture whose variations have nothing to do with allegories of good and evil but arise out of the usual territorial conflicts.

This substitutes for the Spanish account one that is at least as plausible and of a more reliable provenance. But Hulme now worries that his picture of a single, if varied, culture may be at odds with the Arawaks' clearly adversarial report that the Caribs were cannibals. It may require more than a plausible alternative reading to counter the support this claim lends to the colonialist view of things. So Hulme puts the question squarely: "Were the Caribs . . . really cannibals?" (78). His pursuit of a factual answer offers an exceptionally subtle illustration of the logic of discourse-based history.

The first step is to reject the form of the question for being "superogatory" in that the words *Carib* and *cannibal* are derived from one another. To the recast question "Did the Caribs really, as a matter of custom and practice, eat human flesh?" the first answer is, "We do not know," there being no conclusive evidence for or against (79). But then Hulme cautions that by itself this response is misleading. He provides two glosses, one historical, one textual. A rehearsal of the historical literature of anthropophagy provides a series of traditional explanations for the consumption of human flesh ranging from vice to ferocity to primitive superstition to protein deficiency. The discussion has progressed from a question of fact (did the Caribs eat people?) to a factual answer ("we don't know") to an elaboration of this answer taking into consideration what would be implied by interpreting "we don't know" as "possibly yes." And this implication—that the indigenous Caribbeans were ferocious savages or, improbably, desperate for meat—weighs very heavily against contemplating any sort of yes.

At this stage, to counterbalance the racist anthropology he has been rehearsing, Hulme cites the work of the anthropologist William Arens, whose analysis of the fallacies of the literature led him to deny that there was any solid evidence that cannibalism ever existed.[7] With this, the historical answer "we don't know" has become a textual "the reports are false" (my phrase, not Hulme's); and Hulme now discards "we don't know" because "simply to answer 'non-proven,' even to the reformulated question, is still to acquiesce to the implicit violence of colonialist discourse" (81). Thus "the reports are false" slides into something like "we should positively reject the false reports."

This slide marks the transition from the historical gloss to the textual one, the evolution of the concept of cannibalism in modern Western writing. A survey of both the psychoanalytical and the anthropological literatures leads Hulme to observe that there exists a "widespread desire for the existence of some touchstone of the absolutely 'other'" and that this desire is perfectly satisfied by the image of the cannibal. With this second set of qualifications, the material question of whether there were Caribbeans who ate their fellows has moved entirely into the realm of the European imaginary. The passage concludes that "only now . . . is it possible to undertake the specific task of defining the signified of 'cannibalism,' thereby relocating the argument on to the plane of discourse, and reasserting the historical matrix of semantic questions" (83).

This "historical matrix," however, is entirely discursive, composed of "semantic questions" whose material referents dropped out of consideration when "we don't know" turned into "the reports are false." The argument, located wholly on "the plane of discourse," now moves under the impulse of logic, *not history*, to its inevitable answer: "If there is any ground at all [to the claim of Caribbean cannibalism] then the earlier definition of cannibalism can be glossed to the effect that the threat it offers, although figured as the devouring of human flesh, is in fact addressed to the body politic itself" (87). In other words, cannibalism almost certainly did not exist; but if it did, it was a figure of speech and moreover one that points to the guilt not of the Carib but of his oppressor. The discussion closes with the entirely figurative explication of the cannibal as one on whom is projected the violence of the body politic that is about to devour him. If cannibals did exist in the Caribbean, we know who they were.[8]

Figuratively, this seems entirely justified; I have no dispute with Hulme's analysis of the *discourse* of cannibalism. But while he establishes that *cannibalism* "is a term that has no application outside the discourse of European colonialism" (in that it means not just eating human flesh but eating it "ferociously" [84, 83]), he still has not answered his own factual question, "Did the Caribs really, as a matter of custom and practice, eat human flesh?" Indeed he seems to have abandoned this question. He may have decided (reasonably) that the answer is irrelevant. And he is surely right to insist that any historical investigation must take into account the discursive field it crosses; one can even argue that it is finally impossible to cross this field and arrive at a factual answer. But the absence of such an answer ought to be an answer in itself, taking up space as an unknown terrain in the historical landscape and thus helping to map it.

On the contrary, rejecting not only the content but the form of his evidential investigation, Hulme now contends that even acknowledging the absence of a factual answer is complicitous with the racist orthodoxy: "simply to answer 'non-proven' . . . is still to acquiesce to the implicit violence of colonialist discourse." Perhaps. But to answer effectively "proven false" is also to participate in that discourse. Acknowledging the fallacy of reversals, Hulme has performed one. Moreover, as his argument develops, not only do no alternatives to reversal appear, but the ground for them disappears beneath an expanding web of reversed claims that finally chokes the field of possibilities. This certainty is significantly more definitive than would have been the conclusion that since no reliable evidence for cannibalism can be found, it probably did not exist. The presence of cannibals in the region has not been more or less disproven or proven dubious; it has been deconstructed. It is no longer a possibility. In the essay from which I cited earlier, Ginzburg observes that "theoretical naiveté and theoretical sophistication share a common, rather simplistic assumption: they both take for granted the relationship between evidence and reality."[9] It seems as though Hulme's theoretical sophistication has combined with his political commitment to free his own historical narrative of the colonialist bias implicit in the cannibal mythology to mislead him to the conclusion that something for which he finds no solid evidence did not exist.

The question of whether cannibals existed in the pre-Columbian Caribbean is exceptionally resonant. Cannibalism, for all that Europeans have practiced it themselves, became in Western culture the ideal type of alien behavior. Montaigne's essay "Of Cannibals" exploits this typology prophetically. In the colonial situation, the cannibals are ineradicable markers of alterity. Thus their removal from the Caribbean scene in *Colonial Encounters*—again, not as presence but as possibility—erases a particularly sure sign that the Caribbean might constitute a genuinely alternative culture ("alternative" in the sense that while it surely had important elements in common with European culture, Caribbean culture was not directly intelligible or transparent to Europeans, and required, beyond translation, interpretation). By dismissing the possibility of cannibals, Hulme does not just erase this sign of alterity, he writes over it. The Caribs, while remaining mysterious for lack of documentary information, nonetheless lose the most dramatic part of their mystery and with it, symbolically, part of their ability to define themselves as whatever they are.

Yet the recuperation of the self-definition—or more broadly, the agency —of the conquered has been the central principle of the postcolonial scholarship that precisely thereby enlists itself in decolonization. *Colonial Encounters* embraces this principle and, in the absence of contemporary New World texts,[10] exemplifies its unavoidably parochial workings through readings of the European discourse that seek nonetheless to restore the presence of the native inhabitants by exposing the process of their effacement. But this exposure, when it takes the form of promoting with the same certainty an alternative face, is in its turn also effacing. The old mask of "cannibal" gives way to a new one of "noncannibal" while the categories remain the same. The trick would be, as everyone in the field understands, to read in a way that uncovers the agency of the colonized even though the texts one is reading are virtually always and only the colonizers' narratives. In the remainder of this discussion I will propose such a way of reading. In the absence of the evidence a counternarrative would provide, one can still open the historical scene to other possibilities a little more than we have done. The way to do this, speaking in terms of cannibals, is to focus on their "nonproven" status, and instead of reducing the field of the "nonproven" by preemptive glosses, possibly even to expand it.

II

The following describes a situation that is the complementary opposite to the one embodied in the Caribs. The Indians in this encounter are "good Indians," not to be annihilated but incorporated. In terms of Hulme's definition of the cannibal as the projection of those attempting to devour him or her, this is cannibalism, too, but in its benevolent mode. The whites proffer largess rather than force, and the Indians are gratefully sated. The peaceful entry of Indians into the European body politic needs no threatening myths to justify it. In this particular instance of benevolent cannibalism, the English, to expand their empire in Virginia, were seeking an alliance with the powerful Algonquian Chief Powhatan, who, as it happened, was in the early seventeenth century in the process of extending his own hegemony over most of the tribes in the region. The arriving colonists dubbed him the "Great Emperor" and the English, hoping to transform the Indian emperor into a New World vassal, offered him a crown. John Smith, who had his doubts about the whole strategy, reported the incident in *The Generall Historie of Virginia, New England, and the Summer Isles* (1624) and drew this sketch of the actual coronation:

> All being met at Werowocomoco [Powhatan's village], the next day was appointed for this Coronation, then the presents were brought him, his Bason and Ewer, Bed and furniture set up, his scarlet Cloke and apparell with much adoe put on him, being perswaded by [his son] Namontack they would not hurt him: but a foule trouble there was to make him kneele to receive his Crowne, he neither knowing the majesty nor meaning of a Crowne, nor bending of the knee, endured so many perswasions, examples, and instructions, as tyred them all; at last by leaning hard on his shoulders, he a little stooped, and three having the crowne in their hands put it on his head, when by the warning of a Pistoll the Boats were prepared with such a volley of shot, that the King started up in a horrible feare, till he saw all was well. Then remembering himselfe, to congratulate their kindnesse, he gave his old shoes and his mantell to Captaine Newport [the English leader]: but perceiving his purpose was to discover the Monacans [a nonallied tribe], he laboured to divert his resolution, refusing to lend him either men or guides more than Namontack; and so after some small complementall kindnesse on both sides, in requitall of his presents he presented Newport with a heape of wheat eares that might containe some 7 or 8 Bushels, and as much more we bought in the Towne, wherewith we returned to the Fort.[11]

This is a very complicated story with foreground, background, and even underground. In the foreground there is the astonishing spectacle of Powhatan suspiciously tolerating scarlet cloak, basin, ewer, and bed, but, no matter what anyone says, absolutely drawing the line at kneeling to receive his crown, which requires three men to place it on his head. Made to bend but not bow, the new king reciprocates by making the English captain a gift not just of his mantle but of his old shoes.

In the background there is the Indians' growing recognition that the English visitors are invaders rather than visitors and the attempt led by Powhatan to present a united front, while for their part the English do everything they can to divide and conquer. Underground is Smith's untiring self-promotion, served in this instance by the manifest ineptitude of Christopher Newport who just does not understand Indians as well as Smith.

Underground and background present no real analytical problems. That is, the emergence of individual self-making as part of empire building has been frequently observed; and the treacheries of European-Indian relations are no surprise. On the contrary, we have very little to go on in dealing with the foreground of the coronation anecdote that is curiously out of ideological focus. The ambitious spokesman of a brand-new imperial creed, Smith describes a scene in which not just Newport but the English as a whole and their coronation ritual appear ridiculous. To be sure, Powhatan also looks silly, but that makes sense to the English. The puzzle is why Smith punctiliously records a series of moves that make so solemn a white ceremony seem ludicrous? For if the English expostulations and maneuvers, not to mention the culminating clapping of the crown on that stubborn Indian head, have the aura of slapstick today, it must have been at least latent back then as well. Readers may bring much of its meaning to a text, but they do not bring it all. If, reading this passage, we laugh at the English, somewhere, to some degree, Smith knew they were laughable.

We do know something of the historical context of Smith's account that partly illuminates the situation. Smith was not in charge of the coronation; the ceremony was overseen by his rival, Newport, with whose policies Smith was in scornful disagreement. The discomfiture of this rival was very likely pleasing to Smith, as was the evidence that other ways would have to be found to bend the overproud Indians to the English crown. This is certainly one explanation, but my point here is that it is not sufficiently powerful to account for the subversive force of the anecdote in which the Indians assume an authority that Smith elsewhere assiduously denies them. Except for the moment in which he is startled by the unexpected volley, Powhatan stands firmly and immovably at the center of the scene. In Smith's telling, Powhatan dominates the action throughout, has the last word and performs the last gestures that send the English back to their fort bested, at least in dramatic terms. When we recall that Smith is always a self-conscious writer—that he certainly considered language "the perfect instrument of empire," being perhaps the first empire builder to adapt the bishop's proposition to individual use—the power the scene lends Powhatan is puzzling, for it is not Smith who stars in it, but Powhatan.

One explanation for this lapse in authorial control would be that it represents a sort of textual rupture, a moment in the text when Smith responds sufficiently to the force of the other he is describing to permit us to hear the other's resisting voice. But essentially the same problem arises with this explanation as with the basic assumption that the texts of colonization are "perfect instruments" of empire. In both cases one assumes that these texts are, by nature, wholly about control, and then calls those places where they are not, "anomalies." The literature of colonization is about control, of course, but possibly not wholly; or perhaps control itself is a divided enterprise.

There is, anyway, little evidence in the Smith passage of loss of control; its voice is quite firm and characteristically impatient. The context of the coronation episode suggests moreover that Smith is fully in charge, confidently deploying his authorial skills and literary knowledge. The episode follows, in the *Generall Historie,* an elaborate description of an Indian ceremony that Smith recasts explicitly as an English masque, closing, for good measure, with two lines from Homer. The cause of Western civilization is advancing on all fronts and the fiasco with the crown seems clearly intended to measure Powhatan's savagery. Yet, while the chief's comic refusal does measure, for the English, the limits of the savage mind, it also delimits and bounds English concepts of civilization. Mark Twain would one day perfect the mechanism in the Smith passage whereby a detailed physical description of the garb or ceremony of social dignity calls its bluff or, as we say in America, deconstructs it.

This deconstruction is not a transhistorical effect of language as such. Smith's exposure of English ceremonial constructions responds to a particular historical moment, offering an account whose narrative authority is limited precisely by Smith's own historical involvement. The self-deconstructing tendency of the coronation passage reflects its historical indeterminacies. Smith is uncertain about his situation, meaning that he is neither sure what the story unfolding around him is, nor how to tell is, nor even how he wants it to come out. So he effectively tells several stories composed of overlapping but not identical events. I would suggest that such narrative moments in which several histories can be and are being written (told) are the very stuff of historical process, and further that in themselves, and especially at their intersections and in their conflicts, they produce materials for an alternative imperial history that escapes the trap of reversing the orthodoxy.

Here is another narrative moment that describes Powhatan's reaction to certain English blandishments in terms that appear wholly irreconcilable with Smith's. Smith quotes Powhatan as saying,

If your King have sent me Presents, I also am a King, and this is my land. . . .
Your father is to come to me, not I to him, nor yet to your Fort, neither will I
bite at such a bait: as for the Monacans I can revenge my owne injuries, and as
for Atquanachuk, where you say your brother was slaine, it is a contrary way
from those parts you suppose it; but for any salt water beyond the mountaines,
the Relations you have had from my people are false.[12]

The fact that it is difficult to imagine what Smith could possibly reply to this
eloquent, lucid statement represents the same paradox as in the earlier passage:
Powhatan's understanding of European-Indian relations directly counters
Smith's, while it is only through Smith's telling that we know anything of
Powhatan's understanding. The obvious question is why Smith wants to
communicate a powerful refutation of his own view to his English readers. I
have already suggested one explanation: Smith tells us something he should
not have out of uncertainty over how to organize his historical narrative. This
uncertainty leads him to report as often as he interprets and sometimes to report events and aspects of the scene that are at odds with his own tentative interpretation. In one sense, of course, anything Smith reports is part of a narrative in that he sees everything inevitably in relation to a story of some kind.
But this is a weak story unable to fully transform its materials to make them
cohere with its argument. These materials remain, as it were, undigested or
semidigested; they retain a quasi-independent and possibly rebellious life, as
does the quotation of Powhatan's speech above.

We have become accustomed to invoking various fictional genres as ana-
logues for historical narratives. But semidigested, discordant pieces of reporting, like Smith's description of the coronation and Powhatan's rebuttal, bear
little resemblance to the story parts of imaginative fiction. Instead, they recall
the components of another kind of story, the story of the scientific process.
Smith's descriptions are effectively scientific observations, a comparison that
is suggested also by the fact that the rise of the empire that Smith recounts was
concurrent with the rise of empirical science.[13] Prompted by this comparison, I want to turn from the literary model to the scientific in search of a way
to understand the peculiarities of Smith's history writing. (Charting the progress of science and of the empire presents similar intellectual problems also in
that the rise of a global European empire has appeared for half a millennium
as inevitable as the discovery of the double helix.) The narrative model I want
to borrow has been sketched especially clearly by Bruno Latour, and although
he ultimately derives from it a different argument, his terms seem to me autonomously applicable.[14] Many historians of science have labored to demys-

tify science in much the same way historians of American colonization have been attempting to demystify the discovery. The effort to write the history of science otherwise than as a series of epiphanies—to write a *history* of science, not its bible—has produced newly procedural accounts of the emergence of scientific knowledge. In Latour's terminology, there are two ways to define science: "science in the making" and "ready-made science." The first definition describes a process of finding or making scientific advances fraught with uncertainties, redundancies, and contingencies. Scientific progress is thus *underdetermined:* there is never enough evidence to make certain an explanation of observed phenomena. An explanation becomes certain only after it is made, at which point it appears "just enough determined" and seems forevermore the inevitable outcome of an entirely coherent and meaningful evolution.

This distinction between states of scientific knowledge before and after discoveries, and especially the notion that progress toward a discovery is underdetermined up to the moment the discovery occurs, seems to me highly pertinent to the problems of writing an alternative colonial history. "Science in the making" and "ready-made science" suggest analogous kinds of history, "history before the fact" and "history as the past." Like science in the making, history before the fact is uncertain, apparently redundant, and contingent; only retrospectively does it take on direction and determination. The Smith passages can be seen to represent history before the fact, and it is governed not by excessive but by insufficient determining forces. (I should perhaps stipulate that by *fact* I mean an accepted account of things, and that while I would maintain that there is a world out there and that it contains objective conditions we do not create, I do not refer here to such objective conditions but to the hybrid we call a fact and which fuses the material and the ideal such that we are unable to extricate them.)

Registering Powhatan's resistance, Smith writes with political intention but also in considerable doubt about his ability to carry out his intention—to make the Indians submit to the rule of the English crown and also to win for himself the rewards of such a victory. Uncertain and needing not only to persuade others but to understand for himself, he describes more of the elements of the situation than fit into his favored interpretation, including some elements that will turn out, once the incident is closed, to have led toward its outcome, while others will in retrospect appear contrary to historical tendency or just insignificant, ephemeral.

In short, Smith's language is *not* the perfect instrument of empire. He tries to make it so, but he is never perfectly successful. On the other hand, if he were successful, if there were a perfect *instrument* of empire, would this not imply that there were also perfect *objects* of colonization? A great deal has been written about the mutuality of colonizer and colonized. But most of it is about either ideology or psychology, or at any rate about the content of the relationship. The form is equally at issue and in one respect still more radically defining. For it is in the formal definition of the dyad of conqueror and conquered that the third party to the analysis, the scholar, is also inevitably and organically engaged. And just as it is becoming evident that the authority of the colonizer to define the empire must be curtailed before a new account can be produced, so must the authority of the scholar. The impulse that drives *Colonial Encounters* to produce an *authoritative* counternarrative is both admirable and ultimately self-defeating.

This contradiction has two sites: one in the effective appropriation of the voice of the dispossessed in order to speak on their behalf, a second in an appropriation of the imperial discourse in order to condemn it. Decolonization must begin at home with the recognition that the desire to recuperate the contingency of the European hegemony is not disinterested. We find ourselves, in the twilight of the empire, with the urgent task of establishing that Europe's global dominion was not in the nature of things; that whatever brought about five centuries of Western rule, it was not, as the founders of the United States claimed for their own empire, "Nature and Nature's God"; that civilization can exist under different auspices. If, contemplating a world without the European empire, we take seriously the repudiation of its universality—of its sufficiency for all truths and political realities—this should be reflected in the form as well as the content of our revisionary narratives. An omniscient counterhistory in this regard is a contradiction in terms.

The latter-day scholarship of colonization has focused on the way the empire builders acquired control. But in the acquiring, in the process of acquisition, control is not yet at work. John Smith does not control the history in the making that he records; he records the history in order to control it. He is not wholly confident that Powhatan can be brought under the English aegis. Hernán Cortés, whose conquest of Mexico seems inevitable to Tzvetan Todorov in his *Conquest of America* (1982), was himself so far from thinking the conquest certain that before marching on Mexico City he burnt his ships to preclude retreat.

Smith's description of the coronation of Powhatan and his report of Powhatan's rebuke to the English king are chronicles of uncertainty that bear witness to material uncertainties. These chronicles' lapses and incoherencies, their redundancies and paradoxes, represent the limits of discourse, the moments in which discourse does not know what to say. These are moments when alternatives coexist, when their futures are underdetermined. When, at such moments, many forces, intentions, and effects combine, interact, parallel, or counter one another, they do not yet add up to causality. They are all insufficient, singly or in any combination, to cause the reality that ultimately ensues. Historical evidence is thus doubly problematical not only because it is always read through an interpretive lens but because even before that it may not explain or it may explain only partially. This second problem is particularly intractable when the evidence is entirely narrative and likely to present entire plots. The uncertain play of historical evolution is more evident when different kinds of evidence have to be related to one another. But the suggestion I am making for the recognition of uncertainty is meant to apply to any historical method. The problem raised by reading evidence with relation to reality, in my view, is not just that we are uncertain about how to interpret the evidence but that it may not relate to the reality we seek to explain.

For what these underdetermined and therefore incoherent moments inscribe is not historical direction but human agency. And to read these moments it is not enough to recognize the colonizer's limited authority over history and the text; that recognition leads only to reading textual ruptures, which perversely confirms the wholeness of the *reader's* understanding. If an account of the past includes its indeterminacies, parts of the account are very likely to remain terminally "nonproven" and others incoherent. About the crowning of Powhatan we can say with certainty neither that the English crown appropriated Powhatan's authority nor that it failed. In fact, the major event in these scenes is not the outcome at all but the interaction.

As we look back to the seventeenth century, seeing interaction in the course of empire building makes it seem less destined and the empire builders less entitled—a welcome implication. We are pleased to see the authority of Cortés and Smith diminish as their narratives of the rise of the empire prove uncertain. On the other hand, stressing the uncertainties and incoherences of imperial chronicles may also have a less welcome implication for how we see ourselves in relation to the twenty-first century. The underdetermination of the empire's rise is a ground for denying definitive authority to the narratives of Cortés and Smith. But underdetermination also limits the authority of current historians of the empire's fall. We too write chronicles of uncertainty, of which we are just the coauthors.

Although virtually everyone now agrees that histories are unavoidably interested fabrications, much of the current historical scholarship is dedicated to setting the record straight. A
striking paradox but perhaps not a surprising one. Skepticism
is a hard act to follow but even harder to sustain. Granted that
no account of things is ever definitive, it is nonetheless difficult, once launched on an interrogation, not to seek a definitive answer. It has become routine to stipulate that the most
faithful historical narrative interrogating the past is still only
an interpretation; that, far from telling the exact truth as the
author of the treatise discussed in this essay boasts, histories
present an inevitably biased selection of facts and indeed, in
claiming objectivity, effectively lie. However, while the argument that histories invent rather than discover has mostly
done away with the duplicities of empiricism, it has developed its own contradiction by often serving as a ground for
revisionary accounts presented not just as new narratives but
as corrections of the old. Exposing history writing's aptness
to prevaricate, revisionist historians prove the point by exposing specific misrepresentations—and not infrequently go
on to propose in their place new exact truths.

If this paradox is generic to any skeptical intellectual
practice, its present form seems particularly acute. Past or traditional accounts get remarkably little credence today, while
they are replaced by new ones whose authority seems as remarkably unimpeachable. Reestablishing authority was not
the way postmodern disassemblies of received historical truth
were meant to work of course, quite the contrary. However,

it might have been expected that an epistemology stripping authority so thoroughly, not only from earlier histories but from their sources, would create a vacuum of authority that would inevitably suck in the only author available to fill it, the present historian. I want to be clear that my objection is not that recent historical narratives assert the authority of their own engagement, being myself persuaded that engagement as such is a good and even necessary thing in a historian as in anyone else. The problem I want to take up arises from method rather than politics. It expresses itself first in the contradictory effect by which radical skepticism in history writing has been tending to reconstitute the claim of objectivity in terms that are, if anything, more absolute than previously. For in showing the falsity of earlier histories and their sources, the new narratives have acquired an unprecedented autonomy, not just of interpretation but of vision. Here I am mainly concerned with a secondary effect of this autonomy of vision: the way it can fail to reveal or even obscure aspects of a past scene that contradict our present view.

Historians of the colonization of the New World have more reason than most to see the past their own way because the traditional accounts have exceptionally little authority. In the main, the sources upon which colonial histories draw are either unusually compromised or exceptionally difficult to decipher. The preponderance of these sources are writings and records left by imperialists who have now lost their credibility. After five centuries, the European empire is in ruins and, its intellectual hegemony having crumbled concurrently, its account of colonization is everywhere radically discounted. There exists another set of sources in the relics of the colonized but these are much scarcer because most New World peoples had no system for writing while other manifestations of their civilizations were largely destroyed, either systematically or through the general holocaust of conquest. In short, for the colonial era, historical interpretation encounters very little resistance from the materials of history themselves.

Moreover, probably the majority of the historians today are anticolonial and thus prone to disbelieve the accounts and justifications of the colonizers while more or less aligning themselves with the colonized. These historians, facing an established view of the past that cannot be trusted and armed only with fragmentary and indistinct subaltern account, have proceeded in two ways that are at once logical and contradictory. First, they have exposed the complicities of such works as Walter Raleigh's *Discovery of Guiana* or John Smith's several histories of America. Then, or rather concurrently, they have projected a revisionary account woven from the stuff of exposure. I have elsewhere[1] discussed an instance of what I took to be an overly conclusive revi-

sion. Here, hoping to illustrate the shortcomings of what I called above an autonomy of historical vision, I would like to try my hand at a less conclusive revising while reading a text that, admittedly, does seem to be asking to be set
right. I will try nonetheless to unsettle its claims without settling my own.

The text is a mid-seventeenth-century English work by an English writer
named Richard Ligon. For a revisionist historian, Ligon is an especially attractive interlocutor in that he was not a pillar of English society. He was neither a Walter Raleigh nor a William Bradford. His personal story was quite ordinary. Having lost all his property through the vicissitudes of political
alliances, he did what many did in his time, he set off to recover his fortune in
the West Indies. Barely established, however, he fell ill of a wasting fever and,
forced to return to England as poor as when he left, he soon found himself
imprisoned for debt in Newgate. There, hoping to earn enough to free himself, he wrote *A True and Exact History of Barbadoes,* which had considerable
success when it was published in London in 1657.[2]

The *True and Exact History* is known today mainly as the source of a story
retold by Richard Steele in *The Spectator.*[3] However, this well-known story, to
which I shall return later, is not among the passages I want to read closely. Instead my selections are chosen almost at random for their ordinariness, because the paradox I want to explore, the way a radical skepticism is in danger
of engendering as radical an orthodoxy, turns on ordinariness.

The first selection, thus, is an account of the routine that attends the arrival of new slaves; this is the way, Ligon tells us by his tone as well as his story,
things usually go:

> When they are brought to us, the Planters buy them out of the Ship, where
> they find them stark naked, and therefore cannot be deceived in any out-
> ward infirmity. They choose them as they do Horses in a Market; the
> strongest, youthfullest, and most beautiful, yield the greatest prices. Thirty
> pounds sterling is a price for the best man Negre; and twenty five, twenty
> six, or twenty seven pound for a Woman; the Children are at easier rates.
> And we buy them so, as the sexes may be equall; for, if they have more men
> then women, the men who are unmarried will come to their Masters, and
> complain, that they cannot live without Wives, and desire him, they may
> have Wives. And he tells them, that the next ship that comes, he will buy
> them Wives, which satisfies them for the present; and so they expect the
> good time: which the Master performing with them, the bravest fellow is to
> choose first, and so in order, as they are in place; and every one of them
> knowes his better, and gives him the precedence, as Cowes do one another,

in passing through a narrow gate; for the most of them are as neer beasts as may be, setting their souls aside.[4]

Nothing could be more ordinary to Ligon, but it is for us impossible to read as ordinary. In the way we find ordinary, we can only read this passage with revulsion compounded by the matter-of-factness of the narrator. *Our* ordinary assumptions render *his* ordinary assumptions outrageous and unacceptable; at the same time, the passage makes it clear that it never even occured to Richard Ligon to find this unloading of human beings for the stocks an occasion for regret, let alone outrage.

Of course, this absence of recognition of the horror of slavery is one of the features the current historiography seeks to highlight about the past. Thus, from the perspective of revising the historical record, the clash of two ordinarinesses that occurs when one reads this passage today poses no real problem. From that perspective, one has succeeded when the passage is made to expose its own inhumanity. My argument begins here, for the exposure has a double effect—it reveals, but it also conceals. The text a revisionist reading brings to self-exposure betrays itself in both senses of the word, in the sense of acknowledging something hitherto hidden, but also in the sense of denying its own principles. When Ligon's account of the slave auction is made to admit to the human reality it suppresses, as a historical account, it does not only expand, it also shrinks. The loss is difficult to describe or even name in the abstract, but it is sensible in the flesh of the text: "For the most of them are as neer beasts as may be, setting their souls aside."

What I am after here is contained in the tone of the sentence and in its grammar. Up to the comma, Ligon is moving forward easily, without friction. Then, at the comma, suddenly, something else occurs to him; although in his memory the Africans being herded along resembled cattle, yet, in a split second pause, it comes to him that they are not really animals. Awkwardly, he acknowledges this second thought, and tags it on at the end of his sentence where it hangs free. The whole sentence has now lost its momentum and arrives limping at a very different conclusion than it had in view when it set out, which was to describe a group of beings made interesting by their distance from the author's and reader's humanity. These beings were to be characterized by their physicality and instead Ligon's sentence has delivered him before the recognition of their souls.

This puts him in mind of spiritual issues in regard to which he reaffirms his initial view: "Religion they know none; yet most of them acknowledge a God, as appears by their motions and gestures." Again his sentence has divided, is divided as if against itself. Trying to recover the main thread of his narrative, not a discussion of African souls but an entertaining and instructive description of the slaves' alien nature, he once more stumbles. They have no religion but, he corrects himself (typing quickly, I first wrote "conceded" instead of "corrected," which conveys my view of the event but would have introduced something into the text that I do not think is there), they reveal some impulse toward divine worship. Again Ligon amends his narrative midway. Launched in a sentence of denial, he pauses here at the semicolon: "Religion they know none; yet most of them acknowledge a God, as appears by their motions and gestures." And now that he comes to think of it, they do acknowledge a God, he has a vivid memory of seeing them doing so: "For, if one of them do another wrong, and he cannot revenge himself, he looks up to Heaven for vengeance, and holds up both his hands, as if the power must come from thence, that must do him right" (47).

Now, this sentence projects an entire drama. A dispute or a fight between two Africans has left the one who is probably in the right defeated. The victim lifts his hands to heaven and calls down its vengeance upon his aggressor. Meanwhile the scene is being observed by an outsider able to understand only its gestures. For him the drama unfolds in mime, but its vividness implies voices behind the veil of incomprehension.

My worry is that the vividness, indeed the completeness, of this account emerges in large part precisely from the perspective that prevents Ligon from representing it as we now understand it must have unfolded. Instead of the terrible pathos of men rendered helpless and yet still aspiring to justice, he sees an interesting charade. The two hands held up to the sky signify for him nothing beyond a degree of religiosity he finds important to report. But though unresponsive in our sense, he nonetheless captures the scene as a more sympathetic observer might not have done, communicating not just the meaning but the terms of the situation by embedding them in his own narrative. The slave dispute unfolds silently—there is no question of Ligon lending the participants a voice—in a mimicry that is, however, the more telling for the absence of words. Look again at the texture of Ligon's language. "He looks up to Heaven for vengeance . . . as if the power must come from thence that must do him right." The repetition of the "must"—"the power *must* come that must do him right"—even, it seems to me, the formula "as *if* the power must come," instead of a more direct statement like "expecting the power to come," these capture the emotional force of the situation more fully *because* the observer has no stake in it.

There is something else going on in this scene that it would be easy to lose

in a revisionist reading based on recognition of the slaves' humanity and condemnation of Ligon's imperviousness to it: the effect of the scene on Ligon
himself. For while he is not moved to protest, he does not remain altogether
unmoved. Indeed the sentence I have just read betrays, again in both senses, a
surprisingly strong response and a spontaneous one. The passage opens with a
flatly declarative statement: "When they are brought to us, the Planters buy
them out of the Ship, where they find them stark naked, and therefore cannot
be deceived in any outward infirmity." The logic expressed in the "therefore"
is purely formal, uninflected by any awareness that the beings whose possible
outward infirmities stand to be revealed might possess an inwardness as well.
On the contrary, however, the logic of Ligon's subsequent reasoning about religion develops within the slaves' own thinking: "Religion they know none,
yet most of them acknowledge a God."

Ligon himself is a member of the group of observers and his own involvement is a major component of his text. But it is also the most fragile
component. The sentence I parsed earlier with the two "musts," suggesting
that it captured the emotion of the slave dispute the better for Ligon's philosophical detachment, at the same time reflects an emotional involvement the
more resonant and evocative for not being based on identification. Another
moment to which Ligon responds, again out of a delicate balance of careless-
ness and fellow-feeling, is equally fragile and telling. When an African woman
bears twins, he reports, her husband concludes that she has been "false to his
Bed, and so no more adoe but hang her." On one occasion, this occurring, the
master "used all persuasions that possibly he could, to let him see, that such
double births are in Nature."

> But this prevailed little with him upon whom custome had taken so deep
> an impression; but resolved, the next thing he did, should be to hang her.
> Which when the Master perceived, and that the ignorance of the man, should
> take away the life of the woman, who was innocent of the crime her Husband
> condemned her for, told him plainly, if he hang'd her, he himselfe should be
> hang'd by her, upon the same bough; and therefore wish'd him to consider
> what he did. (47)

The same feature of this passage—the sheer irritation, the impatience, one
hears in his voice, directed at the stubborn slave who refuses to believe that his
wife has not been unfaithful—conveys at once the plenitude and the absence
of Ligon's understanding. His irritation, blindly superficial from a twenty-
first-century perspective, is wholly responsive in its context. The episode

conveys a sense of one kind of relation between slave and master that we have no way of reconstructing, either in its positive or in its negative aspects, in our more enlightened terms. For the traffic of irritation, incomprehension, mockery, disinterested interest, indifference, and sympathy that defined slave-master relations, comprised emotions and modes of understanding that arose on a ground of assumptions we can no longer contemplate as even possibly valid.

Michel Foucault's concept of discourse has for some time now offered a way to map this ground while also excavating it. By explicating Ligon's thinking in the terms of a coherent or at any rate cohesive discourse, it should be possible, according to this concept, to read him dynamically, for the way he manipulates concepts and values with which one need not agree. But I want to suggest that the notion of discourse only postpones the problem, and may even exacerbate it. Reading Ligon in the larger context of a seventeenth-century discourse of colonization and slavery places a twenty-first-century reader in a globally critical position from which the *True and Exact History* appears even less authoritative; as if less authored. For the issue is not whether to accept what it tells us as truth—its truth can never be ours—but rather to engage with it as an interlocutor. But when we read it as part of an overall discourse and as evidence for it, we are less able to read it in its own terms, which have vanished into our translation of them. Ligon's writing itself becomes, oddly, less text than context, and on this level, exactly in the act of defining Ligon's normal terms, we have denormalized them. And while denormalizing a slavery discourse is in itself worthwhile and even necessary, it may undermine the other purpose for reading such works, which is, precisely, to recapture a lost and alien normality; to juxtapose them to current norms, not only as outrage but as ordinariness.

Hannah Arendt's exposition of the banality of evil does not explain how we are to see this banality banally. Yet if we do not see it banally, we do not to that extent understand it. Of course if we do see it banally, we also fail to understand it. Not to shudder at the picture of human beings brutalized and yet retaining their humanity, would be to miss the point. Is it possible, nonetheless, at the same time, or rather, in terms of the same explanatory paradigm, not to overlook the fact that Ligon also sees the humanity of his victims? that for him there is no incoherence between stripping the slaves like animals and recognizing their human modesty? that he participates calmly, without advocacy in relation to either, in both representations?

I would like to carry these questions into the considerations of a second passage, which actually comes earlier in the text, and indeed treats the an-

tecedent issue of the very ground of slavery. "It has been accounted a strange
thing," Ligon begins in the tone of disinterestedness, "that the Negroes, being
more then double the numbers of the Christians that are there, and they accounted a bloody people, where they think they have power or advantages;
and the more bloody, by how they are more fearfull than others: that these
should not commit some horrid massacre upon the Christians, and thereby to
enfranchise themselves, and become Masters of the Iland" (46). This is a most
remarkable sentence and, I think, truly incomprehensible today; not what it
states, but the status of the statement, which for Ligon is wholly commensurate with the problem of slavery while for us it fails to even raise the central issue. The problem of slavery, as Ligon names it here, is not how certain human
beings justified buying, selling, and owning others, a problem of ethics and
politics, but how, practically, the slaves were made to submit. Someone today
could explain slavery in something like Ligon's terms by averring that brute
power is the motor of human relations; but the fundamental difference even
in meaning between such apparently similar assertions is manifest in the fact
that the power explanation could never be proposed today with Ligon's calm
and unjudging acceptance. On the contrary, offered without adjectives or
context, it would still read as accusation, reproach, denunciation; indeed, if
we allow ourselves to pull Ligon's question into our context, it reads as
rhetoric or possibly even as injunction. But that is not how Ligon seems to
have written it.

It is as a genuine question that he asks why in practical terms the Africans
allow themselves to be enslaved, and he offers a genuine, that is, a sufficient,
answer that in his view clearly encompasses the whole of the problem. The
first part of the answer is least alien to our own thinking: The unarmed slaves
are intimidated by constant shows of force. The second part, that the slaves,
drawn from different parts of Africa, lack a common language, is more difficult for us to read in a neutral tone in that it blandly acknowledges, but makes
nothing much of, what we consider a charged and revelatory fact, the linguistic complexity of the slaves' culture, of itself testifying decisively to the inhumanity of slavery.

The third part of the answer, however, presents a categorical difficulty for
a latter-day reader, invoking for us inescapable assumptions about the nature
of human beings and of society. Ligon suggests that the slaves accept their status in relation to Europeans because they recognize it as a more or less normal human situation, Africans themselves having their own practice of slavery. "In some of these places where petty Kingdomes are," Ligon explains,
"they sell their subjects, and such as they take in Battle, whom they make

slaves; and some mean men sell their servants, their Children, and sometimes their Wives; and think all good traffick, for such commodities as our Merchants sends them" (46). Thomas Hobbes had already published his *Leviathan* when Ligon wrote this account of slavery's origin, and it is thus the more difficult and important to recognize the absence in it of any concept of inalienable self-possession. Subjects and prisoners of war are made slaves without any apparent rupture of social norms. The men who sell their servants, children, and wives are "mean," they are greedy therefore and no doubt cruel, but it is not suggested that they are in violation of basic or natural laws. They engage in a despicable commerce and Ligon is clearly shaking his head in the phrase "and think all good traffick"; on the other hand, "our Merchants" are not condemned, they are simply taking advantage of a commercial opportunity. After all, it is not their servants, children, and wives they traffic in. In other words, this passage has no ontological concerns over human beings being bartered nor broaches any ethical issues beyond the desirability of being decent to one's family. If it is regrettable to find groups of enslaved human beings, the issues this raises and the moral violations it represents are hardly fundamental.

The end of this passage beings us to the beginning of the one read earlier, which began, "When they are brought to us." The unproblematical implication of this dependent clause rests easily on the preceding explanation of a slavery that seems to pose only ordinary questions of administration or possibly of negotiation. The dependent clause "When they are brought to us" thus posits the three-part explanation immediately preceding, permitting the freedom of conscience of the main clause: "the Planters buy them out of the Ship." The Barbados slave market is in Ligon's treatment the most ordinary of markets, a totally banal market. In Arendt's concept, the banality of evil flows from a pathological superficiality: Eichmann knew only the surfaces of life and at his most evil never plumbed the moral depths he defiled. I am suggesting that Ligon need not have been a superficial man to have viewed a slave market in the banal terms of this passage; our depths were not his and he did not need to fail to plumb them.

By the same token, however, his depths were not ours and at least one point of writing history is precisely to enter other depths than our own. To that end, let us consider a third passage from the *True and Exact History,* offering another representation of slavery and one that seems at first more congenial. Ligon here describes a visit he paid to the governor of a nearby island where he had the pleasure of meeting the governor's mistress, a black woman who is also his slave. Ligon is much impressed by the beauty of this mistress

whose personal attractions and wonderful attire he describes at length. She
was, he tells us,

> A Negro of the greatest beautie and majestie together that ever I saw in one
> woman. Her stature large, and excellently shap't, well favour'd, full eye'd, &
> admirably grac't; she wore on her head a roll of green taffatie, strip't with
> white and Philiamort, made up in manner of a Turban; and over that sleight
> vayle, which she tooke off at pleasure. On her bodie next her linen, a Peticoate
> of Orange Tawny and Skye Colour; not done with Straite Stripes, but wav'd;
> and upon that a mantle of purple silke, ingrayld with straw Colour. This Man-
> tle was large, and tyed with a knot of verie broad black Ribbon, with a rich
> Jewell on her right shoulder, which came under her left arme, and so hung
> loose and carelessly, almost to the ground. On her Legs, she wore buskins of
> wetched [sic] Silke, deckt with Silvr lace, and Fringe; Her shooes, of white
> Leather, lac't with skie clour; and pint between those laces. In her eares, she
> wore Large Pendants, about her neck; and on her armes, fayre Pearles. But her
> eyes were her richest Jewells: for they were the largest, and most orientall, that
> I have ever seene. (12)

Despite this extraordinary catalogue of her physical attributes and posses-
sions, Ligon does not see the woman as just a body. He wants also to hear her
speak and contrives a plan which enables him to be shortly even more impressed by her "language & gracefull delivery." His admiration now raises her
to the pinnacle of womanhood: She moves "with far greater majesty, and
gracefulness, than I have seen Queen Anne descend from the Chaire of State,
to dance the Measures with a Baron of England, at a Maske in the Banquet-
ting house."

This passage presents the opposite difficulty from the other two. Granted
a voice of her own and rendered comparable to an English monarch, the
slave-mistress tempts a postcolonial critic to see her as a rupturing, subversive
figure who has overcome her author's bigotries. I think this would be as mis-
taken as taking the description of the slave auction earlier as a sign of Ligon's
inhumanity. The governor's mistress has real status and dignity, and her linguistic sophistication is genuinely empowering. None of these attributes
bring Ligon to reflect upon her slave status; they enter into it only insofar as
they make the governor a lucky master.

But I would go further and suggest that it is in part by *not* reasoning from
the woman's evident equality if not superiority to everyone around her to the
conclusion that her status as a slave is therefore wrong, that, in a context deny-

ing basic laws of human relations, Ligon is brought to feel warmth, generosity, empathy, and in short the whole panoply of humane feeling. This is one instance, indeed, when he may well see more humanely than we do, or rather when he may better see aspects of a human experience obscured for us by another we find more vivid. In other words, there is both less and more to Ligon's view of Barbados than is evident from our perspective.

Both the less and the more are particularly evident in the anecdote for which the *True and Exact History* is best-known for having been retold later in *The Spectator.* This is the story of Inkle and Yarico. Inkle (vernacular for "English") is a sailor who, on a trip to the Indies, lands on a small Caribbean island where he is attacked by Indians and gravely wounded. Yarico is the Indian girl who saves him and nurses him back to health. Falling in love, they pass their days in pastoral bliss until a passing ship stops at the island offering rescue. Inkle asks Yarico to accompany him back to his country and she accepts. "But," writes Ligon, "the youth, when he came a shoar in the Barbadoes, forgot the kindness of the poor maid, that had ventured her life for his safety, and sold her for a slave, who was as free born as he: And so poor Yarico for her love, lost her liberty" (55).

In exchange, however, Yarico acquires the status of a full-fledged heroine while the tale renders the sailor an utter villain. The problem is how to read this story of betrayed love, pathos, and the pursuit of empire. In showing Inkle to be a thorough scoundrel, does the story denounce the colonial system he represents? Does it warn against the dehumanizing effects of racism? Does it represent a "subversion" of the "colonial text"? Should we invoke Montaigne?[5]

I think not. Ligon no more protests here than he condones in the earlier passage about the slaves. Moreover his failures either to protest or to condone are complementary, and together they express an understanding of colonization that simply does not raise fundamental issues of being. As with his celebration of the slave-mistress, Ligon here displays a discursive coherence that does not connect the British sailor's mistreatment of Yarico to the morality of England's takeover of Barbados. Abuses, excesses, wrongs, or alternatively, flirtations, amusing encounters, and sentimental episodes: sad or spirited, Ligon's tales of slavery treat it as another of life's vicissitudes. His treatment of slavery neither is inhumanly callous nor vindicates the brotherhood of man. His understanding of slavery appears to differ from ours exactly in not seeing that it raises fundamental issues.

By insisting on recognizing this difference and proposing to read accordingly, I do not mean to invoke, for instance, Hayden White's notion that interpretive models simply generate the history they posit. On the contrary, I am persuaded that the current accounts of the colonial past are substantially truer than those they replace. This is, therefore, not an argument for relativism. Nothing prevents our judging the universe of Ligon's discourse by the values that order ours. It seems impossible, indeed, not to judge Ligon's view of the world, in the same measure and for the same reason that it is impossible to entirely recapture it. If slavers did not find slavery an abomination, this is no reason not to condemn them of one. Taking sides is an expression of intellectual integrity. The problem for historical scholarship arises not in judging the past but in recasting it congruently with the judgment. The men and women dragged up out of the slave ships to be auctioned in Barbadoes suffered abominably, and Richard Ligon, as a member of the slave-owning class and an aspiring slave owner, was implicated in that suffering. That is history as we know it today. To know Ligon's history as he knew it then, however, requires allowing the possibility that he was also not implicated, or not in the way we understand him today to have been.

Seventeenth-century thinking about slavery overwhelmingly justified it on grounds of both principle (derived from ancient philosophical tradition) and expediency. Plato and Aristotle had approved the practice, Thomas More incorporated it into his *Utopia;* David Brion Davis observed that "the great seventeenth-century authorities on law" would seem to have concurred, and that the period's great philosophers, Descartes, Malebranche, Spinoza, Pascal, Bayle, or Fontenelle, did not dispute the traditional view;[6] Hobbes assumed its inevitability and did not find it precluded the good society. Locke opposed slavery in principle but not in the practical instance of African slaves, being himself an investor in the Royal African Company. It is true that some in the seventeenth-century opposed slavery. To recuperate Ligon's history, one needs to project him against the contemporary opposition, as defined for instance by Thomas Tryon, who denounced slavery in his 1684 *Friendly Advice to the Gentlemen-Planters of the East and West Indies,* but counseled "Sambo," once well-treated, to obey his masters and thus find happiness. The governor's mistress in Ligon's account might have been the sister of Tryon's Sambo; which is not to suggest that Ligon is a crypto-abolitionist, but rather that Tryon's abolitionism was also not ours.

Some degree of incoherence must ensue from the double sight of Ligon in his time and ours. But there is no reason outside of the historian's sense of authority why historical narratives need resolve into single accounts. A scholarly history can be structured, rather than by a unified logic of its own, by an exposition of the known, the known in different versions, and the perhaps irrevocably unknown. The goal of a critical analysis is at any rate not a solution in the mathematical sense; rather, critics and historians produce useful descriptions or redeployments of texts and materials such that they are more accessible to being thought about. Of course, a useful description is not an empirical account since it begins by rearranging facts and even second-guessing motives. Still, it seems useful to remember that while we are in dialogue with the past, the past was not in dialogue with us; and that if, for us, today's universalities apply to the seventeenth century, this does not mean they were universal then. In short, true and exact histories, while neither true nor exact, are not exactly false either.

In 1915 Virginia Woolf published her first novel, *The Voyage
Out,* the story of a young woman who accompanies her
father on a voyage to the Amazon, becomes involved with
a group of English people vacationing in a village at the
mouth of the river, falls in love with one of them, and is engaged to him.[1] They plan to marry upon their return to England but just before they are due to leave, on a trip up river,
the young woman falls ill of a fever and dies. The preternat-
urally thoughtful heroine, Rachel Vinrace, is continually occupied in scrutinies of her own inner dramas and speculations about those of others, for the psychic landscape off this
first novel is already recognizably a Woolf universe. Clarissa
Dalloway, as a young wife, appears briefly but memorably
and, on leaving, promises to return.

We know where we are in *The Voyage Out;* except that its
familiar ground is also significantly foreign, the drawing
rooms and gardens arising on the other side of the world.
Still, the drawing rooms and gardens are the novel's most interesting sites where characters elaborate their intricacies,
problems unfold, and things happen. Except on two occasions, the surrounding Amazonian life remains marginal to
the concerns of the story whose stage consists of a villa, a hotel, and the paths linking them. Neither the novel's central
character nor its center stage have much to do with Amazo-
nia. Rachel, who had planned to accompany her father further inland, is persuaded to remain in her aunt's villa by the
promise of "a room cut off from the rest of the house, large,
private—a room in which she could play, read, think, defy

the world, a fortress as well as a sanctuary" (123). The best thing South America has to offer her is a room of her own.

Most students of Virginia Woolf therefore read the title of *The Voyage Out* figuratively, to signify a voyage in, the route of all of Woolf's writings. But why go so far to explore one's own interior? I will suggest that in this first of Woolf's journeys to the heart of the self, South America is neither incidental nor metaphorical; that Woolf had reason to set her first novel in the Amazon, and that the interior life of her heroine is intimately involved with far-flung lands she has never visited and peoples she never meets.

At one level of the story, the connection between foreign lands and English girls is explicit. Rachel's father, Willoughby, is captain and owner of a freighter plying a trade route between London and the mouth of the Amazon. Bringing out dry goods and returning with rubber, he has grown rich enough to contemplate a career in government. On this trip, he has brought along, besides his daughter Rachel, his sister-in-law Helen Ambrose and her husband to spend a few weeks in the town at the mouth of the river in a villa belonging to Helen's brother. In the last ten years, this town, Santa Marina, has become the site of a small English colony, at first schoolmasters on holiday, then a more varied group in search of something a little different from Spain or Greece. Woolf's sketch is spare but complete. Willoughby Vinrace's asymmetrical commerce; the English tourists seeking something exotic and cheap; Santa Marina which has recently converted an old monastery into a hotel for its growing trade; the history of the area which includes a brief English settlement in the seventeenth century lost to the Portuguese and Spanish who established more lasting ties by intermarrying with the Indians: these are the features of an early-twentieth-century imperial Britain whose portrait is as distinct as the characters'.

In fact, the beginning of the story gives the Empire a leading role. When the outbound freighter docks at Lisbon, Richard and Clarissa Dalloway come aboard. The Dalloways have been traveling "chiefly with a view to broadening Mr. Dalloway's mind" (39) during an interlude in which he finds himself not a member of Parliament. They have been to "the Latin countries" but were frustrated in their desire to penetrate Petersburg and Teheran. "In Spain," we learn, "[Mr.] and Mrs. Dalloway had mounted mules, for they wished to understand how the peasants live. Are they, for example, ripe for rebellion?" Richard Dalloway is rather ridiculous and in connection with him, his wife only slightly less so. She confides to her diary that upon visiting Fielding's grave, she "let loose a small bird which some ruffian had trapped, 'because one hates to think of anything in a cage where English people lie buried'" (39–40).

Together the Dalloways caricature conventional, conservative England. Richard is the soul and voice of the British empire. He has been to both Oxford and Cambridge because his father wished for a maximal broadening of his son's mind (broadening the mind is Richard's constant and not innocent phrase). "I can remember . . . settling the basis of a future state with the present Secretary for India," he tells Rachel, musing over his career. Has he fulfilled the ambitions he acquired at what he has described simply as "both universities" (64)? Well, he has not lowered his ideal which, prompted, he names as "Unity. Unity of aim, of dominion, of progress. The dispersion of the best ideas over the greatest area." By which, prompted further, he admits that he means the dispersion of the English who are "on the whole, whiter than most men" (64). In short, "I can conceive no more exalted aim—to be the citizen of the Empire" (66).

Neither can his wife. The conversation between Richard Dalloway and Rachel Vinrace from which I have been quoting ends at a cry from Clarissa who has been looking out over the sea. "'Warships, Dick!' she calls out excitedly. 'Over there! Look!' . . . 'By George!' he exclaimed, and stood shielding his eyes. 'Ours, Dick?' said Clarissa. 'The Mediterranean Fleet,' he answered. The *Euphrosyne* was slowly dipping her flag. Richard raised his hat. Convulsively Clarissa squeezed Rachel's hand. 'Aren't you glad to be English!' she said" (69). But describing what Clarissa has seen, Woolf pictures "two sinister grey vessels, low in the water, and bald as bone, one closely following the other with the look of eyeless beasts seeking their prey" (69).

Earlier the Dalloways have been speaking of their desire for a son who might be inspired by his father's career also to become a leader of men. This possibility moves Clarissa to ponder "what it really means to be English. One thinks of all we've done, and our navies, and the people in India and Africa, and how we've gone on century after century, sending out boys from little country villages—and of men like you, Dick, and it makes one feel as if one couldn't bear *not* to be English!" (50–51) Her husband has "a vision of English history, King following King, Prime Minister Prime Minister, and Law Law. . . . He ran his mind along the line of conservative policy, which went steadily from Lord Salisbury to Alfred, and gradually enclosed, as though it were a lasso that opened and caught things, enormous chunks of the habitable globe. 'It's taken a long time, but we've pretty nearly done it,' he said; 'it remains to consolidate'" (51).

Being lassoed sounds painful and possibly deadly for the captured chunks and, already in 1915, consolidating the empire had triggered a slaughterhouse of a war. Dalloway is a most unpleasant sort of humbug. Earlier, at the thought that he was a leader of men, the narrator has told us, "The chest slowly curved beneath [Richard Dalloway's] waistcoat" (50). Richard Dalloway is being darkly mocked and, along with him, his precious British empire.

Other versions of the colonizing fervor, propounded by different characters, are no more attractive. Evelyn Murgatroyd, all in white and looking "like a gallant lady of the time of Charles the First leading royalist troops into action" (128), is moved, upon hearing that "South America was the country of the future" (136), to wish she were a man so she could "raise a troop and conquer some great territory" (136). She yearns also to have accompanied Garibaldi, but her dearest wish is imperial conquest. She detests modern life and would give anything to have lived in Elizabethan times, "to be one of those colonists, to cut down trees and make laws and all that . . ." (197). Mrs. Flushing, a disastrous amateur painter who hates Shakespeare and bullies her servant, boasts to Rachel that Mr. Flushing has made quite a tidy job of acquiring art objects from the Indians who are too stupid to know the value of their property.

But these folk and their grotesque love of the empire are there as if for comic relief, the author's as well as the story's. The business of *The Voyage Out* is with another group of characters who inhabit the South American landscape differently. Rachel Vinrace is the central figure in this group which includes her aunt Helen and her eventual betrothed, Terence Hewet. When they do not ignore their colonial situation altogether, Rachel and her likes relate to their colonial situation only distantly, even abstractly. Distance and abstraction are essential to one of the novel's crucial scenes, the first of the two occasions on which the story leaves the domestic setting of villa and hotel.

Hewet has planned an excursion, a picnic at the top of a nearby mountain, Monte Rosa, the invited guests to make the long ascent on donkeys and be rewarded by what is reported to be a magnificent view. Rachel and Helen are of the party as well as several others whose gathering at the point of departure might well be taking place in the English countryside. Natives are mentioned as busy about the animals and the ferrying of supplies but they are voiceless and one does not suppose that, were they to speak, they would sound any different from their English counterparts (who one surmises would be equally unheard). Indeed the climb carries the party ever further from any specific location: "Higher and higher they went, becoming separated from the world. The world, when they turned to look back, flattened itself out, and was marked with squares of thin green and grey" (129). They might be anywhere, as social or political specificities are eclipsed. "Towns are very small," Rachel observes, "obscuring the whole of Santa Marina and its suburbs with one hand." Even the solidity of land dissolves, for, when she has covered over Santa Marina, instead of its surrounding landscape, Rachel sees only "the sea [filling] in all the angles of the coast smoothly, breaking in a white frill, and here and there ships . . . set firmly in the blue" (129–130). The air is "amazingly clear" but all it reveals is generic nature.

At this point, Evelyn Murgatroyd wonders whether Garibaldi was ever up this mountain, but her silliness only emphasizes the irrelevance of such concerns to what the more intelligent characters understand to be a transcendent place and moment. This is *not* history but reality, life.

The journey grows hot and wearisome, the sun beats down equatorially and we get a brief glimpse of where we are when the suffering English on their donkeys fall silent while the natives walking beside them "broke into queer wavering songs and tossed jokes from one to the other" (131). We are immediately restored to British consciousness, however, in the person of Hewet who promises that "the view will be wonderful" (131); the explorers press on and reach the summit. "One after another they came out on the flat space on the top and stood overcome with wonder. Before them they beheld an immense space—grey sands running into forest, and forest merging in mountains, and mountains washed by air, the infinite distances of South America." Hewet, who has planned this trip to bring more breadth into his own life and into those of a group of people he finds rather narrow, has succeeded brilliantly. The "immense" view of South America, the whole situation—Hewet's project, the properly awed assembly of English men and women, nature itself—is the genuine article in the category of broadening visions about which Richard Dalloway only pontificated.

The scenery does everyone credit; they show a proper sensibility: "The effect of so much space was at first rather chilling," the narrator notes, adding approvingly, "They felt themselves very small, and for some time no one said anything." When Evelyn M. breaks the reverent silence, even she says the right thing: "Splendid!" And Hewet, "gone a little in front, looked up at his guests as if to justify himself for having brought them" and sees them grow monumental: "On their pedestal of earth they looked unfamiliar and noble. . . ." That we are meant to see them the same way and to understand that they have transcended themselves is clear from the second half of the sentence, ". . .but in another moment they had broken their rank, and he had to see to the laying out of food" (131–32). The move to the mundane seals the interval just passed and makes it proof against debunking; the narrator mocked Richard Dalloway's vision but endorses Hewet's. She is not against visions as such.

The scene is not over, however. The picnic begins and, in the classic way of picnics, it is invaded by ants. Hewet suggests "[adopting] the methods of modern warfare" to repel the ants and the party throws itself happily into the game. Too happily, for these Lilliputian revels soon depress Hewet who grows disillusioned: "'They are not satisfactory; they are ignoble,' he thought. . . . Amiable and modest, respectable in many ways, lovable even in their content-ment and desire to be kind, how mediocre they all were and capable of what insipid cruelty to one another!'" (134)

Looking about him in his irritation, Hewet sees Rachel. "Her eyes were fixed rather sadly but not intently upon the row of people opposite her." Hewet asks her what she is looking at. "She was a little startled, but answered directly, 'Human beings'" (135). The last sentence of the chapter is this pa-tently right answer. Shy, inward, innocent, and wise, Rachel draws the moral of the dichotomy that has bewildered Hewet. Human beings are both: noble and mediocre. Wise but a little disappointing. All those eyes gazing at infinity from atop a mountain and then (the reader following closely) the eyes turned down, fixed on the ground where there rages the war of the ants, seems a lot of metaphor for such a tame meaning. Woolf herself may have felt let down: in the next chapter, still atop Monte Rosa, Hewet and Rachel walk away from the group and continue to explicate the scene. Once again, they gaze out at the view. This time Hewet seeks adequate expression in the language of art. "Isn't it like a water-colour too—you know the way water-colours dry in ridges all across the paper—I've been wondering what they looked like." But it is Rachel's unspoken reflection that finally says it all:

> She sat beside him looking at the mountains too. When it became painful to look any longer, the great size of the view seeming to enlarge her eyes be-yond their natural limit, she looked at the ground; it pleased her to scrutinize this inch of the soil of South America so minutely that she noticed every grain of earth and made it into a world where she was endowed with the supreme power. She bent a blade of grass, and set an insect on the utmost tassel of it, and wondered if the insect realized his strange adventure, and thought how strange it was that she should have bent that tassel rather than any other of the million tassels. (141)

This brief paragraph encapsulates all the meanings not only of the excur-sion but of the entire novel. Like Richard and Clarissa Dalloway in their de-based way, like Hewet in his worthier way, and like her companions generally on this excursion, Rachel is inspired by an infinitely expanding horizon. But beyond her companions, she understands and acknowledges the limits of her reach. When the view exceeds this "natural limit," she looks down, at the ground. Though she renounces infinity, however, she does not abandon the ambition represented by an outward gaze. On the contrary, reducing the universe at issue enables Rachel to fulfill her desire to impose herself. "It pleased her," writes Woolf, in the idiom of the deity looking over his creation, "to scrutinize this inch of the soil of South America" and possess it entirely as "a world where she was endowed with the supreme power." In the microcosm she thus possesses entirely, she controls the entire destiny of inferior beings incapable of understanding the forces—her will and whim—that rule them.

One discerns, expressed in Rachel's gesture of turning from the cosmic to the microcosmic, Woolf's belief that the largest meanings can inhere in the smallest events. But it is also clear that the diminution of the theater in no way diminishes the drama. To begin with, offsetting any notion that Rachel has lowered her sights along with her eyes, is the fact that, in relation to an inch of South American soil, she is a colossus. If anything, her image of herself looms over her world larger than Richard Dalloway's over his. And she wields a more absolute power; passing beyond king and emperor, Rachel is a god to her world and its creatures. But the greatest obstacle to reading the passage as Rachel's discovery of an alternative realm of meaning—a woman's discovery of America—is its plot. This plot, reproducing on an inch of soil the drama of global conquest, links imperial possession and self-possession as closely as ever did Richard Dalloway. Indeed, having roundly mocked Dalloway's vision, Woolf seems now to be transcribing it whole into Rachel's, and endorsing it as an image of quite admirable self-fulfillment.

For as Rachel surveys a world of her own lying at her feet, she is coming into her identity, realizing herself on that South American mountain. Immediately after the end of the passage above, Hewet, who has until now called her only "Miss Vinrace," asks Rachel her Christian name. And shortly after that, in the same chapter, they confess their love. Rachel has achieved the supreme power of self-dominion through supreme power. Her earlier response to Hewet, which implicitly affirmed mediocrity as also worthy, was not the right answer after all.

Of course, the fact that Rachel's own world is an inch of ground matters a great deal. I do not want to suggest that her imperialism is in substance the same as Richard Dalloway's, but only that its form is the same, that it structures identity according to the same model. The excursion to the summit of Monte Rosa takes up two chapters of which the first opens with the information I cited earlier, that Helen had enticed Rachel into staying at the villa by promising her a room of her own, "a fortress as well as a sanctuary." The self-possession represented by this room realizes itself in her vision of a world of her own. The same categories organize Rachel's interior world and Dalloway's imperial universe; the individual psyche, and of a woman at that, appears to share an order with the mind of the Empire.

Fredric Jameson's nice concept of a "political unconscious" describes assumptions about the nature of things that lie so deep in the mind of an author that they seem to that author without content. Rachel is critical of Dalloway's imperial program. Unlike Clarissa, Rachel seems an unlikely booster of English expansionism. There are very different political implications to imagining yourself ruling an inch of ground and conquering a continent. But both participate in the same universe of discourse, share certain assumptions, and fail to envision others. No one in *The Voyage Out,* not even the author, thinks to imagine the lives or still less the private selves of the natives; once the top of the mountain is reached, the natives we heard briefly singing "queer" songs, disappear altogether. With all their differences and indeed oppositions, both Dalloway's and Rachel's visions are creatures of empire, hers as much as his.

Hers, however, more problematically than his, as becomes evident on the second occasion when the story ventures into its foreign setting. This is the fatal trip up the Amazon and, along with the excursion up Monte Rosa, it casts the English company into both classic colonial postures: overlooking vast territories from high mountains and penetrating deep inland along claustrophobic rivers. The trip provides the novel's only material account of colonization and it is certainly not a celebration. The Dalloways' enthusiasm was both abstract and idealistic; the Flushings, who replace them on this voyage as imperial visionaries, are vulgarly unscrupulous. The landscape unrolling along the shores as the boat steams slowly upstream is vaguely threatening and decidedly unwholesome. For the first time, natives come into focus in a village where the English are followed everywhere by staring eyes that "followed them, passing over their legs, their bodies, their heads, curiously not without hostility, like the crawl of a winter fly" (285). The colonial world has at last entered the story, and this bodes ill.

Rachel and Hewet are mostly appalled by the Amazon landscape: "it makes us seem insignificant, doesn't it?" he sighs, wishing them back in the coolness and clarity of England (285). There are tales of Europeans who have died along the river; Helen has an ominous vision. As it happens, the trip upriver has doomed Rachel and Hewet's happiness for Rachel will soon be dead of a disease caught in that toxic interior. Why? Why did Woolf, having brought Rachel so far into self-realization, kill her off before the culmination of her marriage? Rachel's death is puzzling because it lacks tragic necessity and responds to no apparent problem. In fact, its arbitrariness has been largely taken as its key, revealing Woolf's categorical inability to imagine her self-possessed heroine in the role of a happy wife.

A great deal is made at the beginning of the story of Rachel's virginity. At the age of twenty-four, she seems not entirely certain how babies are made. Her aunt takes her education in hand but is unable to breach an adamantine innocence. This innocence, which Helen attributes to her niece's situation as the motherless daughter of a sea-captain, is also somehow associated with being an English girl, that is, with her Englishness. At the end of one of their interviews in which Richard Dalloway has promised to send Rachel something of Burke's—"*The Speech on the French Revolution—The American Rebellion?* Which shall it be, I wonder?" (75)—Dalloway becomes strangely moved by Rachel's pointing out that her interests are different from his because she is a woman. "How strange to be a woman!" he exclaims. "A young and beautiful woman . . . has the whole world at her feet. That's true, Miss Vinrace. You have an inestimable power—for good or for evil. What couldn't you do—" He breaks off, and kisses her "passionately" (76).

This is the first time she has been kissed and Rachel is thunderstruck. "Her head was cold, her knees shaking, and the physical pain of the emotion was so great that she could only keep herself moving above the great leaps of her heart." She is "possessed with a strange exultation. Life seemed to hold infinite possibilities she had never guessed at. . . . something wonderful had happened" (76). She is not nearly as moved later by the embrace of Hewet with whom she is in love. That potentially conjugal embrace is curiously muffled, awkward, and unimaginable to the point that, from its perspective, one begins to see the inevitability of her death, since it is impossible to imagine a sexual consummation. With Dalloway, on the other hand, while there is no question of anything further occurring, there is no need of it; the consummation seems to have already occurred: "something wonderful had happened." What has happened, I think, is that Dalloway has activated Rachel's virginity, awakened it and her to its force, the force of a woman. It is to her virginity—to her intact autonomous womanhood—that Dalloway responds rather than to any possibility for sexual fulfillment, while Rachel experiences his kiss as the fulfillment of her sexual being in its virgin self-sufficiency.

I would like to turn to another account of virginity and the British empire. In 1595, three centuries before Rachel Vinrace, Walter Raleigh came to South America and sailed up the Amazon. *The Voyage Out* briefly tells his at-

tempt to establish a colony. About this expedition, Raleigh wrote a lengthy
document entitled "The discovery of the large, rich, and beautiful Empire of
Guiana."[2] The document describes "the most beautiful country that ever
mine eyes beheld" filled with treasures of every kind, and more or less concludes this way:

> Guiana is a country that hath yet her maidenhead, never sacked, turned,
> nor wrought, the face of the earth hath not been torn, nor the virtue and salt
> of the soil spent by manurance, the graves have not been opened for gold, the
> mines not broken with sledges, nor their images pulled down out of their
> temples. It hath never been entered by any army of strength, and never con-
> quered by any Christian prince. It is besides so defensible, that if two forts be
> built in one of the provinces which I have seen, the flood setteth in so near the
> bank, where the channel also lieth, that no ship can pass up but within a pike's
> length of the artillery, first of the one, and afterwards of the other. Guiana
> hath but one entrance by the sea (if it hath that) for any vessels of burden: so as
> whosoever shall first possess it, he shall be found unaccessible for any en-
> emy. . . . (96–97)

This extended image of the rape of Guiana is addressed to Elizabeth I, the
Virgin Queen. Recalling that it is not unusual to regard the rape of enemy
women in wartime as part of the defense of one's own country and of the
women who embody its integrity, begins to explain Raleigh's logic. The rape
of Guiana is to protect Elizabeth's virginity, taken as symbol and guarantee of
her nation's honor. Raleigh proposes to rape Guiana as homage to Elizabeth's
virginity. The despoilation of the South American country will pay tribute to
England's wholeness.

Unsavory but clear, this logic is also familiar. I do not suggest that it is
Woolf's, nor indeed that Rachel's virginity is part of any such program. It remains true that Woolf puts great stress upon this virginity. Rachel is not just an
English girl, nor even just a naive English girl inexperienced in the way of the
world; she is an English virgin of exceptional, even improbable innocence.
And she awakens sexually, which does *not* involve losing her virginity, to the
kiss of a man who, by his own account as well as the author's, is the very incarnation of the British empire. She then dies from a disease caught on a trip
up Raleigh's river, playing out, not an imperial ideology to be sure, but a psychological logic which seems to make it impossible for her to survive as a
character if she marries.

I proposed earlier that the world-order Rachel projects onto her microcosm reflects Woolf's political unconscious which is shaped by the values and concepts of British imperialism. The meaning of her heroine's virginity derives from the same source. At the level of the unconscious, values and concepts express themselves formally rather than as concrete entities. When Rachel happily imagines herself the supreme power in her world, she is not embracing an imperial program but rather projecting an individual vision in a universe whose imperial order she assumes. She does not need to reflect on whether having supreme power over the world is connected to personal autonomy; she does not ponder the link between virginity and public power. Of course Woolf need not have shared Rachel's vision of the world; but there is evidence that it is the author's own unconscious guiding Rachel, and not just one consciously created for the character, in the fact that that relation between virginity and public power comes to Rachel as a revelation, a truth Richard Dalloway reveals to her and that the author makes no move to deny.

Virginity, then, is both a room of one's own and an empire of one's own. Dalloway's apostrophe to womanhood follows upon what seems to be Rachel's relative undervaluing of this condition. Richard has been asking her about herself, "What are your interests and occupations? I should imagine that you were a person with very strong interests. Of course you are! . . . When I think of the age we live in, with its opportunities and possibilities, the mass of things to be done and enjoyed—why haven't we ten lives instead of one? But about yourself?" The error of Rachel's answer, "You see, I'm a woman" (76), will become apparent in the next minute when Dalloway's kiss shows her that being a woman holds "infinite possibilities she had never guessed at"; but on condition that she remain a woman, which seems to mean not a wife. Richard who is trying to decide which Burke text he should send Rachel first (demanding her promise that she write to him to tell him what she has thought of it) has earlier explained to her that "I never allow my wife to talk politics . . . For this reason. It is impossible for human beings, constituted as they are, both to fight and to have ideals. If I have preserved mine . . . it is due to the fact that I have been able to come home to my wife in the evening and to find that she has spent her day in calling, music, play with the children, domestic duties—what you will; her illusions have not been destroyed. She gives me courage to go on. The strain of public life is very great" (65).

There are women to whom one counsels Burke, and there are wives. Both have great powers but only the first, the young and the beautiful, the virgins, can have the world at their feet; the others sit at their husbands' feet. There was no need to voyage to another hemisphere to discover this home truth of course; but sometimes, to see things really clear, it helps to go back to their origins. Virgin, therefore not yet diminished into the ancillary status of a wife, autonomous and self-ruling, holding unquestioned dominion over a tiny world that is nonetheless all hers, Rachel is a creature of her imperial nation who has realized herself the same way as all her compatriots: in the process of colonial exploration and conquest. But she cannot bring it all—her whole expanded imperial self—home. Home for a woman is where another holds the scepter. Elizabeth would not have retained her power either had she married. She could stay in London so long as she remained a virgin for then she could also have her empire; Rachel cannot return to London because she would lose hers, her virginity and her empire. The voyage in for Rachel Vinrace and for Virginia Woolf is, no less than for Richard Dalloway, a voyage out.

I have a recording of Lotte Lenya singing "The Song of Bilbao" about Bill's Ballroom in Bilbao where once were held the best dances in the world, despite a roof that let in moonlight and floorboards through which the grass grew thick. With the chorus "Bilbao, Bilbao" stuck on my mental turntable, I recently drove through undistinguished streets looking for a new building that has made "Bilbao" the last word in architecture. The Basque capital has been receiving an abundance of reporters, critics, and tourists come to view the Guggenheim Museum opened in October 1997, and almost all the visitors have been impressed. They have largely agreed that the building is not only one of the great buildings of our time but that it speaks for the others and "ends the century by summarizing the era's achievements." Since the century happens in turn to end the millennium, there is a millennial aura to the praise of a structure its builders have projected as a site of pilgrimage. I was having difficulty reading the map and turning corners more or less at random when I looked down the Calle Iparraguirre and there it was.

The building filling the view at the end of the street with a configuration of luminescent curving metal plates looked as if it had just arrived from a larger smoother world. Lined with late-nineteenth/early-twentieth-century brown stone houses and shops, the Calle Iparraguirre is very crowded. Cars back up because the street ends and all traffic turns right at the corner onto the Alameda de Mazzaredo running in front of the museum. Pedestrians slow down staring. The building appears serenely self-contained. You approach it transfixed, until distracted by the large Jeff Koons Puppy installed, courtesy of Hugo Boss, to the right of the entrance plaza. The Puppy, clad in multicolored pansies, sits up on its haunches and at first looks as tall as the museum, but this is an illusion fostered by a plaza which steps down toward the entrance.

It is appropriate to ponder size when first looking at the Bilbao museum since size was a primary concern for Thomas Krens who commissioned it as director of the Solomon Guggenheim Foundation. The Foundation's two museums in New York City, on Fifth Avenue and on Lower Broadway, lack room to exhibit its collection of oversized late-modernist works. Also, Krens wanted to be able to mount and maintain large-scale installations, and, when he invited three architects to submit designs for a new museum, he was looking for, in the words of the winner Frank Gehry, "big industrial volumes of space."

The Bilbao Guggenheim is big and feels bigger than it is. Immediately on stepping into the lobby, one cranes to see to the top of a great central atrium rising half again as high as the one in the original Guggenheim, designed halfway through the century by Frank Lloyd Wright. Gehry's atrium soars past catwalks and balconies (over one of which Claes Oldenburg and Coosje van Bruggen's *Soft Shuttlecock* droops like a bleached banana tree), up pillars and towers, to skylights almost out of sight. Yet it is less this atrium that makes the museum seem huge than a gallery plunging off from the lobby and extending farther than a football field.

At the lobby end of this gallery, I passed through Richard Serra's *Serpent,* the museum's signature piece, 172 tons and 104 feet of iron in three sheets undulating to form two not quite parallel paths along which the viewer walks the length of the sculpture sensing its weight in the looming walls. My destination at the far end was Oldenburg's *Knife Ship,* a Swiss Army knife equipped with blades, a corkscrew, and oars; along the way, Andy Warhol's white Mona Lisas, not too big not too small, almost seem conventional.

The first sight of the astonishing building had been disorienting and the dizzying atrium had offered few repairs but the clear accord of Brobdingnagian gallery and art was calming and, on returning to the central lobby, I looked about confidently for the staircase to the second floor and the Kandinskys, de Koonings, and Rothkos. On the way to the stairs I passed one of those large installations for which Krens had the museum designed. Jenny Holzer composed *Nine Signs* for the Bilbao Guggenheim out of vertical LED signboards scrolling a message in Euskera (the Basque language), Spanish, and English. The text is a series of short declarative sentences like "I say your

Guggenheim Museum, Bilbao (Construction Photos), 1997.
Photograph by David Heald
© The Solomon R. Guggenheim Foundation, New York.

name" and "I run from you." It has been praised for drawing viewers "into an uncomfortable complicity." I have always found the peremptoriness of installations irritating and being decoyed among the 40-foot-high displays put me into an uncooperative mood not conducive to appreciating art. So I got a cup of coffee and took it outside.

I wandered along the walkway, retracing the long gallery whose most interesting feature is visible only from the outside. Miming the oversized art within, the long gallery is overlong and extends under the Puente de la Salve which begins its crossing of the Nervion from the edge of the building site. This slide under the bridge was part of the design from the beginning and practically everyone has found it particularly engaging. Passing under the bridge, I was not sure.

With the underside of the roadway overhead and the wall of the gallery close at my right, I felt crammed in. Already, viewed from a distance, the conjunction of building and bridge had appeared cramped, and suddenly the whole thing—the museum's size, its proportions, its assembly out of those huge metal plates—seemed exceedingly out of scale. Yet, according to the more or less official *Frank O. Gehry: Guggenheim Museum Bilbao* (written by van Bruggen with the cooperation of the directing triumvirate, Gehry, Krens, and the Basque representative, Juan Ignacio Vidarte),[1] the building's relation to its site was a principal concern and Gehry designed the extension under the bridge precisely in order to tie the building to it as to a "gritty anchor." The legend of the making of the Bilbao museum begins with a geocultural revelation. The Basque administration, on inviting the Guggenheim Foundation to build in Bilbao, had proposed to transform an old wine warehouse, but Krens and Gehry did not like the site and they were leaving town when Krens had an "epiphany" that it should be located on the riverfront at the city's vital center. Gehry remembers it as a joint epiphany; they agree that an important building starts with an important site, and that the importance of the site is lent by history and culture.

They agree too that architecture returns the favor in that buildings literally shape the future. The difference between his urbanism and the urbanism of his mentor Le Corbusier, Gehry has explained, is a matter of tone. Le Corbusier was loud and aggressive, Gehry keeps his voice down. There is no need to shout "I'm going to demolish you," he says. "If you understand the forms you are using—by which I mean, if you manipulate form, space, and negative space in relation to other buildings or to the city in order to make compositional relationships—you can start to take over." Quoting this, Coosje van Bruggen does not want us to be disturbed by its "slightly Napoleonic ring";

Gehry, she says, is only talking about the integration of building and site. But the way he develops his idea does have a certain grandeur: "If there was a hole in the ground where Notre Dame is today, and you had a church to build and you were really smart, you would make your church just like Notre Dame. The surrounding space is energized by the sculpture of that building and it co-opts a whole piece of Paris."

The message is in the idiom. If you had a church to build, you would make your church just like Notre Dame: it is in the assumption that a "you" can make a Notre Dame. For Victor Hugo, who wrote a novel named after the cathedral to plead for its careful preservation, the only single "you" who could affect Notre Dame would be an irreverent official ordering disfiguring alterations: "The man, the individual, the artist, is erased from these great unsigned masses," Hugo wrote; "Time is [Notre Dame's] architect and the people the masons." Even Henry Adams, though he was American, took a great cathedral to be the "expression of energy" of an entire historical epoch. Still, van Bruggen is right, Gehry's idiom is not Napoleonic; it is self-reliant. His verb tense is not the imperative but the infinitive: "To be at the bend of a working river intersected by a large bridge and connecting the urban fabric of a fairly dense city to the river's edge with a place for modern art is my idea of heaven." The sentence projects decisive action (creating a new order of things in Bilbao) but not aggressive. A new set of relations will emerge simply as a function of his being there. To be the one on the site realizing these relations is heaven: there is hardly a transitive verb in the passage and almost no causality, or only of the least binding. Napoleon marched out and subjugated; Gehry arrives, does what he does and a desired change comes about.

Elsewhere he talks about "trying to get a sense of movement in my buildings" by which he means "a subtle kind of energy" that can radiate from a building so that it "knits into the larger fabric of the city." Here too integration goes the way of the new architecture: "Buildings are part of living in the city and it changes; there's a transient quality." The champion city-changer, the Baron Georges Haussmann, rebuilt Paris to establish order and to found the stability of a political system he hoped would prevail indefinitely. There appears to be no prior plan to Gehry's transient cityscape; it just keeps changing through the unconcerted efforts of individuals bent on their own projects. Instead of a plan, the buildings embody a force whose nature he first saw clearly one day when he attended an exhibition called "Mirror of Empire: Dutch Marine Art of the Seventeenth Century." Being a passionate sailor, he had looked at marine art before but it was this show of ships built to conquer the world that helped him to articulate his idea of architectural movement.

He became conscious of the sail-like features of his buildings and of their appearing impelled as if on a conquering voyage.

It is never the same thing building an empire abroad as at home. The planners of the Getty Art Center in Los Angeles, with which the Bilbao museum is often paired because they opened at about the same time, did not think in terms of launching ships or direct encounters. The Getty, designed by Richard Meier, is a compound of several buildings stretching over 710 acres of its own hilltop. There are no structures crowding its appending galleries and requiring acrobatic accommodation. The site offers spectacular views of Los Angeles and Meier has everywhere figured them into his design. But while the view of the city out the windows of the Guggenheim exaggerates its ties to the community, the vista commanded by the Getty certifies that it is built on very expensive real estate. The value of art is here underwritten by the value of property and sometimes, in fact, the latter takes precedence. A woman, worried that her swimming pool on a facing hill would be observable from the Art Center, was pacified by a cactus garden to prevent visitors from approaching the sensitive lookout.

On the contrary, visitors are encouraged to appropriate any views surrounding the Bilbao museum, the more previously owned the better. There is a railroad yard next door and through the atrium's tall windows one looks out at tracks, trains, and loading cranes. Gehry had to take steps to preserve this scene for, when he came on the site, the riverfront was to be transformed into a green park. Context matters: Gehry must have imagined his shining metal building set among lawns and trees and seen there was a danger of finding himself in Disneyland unintentionally (he has designed a hotel for Eurodisney near Paris). Instead the titanium invokes the historical Bilbao of steel mills and mines.

But the city fathers had planned a park by the river because Bilbao's heavy industry has mostly died. The titanium and the similarly evocative iron *Serpent* are commemorative. The present-and-future Bilbao is characterized by a mosaic of projects promoted by Bilbao Metropoli 30, an organization composed of business executives, government officials, university professors, nonprofit activists, journalists, and cultural figures, to rebuild Bilbao, in the words of the chairman Alfonso Martinez Cearra, as a capital of "knowledge, culture, and art." Bilbao is to be remade from the ground up. One of the major projects is a spectacular steel and glass subway designed by Norman Foster (one enters it through futuristic glass tubes everyone calls Fosteritos). Another is a new airport designed by Santiago Calatrava. Calatrava has also built a pedestrian bridge like a cat's-paw spanning the Nervion and visible from the museum.

Unlike the railroad, the loading docks, and the cranes, Calatrava's bridge is perfectly in tune with Gehry's museum which is one of Metropoli 30's most important projects.

Cearra likes to cite a book titled *Pittsburgh: Then and Now* in which he showed a journalist before-and-after pictures chronicling the transformation of a Pittsburgh freightyard into a park.[2] Bilbao is breaking with the past by getting rid of its material remains. Old factories are being razed, warehouses leveled. Gehry's enthusiasm for the industrial feel of the site was not naive; he understood that he would not be surrounded by booming industry. So it was rather the preservation of industrial ruins he defended, like that which has become almost routine, for instance, in New England. He had been involved in North Adams, Massachusetts, in MASSMoCA's remaking of a factory into a museum and had designed the Temporary Contemporary (now the Geffen Contemporary) in Los Angeles out of obsolete warehouses. His first attention-getting project, rebuilding his own house, suggests how he would be committed to such preservations, both out of appreciation of an industrial aesthetic and for the additional vocabulary. The "gambrel-roofed bungalow" in Santa Monica that Gehry surrounded on three sides with an angular addition of plywood, corrugated metal, and chain-link fencing retains its distinct dialect in a mutually exegetical dialogue with the addition.

Others have tried to save parts of the old Bilbao, mostly foreigners or people who work for foreign institutions, like the curator at the local branch of the French Institute, Jerome Delormas, and the director of the Fine Arts School of Bordeaux, Guadalupe Echeverria, who have preserved a former electrical-resistor plant by recycling it into an arts compound. But this oddity, Bilbaons destroying their heritage while strangers try to preserve it, is less paradox than parable. One could call it the parable of the two culturalisms.

• • •

Frank Gehry came to Bilbao to create something newer than new, a Guggenheim Museum of modern art more modern than the Guggenheim Museum of modern art. For him there is no conflict between the new Bilbao and the old or between any new and any old, not just an industrial old. He has intimate experience of the way the old nourishes the new. His grandmother, he recalls, gave him the idea of building when she made houses with him from sticks and bits of wood. But it was her cooking that really shaped his career, for his grandmother often cooked fish and ever since the fish shape has been Gehry's aesthetic standard. Proving that childhood impressions are unpredictable, he tells an anecdote that might have had the opposite effect: "We'd go to the Jewish market, we'd buy a live carp, we'd take it home to her house in Toronto, we'd put it in the bathtub and I would play with this god-damn fish for a day until the next day she'd kill it and make gefilte fish." One could understand his never again being able to look at a fish, but instead the fish came to represent the ideal form: "I kept drawing it and sketching it and it started to become for me like a symbol for a certain kind of perfection that I couldn't achieve with my buildings. Eventually whenever I'd draw something and I couldn't finish the design, I'd draw the fish as a notation . . . that I want this to be better than just a dumb building. I want it to be more beautiful."

The fish appeared in Gehry's architecture as soon as he began to develop a personal style. In 1981, he collaborated with Serra (who feels the same way about snakes) in a show illustrating the link between art and architecture, and imagined a bridge one of whose pylons was a fish rising from the Hudson. He has also designed a prison in the shape of a fish for a show on architectural follies; *Standing Glass Fish,* a 22-foot fish sculpture; another still bigger fish sculpture for the Villa Olimpica in Barcelona; a formica lamp in the shape of a fish; and the Fishdance restaurant in Kobe, Japan, resembling a huge fish supported upright on its curved tail. Coosje van Bruggen, who had long conversations with Gehry for the Bilbao volume, sees this culminating in the Guggenheim, where "'fish'—truncated, without head or tail, transformed into leaf or boat-like shapes and applied in some of the side galleries—is endowed with a more elusive metaphorical quality, and comes to signify fluid, continuous motion; it is a tangible sculptural abstraction vivifying the building."

Out of his memory of his grandmother's bathtub, Gehry lifted an image that was psychically and culturally drenched, shook off the personal and historical stuff clinging to it (he did not reject this stuff, he just did not carry it off along with the image), and transported it into his architectural vocabulary. Transported, it became nomadic; translated, it became multilingual, became, in other words, capable of multicultural relations. In the form it takes as the source of Gehry's idea of architectural beauty, Gehry's grandmother's gefilte fish could be served at the Kobe Fishdance with zarusoba; it no longer implies horseradish. It has no automatic adjuncts, is responsible to no grammar of images decreeing what goes with what, has independent relations with other cultural references.

Gehry's grandmother would be very proud to see how far he has gone with her carp, and she probably would not mind that to get to Bilbao he had to put her kitchen definitively behind him. I returned from Bilbao to Paris just as France was winning its first soccer World Cup ever. The hero of the last match was a Kabyle born in Marseilles of immigrant parents and named

Zinedine Zidane, dubbed Zizou. The day after the victory, the television news feature saluted a newborn Gypsy Zidane and Breton Zizou. "Zizou" was already a French-style diminutive. Like Gehry's fish, M. Zidane's name has floated free of its associations with other features of a foreign culture and now enriches French culture as an all-purpose ethnicity.

The night of the game, when there were as many people in the streets as at the Liberation in 1945 and more flags, a television commentator proposed a change of colors from "bleu, blanc, rouge" to "black, blanc, beur": black for the Africans, blanc for the Whites, and beur for the Arabs, the communities represented in about equal numbers on the winning team. The team was mixed, France is increasingly mixed, still the team was French and a more racially inclusive France remains France. There must have been Arab and African inflections in the French game but the French Africans and the French Arabs did not transport their whole cultures into their playing any more than Gehry installed his grandmother's kitchen in Bilbao. The French playing style the commentators talked about exists only as French. German recruiting policy, taking note of France's winning mix, is supposedly changing to include more foreign residents. The German team apparently has a distinctly different way of playing from the French, and if in the future, players of Turkish background alter this way of playing, it will change into another version of a German style. Embracing a soccer player of Kabyle origins, the French press has declared him wholly and gloriously French. For Americans, a French immigrant, J. Hector St. John de Crèvecoeur, defined the new mode of nationality already in the eighteenth century: an American is one who started out from anywhere but came to America. There is no loss of national identity involved for the nation when it includes different ethnicities; naturalization means becoming French, German, American, of Kabyle, Turk, or Korean origins.

Becoming Spanish of Basque origins is exactly what the Basques in Spain have been resisting for generations. They are not immigrants, they have stayed home, why should they not on their own ground be a nation as well as a culture? No doubt they know that the history of nations is largely independent of the history of indigenous cultures. But if a cultural group wants political sovereignty as such, what other argument is there but the rightful identity of nation and culture? Alone in Spain and maybe in Europe, Bilbao's soccer team, the Athletic, has an official policy of restricted recruitment. The Basques do not want to be Basque the way Gehry is Jewish or the way he is American (by way of Canada). They do want his fishlike building to sustain their claim to cultural nationhood, and this compounds the contradiction: however it divides among Jewish, Canadian, and American, the building does not seem at all Basque.

It has escaped no one that there is some lack of clarity in the museum's relation to its purchasers. While I was buying *Frank O. Gehry: Guggenheim Museum Bilbao* in the museum store, I overheard a conversation between a clerk and a French visitor who wanted the book in French and was annoyed to find it could be had only in English. The very polite young clerk snapped in fluent English that not having it in French was hardly the problem, there was not even a Basque version. During preparations for the museum's opening in October 1997, a policeman was killed when he tried to question two florists tending the Puppy's pansies. It turned out that the fake florists had planted twelve bombs to go off during the ceremony. They were members of the radical wing of the Basque separatist movement which has denounced the Guggenheim as an imperial intrusion and a misappropriation of communal resources. They have pointed to the building's cost. After providing the land, the city put up at least $100 million for construction (one interview has Krens saying $150 million); they paid $20 million to the Guggenheim Foundation for advice and the use of its name; provided $50 million for new acquisitions; and guaranteed a budget of $12 million a year for operating expenses. In return, the Basques own a magnificent museum over which they have no artistic control. Everyone agrees that they will have some in time, and that Basque art is to have a prominent place in the collection, but not yet.

Vidarte, who signed the agreement with the Foundation as Director of Tax and Finance at the Regional Council of Bizkaia (the Basque region) and is now Director General of the Guggenheim Museum Bilbao, is aware how it looks but not worried. There will be Basque curators; meanwhile, he says, "to play in this league, you have to be associated with someone in it." To understand the delicacy of the position he and his political colleagues are in, one has to see that for them the idea that you have to have associates to play in the global game does not imply that you should allow strangers on your soccer team. The international status of the Guggenheim is a trophy not an identification.

The delicacy of the balance between leaving the past behind while continuing to press for autonomy may be one source of the puzzling eagerness of Bilbao Metropoli 30 and its associates to remove the physical vestiges of their city's history. If for Gehry there is no conflict between old and new, there is some conflict for the Basques trying to recast Basque cultural identity in terms of industries of art and communication. Basque nationalism arose in the nineteenth century in the factories and warehouses now being leveled and among workers whose descendants have been largely displaced. The struggle between radical and conservative wings of the movement is to an important extent a class struggle: unemployment in the region is still nearly twenty-five percent (in 1998) and includes many who will find it hard to retool for the new industries.

Twelve miles down the road from Bilbao is the town of Guernica or, in Basque, Gernika, martyred for its resistance to Fascism, a resistance in which Basque nationalism confirmed its ties to the working-class culture of industrialism. After Franco's death, as Picasso had decreed, his *Guernica* came to the Madrid Reina Sofia Museum with which Gehry is now negotiating a transfer to the Bilbao Guggenheim. In Guernica itself, meanwhile, there is a Gernika Museoa which retraces the history of the town from the middle ages to modern times. Most of this museum is devoted to displays about the Civil War, including an archive of photographs of the Fascist blitz that inspired Picasso's painting which, in a small faded print, marks the end of the exhibit. If it has been suggested that the *Guernica* go to Gernika rather than to Bilbao, I could not find any reference to it. There may be problems of preservation and security that preclude it, but that the possibility does not seem to have been considered is curious.

Yet Vidarte and his Basque associates, who are pressing the claim for the painting, could reasonably worry about settling it into their museum. In Madrid, it fits into a landscape of antifascism; this is how Picasso must have envisioned it. But in the Basque capital it will be a monument to Basque antifascism specifically and to a past militancy with which the Guggenheim Museum has nothing to do; once in Bilbao, in short, the *Guernica* will look as if it should be in Gernika. Or else the contrary: when it is no longer associated with its journey to a Franco-free Spain and to the city that was the heart of the Spanish Republic, its political character may dim and, taking on the local color of modern art, it will look as if it could as well be on Fifth Avenue. Tipping in either direction, the painting is likely to exacerbate the museum's own ambiguity. Its Basque status will seem still more disputable when the museum places a local icon in the context of a transcendent art-history.

Exposing the Bilbao Guggenheim's political ambiguity will not bother Gehry, since for him the building constitutes the museum and its coherence inheres in his vision of it. And it will rather please Krens precisely in making more evident the way the museum is both local and transnational, with nothing in between. Krens has developed a model of a museum of the future which is no longer located "in the center of the universe" but anywhere the space is good. Travel is now easy, people travel. He visualizes the Guggenheim "as one museum that has a constellation of spaces." So far the constellation has stars in Massachusetts, Venice, and Bilbao, besides the two in New York City; a sixth is being born in Berlin. Some observers of this expansion have called Krens a franchiser, others an imperialist, but both epithets are off the mark. The Guggenheim in Bilbao is not a franchise, like a Benetton, but an extension, a new wing: Bilbao has twice the gallery space of the New York museums combined and less than half the staff. Nor is the Guggenheim Foundation imperialist; Spain, Italy, and Germany are not colonies and modern art is not American, even if American art is modern.

Krens, who described his sudden realization of where in Bilbao to place the museum as an "epiphany," insists in the same idiom that people will "make a pilgrimage" to see significant art. The words "icon" and "cathedral" pepper the talk of the museum's American planners and builders until one begins to wonder why Protestants and Jews should have such a Catholic turn of phrase. Or why purveyors of modern art who claim to have built a museum for the twenty-first century portray it as an edifice from the middle ages, apparently not finding in the intervening centuries another category of building to which their new museum can be as well compared. How is a Guggenheim Museum of modern art like a medieval cathedral? Possibly in that they are both houses of worship. That is, the Guggenheim and Notre Dame are not simply sites of the spiritual life but its politically efficacious incarnations. Medieval cathedrals were built the last time Western society joined spiritual and political authority. Between then and now, the major task of the West's history has been to separate them. But Gehry's abstracted fish and Krens's global museum rejoin the spiritual and the political.

The medieval cathedral is a congenial concept for Gehry and Krens because it has aspirations beyond single nationality or the secularity of modern cultural institutions (Americans, whose religion is within, have never really accepted secularity). The art enshrined in and by the Bilbao Guggenheim is at once personal vision and worldwide institution. Much like European soccer, modern art happens multiculturally and demonstrates how culture can be both immanent and transportable. All the major European nations are in the throes of multicultural redefinition which they often represent as following the American model that fueled the United States' rise to world power. It is hoped that amalgamation, cultural as much as economic, will produce a renewed European ascendance. The powerful nations' nationalism (not the Basques' or Croats') is becoming a matter of transnational cultural influence and multinational markets, a lot like the institutionalism of the Guggenheim Foundation.

Not that chauvinism is dead in these powerful nations. Winning the World Cup brought on paroxysms of patriotism in some very internationalist Frenchmen and women. And, on the other side, for one American critic, Gehry is John Wayne and Henry Ford: his building "is American in its wilderness"; it is "exporting raw, generous, Western vitality to the old world," and besides "represents the first significant architectural idea to land on European shores since Frank Lloyd Wright's Wasmuth portfolio" (containing his Oak Park work). But such fifties talk is almost quaint. Krens's museum-as-cathedral concept enshrines the current consensus that national cultures are powerful in the degree that they command many constitutive cultures: the more catholic, the more travel-worthy, the better-traveled, the more commanding. And, indeed, the less nationally or culturally specific: the Bilbao building looks as if it has landed from outer space because it has landed from Los Angeles.

One group will probably find culture less transportable in Krens's museums: those on very restricted travel budgets. As in the changing definition of Basque identity, there is a class issue latent in the changing definition of museums represented by the Bilbao Guggenheim. The traditional museum, says Krens, is "an eighteenth-century idea, which is the idea of an encyclopedia." The idea of the encyclopedia, expressing the republican idealism of the eighteenth-century revolutions, is to distribute knowledge more widely. Museums have made art accessible beyond the salons of rich patrons. But art in the Bilbao Guggenheim is less widely accessible than in the British Museum, the Louvre, the Metropolitan, MoMA, or the New York City Guggenheims because poorer tourists, unless their destination (like Disneyland) can absorb their entire vacation, generally cannot afford to travel to a place where there is just one thing to do or see. It is likely that Krens's pilgrims will be mainly knights and merchants.

• • •

Krens has not initiated this antidemocratic trend; the coherence of Western society seems generally to have shifted its ground. Economic equality was never achieved in Europe or the United States but for about two centuries a more economically egalitarian society was the political ideal. It does not seem to be any longer except insofar as it enters into the ideal of cultural and racial equality that has replaced it and made difference the basis for social cohesion and of aesthetic order as well. That the Bilbao museum is out of scale with its surroundings does not indicate the builders' lack of sensitivity to the site. Gehry's building is carefully attuned to the site but according to an aesthetic of incongruity. When the architect says that what he finds especially interesting about building in cities is putting "dissimilar projects next to one another" and figuring out "how to include rather than exclude existing buildings," he points to an aesthetic moral, namely, that congruity, as he might paraphrase Ralph Waldo Emerson, is the hobgoblin of small artistic visions. Emerson did not find inconsistency a problem when reasoning in a world destined to unity within one's mind. Gehry does not find incongruity a problem when designing in a world that is becoming one constellation of cultural spaces.

I continue to think that the museum's long gallery crowds the Puente de la Salve and that the flourish of shining metal condescends to the freightyard. Moreover, I doubt the fit of building and site will improve with custom, though one could become used to their not fitting. Fit is very little in the eye of the beholder. Looking up the Avenue de l'Opéra toward the astonishing Opéra Garnier is not disconcerting, like one's first sight of the Bilbao Guggenheim. On the contrary, it cues one at once to the imperial world of Napoleon III manifest in fitly broad avenues converging in state upon the splendid building which looks not too big but of just the right immensity. The colossal Pantheon built by imperial Rome is excessive for the baroque Piazza della Rotonda in which one now finds it but this isn't perplexing either because one recognizes the misassortment instantly as having been arranged by history. The effect is poignant, even tragic, but the Pantheon was there first and the piazza surrounded it in its good time; as Victor Hugo said of Notre Dame, time was the architect of this disproportion and time is an essential order.

Gehry's building is perhaps not disproportionately large but because it contrasts with its surroundings all of it stands out. It is as if the Nervion riverfront did not know how to take hold of it. The building is a dream and a nightmare to photograph, for any angle offers a striking picture and none really captures it. In books and postcards, foreshortened perspectives collapse giant titanium wings onto a dwarfed city; a tangle of curved shining metal looms inexplicably over an assortment of trains; an arrangement of shapes in blue, grey, and gold projects against the sky but has no apparent relation to the ground. Virtually all the photos are both dazzling and unlikely. Only with the river's width for distance is it possible to produce pictures of the whole building. These show a tremendous construction of irregular masses difficult to identify as a building at all.

The pictures do not lie: no one has been able to visualize this building clearly, not even its builders. *Frank O. Gehry: Guggenheim Museum Bilbao* has two appendices. One is a paragraph written by Gehry describing the decision to use titanium, which now gives the building its single visual certainty. The other is called "On the Use of the Computer" and explains how it can be that a building should rise almost incomprehensible to the eye. It is done with computers, in particular with a program called CATIA developed by Dassault Systems, a French builder of airplanes. CATIA's distinction is that it can map entire surfaces rather than points at intervals; since it thus represents shapes, it permits their almost infinite permutation (Jim Glymph, who works for Gehry, describes it as "the most infinitely shapable technology we've ever been presented with"). This allows the architect to propose any shape he can imagine even when he himself cannot quite see how it will work. "Many of the forms [Gehry] is developing now are only possible through the computer," says Glymph.

Before CATIA, these new forms "would have been considered something to move away from. It might have been a sketch idea, but we would never be able to build it." Now the staff takes a sketch idea, investigates and refines it into a model, and returns it so Gehry can deal with "the slightly altered shapes as a thought . . . and as a gesture." And so on, back and forth, Gehry rethinking the shapes and CATIA showing him the full figure toward which he has gestured. Technology has always intervened in architectural design, of course. But this relation of computer and architect seems more involuted. If one said that reinforced concrete, for instance, furnished a new architectural grammar, then, by comparison, CATIA would be finishing Gehry's sentences.

He remains in control of his text however. "Gehry's forms are exciting, but they're not perverse," one critic writes, and goes on to explain away the building's strangeness by asserting that it is skin deep; it "isn't nearly as weird as it appears to be. It's a sheep in wolf's clothing." Given that the museum is everywhere reviewed as visual art, do the clothes in that case not make the wolf? But this aside, it is true that Gehry draws a line between inventive and eccentric. On later looking at the sketch that had won him the commission for the museum, he recalled, "I realized that this stuff was so arbitrary and off the wall. . . ." Doing the sketch "was great, it was exciting, and then I became Mr. Architect." The process he describes of translating an initial vision of skylights into a workable drawing is the opposite of arbitrary: "I have a road map, and I know where I'm going. It frees me too, I decide where and how the pieces fit the site, determine the scale, and start a formal vocabulary, which I then can explain to somebody." Freedom in this account follows from knowing where he is going; he does not define it as permission to wander at will. The formal vocabulary he develops is a code to which everyone works, including him. Mr. Architect is a responsible citizen. Unlike Frank Lloyd Wright of the famously unsuitable spiraling walls, Gehry cares very much that his building work well

Guggenheim Museum, Bilbao (Construction Photos), 1997.
Photograph by David Heald
© The Solomon R. Guggenheim Foundation, New York.

as an art museum. Philip Johnson's dismissal of the issue of utility has become the final word on Gehry's success: "When a building is as good as that one, fuck the art"; but Gehry would never say that. First because many of his best friends are artists, but also because iconoclasm does not seem to be his style.

On the contrary, he assigns the aesthetic of the museum, the a–geometry that makes it so difficult to visualize and that one takes to be supermodern, to the oldest of all formal repertoires. He explained to a reporter that another reason, besides childhood memories, that he designs in the shape of fish is dis-affection from the postmodernist way with traditional shapes: "When every-body started doing Greek temples again," he recalled, "I got mad and said, 'If you really want to go back into the past, why not do fish, which were there three hundred million years ago?'" He was only half joking for on another occasion he speculated "that the primitive beginnings of architecture come from zoomorphic yearnings and skeletal images."

It is unlikely he was proposing a zoomorphic school of design although there are some respectable zoomorphic buildings built in this century: Antoni Gaudi's Battlo House in Barcelona (Gaudi is frequently mentioned in relation to Gehry), Eero Saarinen's bird-shaped TWA terminal at Kennedy Airport in New York, and, more recently, Jean Nouvel's Harbour Exposition Center in Rotterdam and his Vinci Conference Center in Tours, both whalelike. Le Cor-busier's Notre-Dame-du-Haut chapel in Ronchamp has a roof shaped like a conch. Still, zoomorphism is a minor rill in the modern architectural stream.

The Ronchamp chapel is one of the most beautiful buildings of this era and a site of pilgrimage (which relates it to Krens's aspirations for the Bilbao museum). But Le Corbusier led the mainstream movement to an ever more purified geometrism and his Unité d'Habitation in Marseilles for instance, though its proportions are based on the Modulor's natural scale, never mimics nature. Wright's Falling Water does not resemble a waterfall; on the contrary, it incorporates its waterfall in a design whose strict rectangles bring it inside the house's perimeter to serve its architectural vision. The wavelike facade of Alvar Aalto's Baker House at MIT is a theoretical allusion to the Charles. The shells making up the Sydney Opera House (the Bilbao museum is constantly compared to it and Krens asked specifically for a building that would be equally innovative) come closer perhaps to imitation but only so far as to em-body the shell concept, hardly the irregular reality of shells on the beach. Gehry's structure looks enough like a fish to flesh out a dispute with those who see it instead as a boat. So that, even if its weirdness is a matter of surfaces, the incomprehensibility of Gehry's building goes deep; it may not be a wolf but it is not a sheep either.

A few days after returning from Bilbao, I was in the courtyard of the Louvre and realized that I had just traveled to two ends of the world of modern architecture. I. M. Pei's pyramid is the antithesis of Gehry's museum. Its form being instantly grasped, the surprise passes quickly and instead, even on the first visit, there is a sense of recognition. Not itself a building but only the threshold to a building, the pyramid is also liminally incarnate: its glass triangles embody their form only enough to make it visible. This may be all that is needed, for the prestige of the triangle gives even this transparency authority over the solid stone quadrangle it mirrors and refracts. In the middle of the old courtyard, the pyramid seems to offer an explication of architectural form across the centuries. There is a definitiveness to the geometry of palace and pyramid that makes sitting on the low wall around the pyramid's reflecting pool particularly restful.

The Bilbao museum induces continual motion. Since the form is almost impossible to fix in one's mind, its contemplation is a restless business and even the surroundings seem swept up in an eddy of shifting shapes. Gehry's notion that a building ought to express movement is no doubt involved here but movement does not require this radical irregularity in which no two pieces composing the surface are identical. Gothic and baroque geometries can pulse with energy but the energy is directed or at least channeled; even when it aspires to infinity, it flows within and toward predictable ends. But the eye does not foresee the ends of Gehry's organic shapes. They are undecidable in their lifelikeness; there is possibly a whiff of blasphemy in the zoomorphism of Gehry's cathedral.

His advice to postmodernists to "do fish" rather than Greek temples, pointless when directed to them since they want to engage with an architectural tradition, makes sense in relation to the Bilbao Guggenheim where Gehry tried to compose in a natural idiom without transposing it into Pythagorean. It is not harmony with nature he sought; his business was with cities and industry. Beyond that, the search for harmony presupposes division, and in this building, the division between nature and architecture does not seem abrogated (Gehry doesn't think a building is a tree) but unimportant. Stonehenge's vertical defiance of the horizontal field around it challenges nature. Gehry's fish is not a challenge; it is simply his fish that he has made of titanium because he does not work in flesh. With the division between nature and culture attenuated, so is the one between organic and invented shapes. Gehry has not so much abandoned geometry in the Bilbao museum as stopped caring about it: if geometry is the grammar of architecture, the Bilbao museum is a tangle of incomplete sentences, dangling modifiers, and crossed tenses. But Emerson would have approved: nature should be your grammarian, not convention.

It was almost two centuries ago that Emerson thought one should pattern one's creations on nature, and with the accelerating rate of technological evolution, it might as well be four. An architect making a building he himself cannot see whole without the aid of a computer while imagining that he was copying nature seems unlikely. But of course Gehry does not think that when, as he puts it, he does fish, he is following nature directly; he is being an artist. Gaudi, Le Corbusier, Wright (to take three architects often cited as Gehry's precursors) represent the modern enlargement of the architectural mission to include a political dimension. They were each in their way utopians. Not Gehry; indeed his turn toward art can be seen as anti-Utopian: as pragmatic rather than visionary. Gehry wants to rebuild the world according to an image but not a system.

The fish shape is more than an aesthetic opportunity but less than a cosmic scheme. It embodies a conception of self-sufficient and at the same time globally effective creativity; the connection between fish and both the beginning of time and the origin of life (in his own biography and in the history of the race) attests to this conception without extending it into a philosophical program. Similarly Gehry's relation to technology, in contrast, say, to the relation of the Bauhaus to the machine, is personally empowering but does not engage him in a world view. The computer that is enabling him to replace geometric abstraction with zoomorphism has simply made Gehry, in his words, "once more the master builder." "Once more" because the technology had developed beyond the control of an individual builder and now he has regained mastery. The technology remains as powerful or more, but he has become still more so. This makes him a new sort of master builder who need not, in conceiving his buildings, stay within his own limits. He can build what he envisions and not only what he can see. It does not occur to him to build what on their part either the technology or the times project.

Wielding CATIA, then, Gehry sculpted the Bilbao museum as Serra did the *Serpent*. He did not incorporate sculpture into the building, as he had several years earlier when he used a rendition of Oldenburg and van Bruggen's *Binoculars* for the entrance to the Chiat/Day office building in Venice, California. In that arrangement, the sculpture, unperturbed by the swinging doors that have been installed between its lenses, has all the good lines and takes the building as straight-man. Gehry did not repeat this error: Koons's big *Puppy* sits at a distance from the Guggenheim warming up the audience for the main attraction; in Bilbao, the building itself is the sculpture. This makes much clearer Gehry's ambition to treat architecture as art; except that the relation of art and architecture itself remains far from clear.

Wright's Guggenheim opened empty and was its own first exposition. But could it have stayed empty? Falling Water is an exposition, as is Versailles, though they became expositions only after being inhabited: they did not start empty but were emptied. I went to Bilbao to see the building: why should that not be an exclusive end, like the Vermeers at The Hague? The artistic status of architecture has been disputed for as long as it has been recognized. The question is not whether architecture is an art, obviously, but whether it is a fine art. In April of 1998, in Marfa, Texas, the Chinati Foundation held a conference about architecture and art. Several speakers hailed the triumph of Gehry's just-opened museum as signaling the end of the distinction between buildings and sculptures, or its demotion into a distinction without a difference. But there were artists as well as architects in attendance and some of the artists seem to have hesitated. Notably, Oldenburg remarked (loudly enough to be heard by the press) that art has neither windows nor toilets.

Fresh from Bilbao and dazzled by the vision of an architecture apparently unbound from its own necessities, I read the newspaper accounts and was much struck by Oldenburg's invocation of windows and toilets, these being code for the recognition of necessity. The great architectural theorist of the nineteenth century, Viollet-le-Duc, would have approved Oldenburg's quip: for an architect, Viollet-le-Duc stipulated, "purely artistic questions of . . . apparent form are only secondary conditions." The Bilbao Guggenheim embodies an opposite view.

Actually, in elite architecture circles, artistic issues have been primary conditions for some time. Fifteen years ago, I taught on a campus which was an architectural showcase. Philip Johnson had been the supervising architect but the humanities building in which I had my office was by Robert Venturi. The architect, I learned later, thought of this building as an amusing copy of a 1940s high school but no one I knew was amused. In our experience this was a 1940s high school, only modified to add a few additional torments. A major one was the central staircase which set off in the direction of the exit at its foot but, four or five stairs from the bottom, veered 180 degrees to the right so that one now descended heading away from the door and, at the bottom, had to turn around and retrace a distance about half the length of the staircase in order to arrive at the point it would have reached had it gone straight forward.

The U-turn in the staircase was bounded by a low granite wall that one was each time tempted to vault, had its wide rounded top not made any foothold precarious. So, willy-nilly, we walked downstairs as the building directed, but I often wondered whether Mr. Venturi had thought about the possible effect of enforcing detours on the occupants' appreciation of his design; even whether, intent on imagining the form of the staircase, he had imagined occupants at all. But of course he had: the militancy emanating from declarations that architecture is art only expresses everyone's recognition that, however primary their artistic goals, architects can never entirely ignore the practical. It occurred to me, teaching literature on my showcase campus, that the practices of architecture and of language have a basic element in common: at their most aesthetic, both retain an irreducible necessary functionalism. Even writing *Finnegans Wake,* James Joyce had to convey a cognitive message; the building Gehry made for the Fishdance restaurant had to keep out the rain.

Gehry has no ambivalence about his responsibility to keep out the rain. Pointing to the moment in his designing of the Bilbao museum when he passed from artist to architect ("in the . . . sketch, it was great, it was exciting, and then I became Mr. Architect"), he clearly finds it half the fun of the job. Unlike Frank Lloyd Wright with the first Guggenheim, Gehry was anxious that the second accommodate its tasks as an art museum. It is odd, therefore, that he nowhere ponders a relation between the dual aspects of architecture. He has often spoken about his commitment to serve both beauty and utility but nothing that I could find about possible interactions between them. No doubt it is the bias of one whose primary example of the beautiful and the useful has been literature that makes me wonder at this silence on the link between them. Still, it is striking: Gehry embraces architectural necessity and pursues architectural beauty on parallel paths. The fact that to get his building built, he has to straddle the paths does not seem to inspire him to consider how they might be connected. He may even be thinking the contrary, that in making the museum useful, he is abandoning some portion of his artistic ambition. He makes this concession voluntarily and even gladly, but it is a compromise between distinct purposes. In other words, if, due to his conscientiousness, the architect's museum turns out to work well for artists and visitors, this is pleasant but not essential.

In literature at least, the relation between the beautiful and the useful works differently: a poetic phrase is beautiful and precise in the same breath. The beautiful and the precise are not identical but they are reciprocal, and reading Wallace Stevens or Flaubert, it seems obvious that the aesthetic is a way of knowing. The equivalent principle in architecture would make the aesthetic a way of building true to function. Observing, as many have observed, that there is a certain disjuncture between outside and inside in Gehry's building, I wondered whether he were not proving this principle in the breach.

Other than the long gallery whose form and function fuse into a figure as evident from within the museum as from without, the rooms and the overall floorplan are difficult to fit into one's exterior vision of the building. And the same difficulty arises in reverse. The story is repeatedly told that Gehry asked his artist friends how they wanted him to design the museum. They told him to build an architect's building that would be in its way as strong and important as their art. Yet for all the good will on both sides, there is this odd disjuncture between the inside of the building, where the art is, and the outside where the architecture is.

In fact, the disjuncture arose out of the good will. Wright's Guggenheim building, careless of art, is an organic whole, expressing the architect's artistic / architectural vision unmitigated by any of the artists' vision. Gehry's Guggenheim is a building divided between its architect's vision and the vision of the art it houses. Had Flaubert tried to write someone else's ideas in his prose he would have had the same unresolvable problem as Gehry. Gehry has several times cooperated with artists on architectural sketches but these never became architecture and Gehry never became Mr. Architect but remained an artist sketching. When he collaborated with Serra he drew one pylon and Serra the other; in Bilbao, Gehry designed a roof in the form of a flower whose function was to keep the rain off Serra's sculpture.

This was a task destined for disjuncture: as a fine art, architecture becomes primarily a means of individual expression. For the architectural artist, construction's utilitarian aspect is extraneous since it is not he who will make use of it but the sculptors and painters the museum exhibits. As an individual artist, he sculpts a shape in an assortment of materials; the building's windows and toilets are outside this process, "pro bono" work for the community of artists and visitors. I proposed earlier that Gehry's choice of Notre Dame to represent a generically important building by which an architect shapes a city occludes the most important feature of the building of Notre Dame, that no single architect was responsible nor expressed himself therein. While, in this century, it is almost impossible to imagine an act of creation that is not individual, Gehry's inattention to the difference between himself as a singular artist responsible for his project from start to finish, and the builders of Notre Dame has produced a problem reflected not only in the disjuncture of the building's inside and outside but in a set of incongruities of size, material, and outline that combine to impart its spaceship look. Disjuncture (incongruity, even incoherence) is not inherently displeasing; and in this instance it is distinctly attractive: enlivening, energizing. It is a feature rather than a flaw, but a significant feature and moreover one which may point to a flaw in its context.

The flaw would not be in the building but in ourselves, in an ideology that exceeds classic individualism by casting the individual as not only self-sufficient but culture-sufficient. Gehry is not just an individual master builder; he designs indivisibly as an individual and as an incarnation of his culture (North American–Jewish–Los Angeles). Culturally as well as personally global, this individual has only voluntary relations to others. Roofs, windows, and toilets acknowledge that architecture erects its structures for others to inhabit. But the community, in the current cultural thinking, has been internalized: it has become an aspect of selfhood, of individual identity. Actual roofs, windows, and toilets are then without personal significance to the architect and extraneous to his art. The disjunctions, in the Bilbao Guggenheim, between function and form (between inside and out) flow from the paradox that the museum's communal function is fulfilled by the form its architect/artist has designed to reflect his personal cultural-sufficiency. The Bauhaus architects aspired to social reform by inserting their buildings into a political matrix extending beyond them; Gehry, though by all accounts an affable man with a social conscience and no megalomaniac, has absorbed all the relevant politics (history, culture) into his building. It is not just his building, though it is exclusively his; it is also inclusively a whole cultural program.

This sufficiency, however, has engendered another major disjunction, this one in respect to the building's function not as a museum of art but as an element in the reconstruction of the city of Bilbao. There is little in the structure, on the walls, or in the galleries of Gehry's Guggenheim, to identify it as a Basque institution; but this could change. The more intransigent problem lies in the ideology of multiculturalism that informs everything about the Guggenheim, starting with its aesthetic character and extending through its artistic program to its institutional identity and organization. The projection of individual cultural self-sufficiency at the center of this ideology is inimical to the Basque city's cultural nationalism which envisions neither transportability nor personal wholeness but exactly their opposites: a way of being that is locally fixed and specifically delimited. To do the job for which the Basque administration of Bilbao intends it, the new museum would need to project a definition of both art and architecture as the creations not of culture-sufficient individuals but of persons for whom their cultures are sufficient.

• • •

My first amazement on seeing the Bilbao museum never abated but rather deepened with the conviction that its exoticism reacts to very familiar issues. In the hypermodern American building standing proud and incongruous on its historic Basque site, two major disjunctions of recent years seem to have materialized: the first, at once aesthetic and epistemological, is the disjunction of form and function that has rendered form freely expressive but also vertiginously arbitrary. The second disjunction is the political opposition between multiculturalism and cultural nationalism, or between the transnationalism of the rich and the localism of the poor. The Guggenheim Museum in Bilbao absolutely merits the pilgrimage Krens envisages, though not, as to a medieval cathedral, in order to recover a sense of global unity in a catholic God. Frank Gehry's church of art, brilliantly prophesying the gospel that closed the second millennium, celebrates schism: to each era its message.

Notes

CHAPTER ONE

1 All references are to the Library of America edition of the *Autobiography*, in *Benjamin Franklin: Writings,* ed. J. A. Leo Lemay (New York, 1987). The plan for perfection is laid out on pages 1384–85.

2 Robert A. Ferguson, "We Hold These Truths," in *Reconstructing American Literary History,* ed. Sacvan Bercovitch (Cambridge, Mass.: Harvard University Press, 1986), 16–18. Franklin is, according to Ferguson, the only Founder to use humor, irony, and satire. But Ferguson sees him also as the most fearful of discord, because of his emphasis on silence and the nonexpression of contention.

3 Franklin, *Autobiography,* 1307.

4 *The Confessions of Jean Jacques Rousseau,* trans. J. M. Cohen (London: Penguin Books, 1953), 17.

5 Some qualities are so universal in the archetypal individual that they do not warrant mention, maleness being one. Neither Rousseau, Franklin, nor any of the others I discuss ever consider applying their theories to women; on the contrary, women are aspects of the theories that make them practicable by men. I have not wanted to obscure this sexual division in my nouns and pronouns, which are nearly all masculine to reflect the masculinity of the concepts being analyzed.

6 Mitchell Breitweiser, *Cotton Mather and Benjamin Franklin: The Price of Representative Personality* (Cambridge: Cambridge University Press, 1984), 1.

7 I have in mind the astonishing scene in which Michael discovers to Adam the world he and his descendants will conquer (*Paradise Lost,* book 11, 370–411), a catalog of empires that seems to imply England's own as a destined culmination.

8 Mme. de Warens was only 29 when they met but she called him "Petit" and was sufficiently maternal so that in becoming her lover Rousseau felt incestuous. He lived in her house for nearly thirteen years, an idyllic vassalage whose termination he always mourned.

9 Franklin, *Autobiography,* 1308.

10 John Bunyan, *The Pilgrim's Progress,* ed. Roger Sharrock (New York: Penguin Books, 1983), 125.

11 Franklin, *Autobiography,* 1359–60.

12 Ibid., 1321.

13 Ibid., 1321–22.

14 In its focus on the public act rather than the private impulse, this admission is definitely not a Rousseauan confession.

15 Actually, Franklin's description is more sophistic than Socratic. He seems not to have noted Socrates' insistence that truth is more persuasive than falsehood, perhaps because the implication of an ultimate conjunction of form and content collapses the stage of Franklin's actor.

16 Franklin, *Autobiography*, 1321.

17 Ibid., 1359.

18 Ibid., 1385.

19 Lionel Trilling, *Sincerity and Authenticity* (Cambridge, Mass.: Harvard University Press, 1972), 2, 5.

20 Franklin, *Autobiography*, 1393.

21 Ibid., 1363.

22 J. G. A. Pocock, *The Machiavellian Moment: Florentine Thought and the Atlantic Republican Tradition* (Princeton: Princeton University Press, 1975), 462.

23 Ibid., 524.

24 Franklin, *Autobiography*, 1403.

25 Ibid., 1308.

26 Ibid., 1397.

27 Pocock, *Machiavellian Moment*, 4, 56–57.

28 This trust did have its limits, some quite stringent. "Common" and "community" did not encompass everyone by any means. The poor whose incarceration in workhouses he advocated lest they become a burden to their betters were not included, nor were many others. Like its ancestors, Franklin's democratic vision was populated in the author's own image: white men of property were its natural constituents. But he had better expectations from this congregation than did most of his contemporaries.

29 Pocock, *Machiavellian Moment*, 533, citing Jefferson's notes on Virginia.

CHAPTER TWO

1 J. Hector St. John Crèvecoeur, *Letters from an American Farmer* (Garden City: Dolphin Books, n.d.), 46–47. Subsequent page references are cited parenthetically in the text.

2 See the biography by Julia Post Mitchell, *St. Jean de Crèvecoeur* (New York: AMS Press, 1966).

3 Rowland Berthoff and John M. Murrin find this to be the general historical consensus in their seminal essay, "Feudalism, Communalism and the Yeoman Freeholder," in Stephen G. Kurtz and James H. Hutson, eds., *Essays on the American Revolution* (Chapel Hill: University of North Carolina Press, 1973), 261.

4 Despite his protestations to the contrary in the first letter, or rather because of the very language in which these are couched, it is clear that Crèvecoeur was no simple farmer, but a highly educated gentleman whose social and intellectual connections extended far beyond Pine Hill. But if his observations were thus unusually well-informed, this does not mean they were not as linked to the realities of Pine Hill and its environs as those of farmers who knew little of the world beyond. It is an interesting problem whether the greater sophistication of one member of a community undermines his representativeness, or perhaps heightens it, by enabling him to articulate what his neighbors may only feel.

5 Such a revival, interrupted by the Revolution, is discussed by Berthoff and Murrin in "Yeoman Freeholder," 264–76. Indeed the experience of this revival and his opposition to it may well have contributed to Crèvecoeur's loyalism, for, led in Pennsylvania by Benjamin Franklin, the opponents of feudalism sought to persuade the English crown to rule the colony directly in lieu of large proprietors: thus would the monarchy protect the equality of its subjects.

6 Crèvecoeur, *Sketches of Eighteenth-Century America* (New York: Signet, 1963), 262−63.

7 Ibid., 260−63.

8 William Smith, ed., *Dictionary of Greek and Roman Biography and Mythology* (Boston: C. C. Little and J. Brown; London: Taylor, Walton, & Maberly, 1849), 479−80.

9 Crèvecoeur, *Sketches,* 384−86.

10 Ibid., 308−9.

11 Ibid., 253.

12 *The New Science of Giambattista Vico,* translated from the third edition (1744) by Thomas Goddard Bergin and Max Harold Fisch (Ithaca: Cornell University Press, 1970), 8.

13 James Henretta has made the interesting suggestion that another model for Crèvecoeur's notion of a distant monarch might be found in contemporary Deism. Again the issue addressed by the model is the assurance of order without intrusive controls.

14 Crèvecoeur, *Sketches,* 259.

15 This seems to be the assumption even of those scholars such as Jesse Lemisch in his essay, "Jack Tar in the Streets: Merchant Seamen in the Politics of Revolutionary America," *William and Mary Quarterly* 3 (July 1968), 371−407, who challenge the view that such men as Washington and Jefferson represented a revolutionary consensus that included all classes. The discovery that certain groups dissented from this consensus and sought to change the character of the Revolution to better represent their interests and social vision might suggest the possibility that some who felt misrepresented by its leadership may have demurred from the Revolution altogether.

16 Jackson Turner Main, *The Sovereign States, 1775−1783* (New York: New Viewpoints, 1973), 272−73. For a more complete treatment of the Loyalists see chap. V, "The Tory Rank and File," in William H. Nelson, *The American Tory* (Boston: Beacon Press, 1971). Nelson argues that "Taking all the groups and factions, sects, classes, and inhabitants of regions that seem to have been Tory, they have but one thing in common: [being neither unusually rich, nor English, nor colonially connected] they represented conscious minorities, people who felt weak and threatened" (91).

17 Berthoff and Murrin, *Essays on the American Revolution,* 276.

18 What Crèvecoeur feared from the Revolution, what he had hoped America would never become, is just that Yankee society Richard L. Bushman describes emerging in Connecticut and setting the scene for the coming Revolution. It was a society in which "the avid pursuit of gain" had become an acceptable goal of life, which "found an honorable place for self-interest in the social order," and which interpreted that order as orderly competition. See Bushman, *From Puritan to Yankee: Character and Social Order in Connecticut, 1690−1765* (New York: W. W. Norton, 1970), 287.

CHAPTER THREE

1 Leslie Fiedler, *Love and Death in the American Novel* (New York: Delta Books, 1966), 25.

2 Richard Chase, *The American Novel and Its Tradition* (Garden City, N.Y.: Doubleday Anchor Books, 1957).

3 Herman Melville, *Moby Dick or, The Whale,* in *Herman Melville, Redburn, White Jacket, Moby Dick,* ed. G. Thomas Tanselle (New York: Library of America, 1983), 1406.

4 Ibid.

5 The stark alternative has not always been clearly stated by Melville's critics.

6 Raymond Williams, "Base and Superstructure in Marxist Cultural Theory," *New Left Review* 82 (November−December 1973): 8.

7 Georg Lukács, *The Theory of the Novel* (Cambridge: M.I.T. Press, 1971), 66.

8 Ibid., 56, 60.

9 Quentin Anderson, *The Imperial Self* (New York: Alfred A. Knopf, 1971), 167.

10 J. Hillis Miller, *The Form of Victorian Fiction* (Notre Dame, Ind.: University of Notre Dame Press, 1968), 96.

11 Melville, *Moby Dick,* 916–17.

12 Melville indeed toys with Promethean notion and abandons it in the character of Bulkington whose main value to the book may be to establish what Ahab is *not.*

13 Ralph Waldo Emerson, "Self-Reliance," in *Emerson, Essays and Lectures,* ed. Joel Porte (New York: Library of America, 1983), 259.

14 Emerson, "The American Scholar," ibid., 54.

15 Emerson, "Self-Reliance," 262.

16 See the "Discipline" chapter of "Nature" in *Emerson, Essays and Lectures,* ed. Joel Porte (New York: Library of America, 1983) for Emerson's linking of morality and economy. For example:

> [Instilling us with discipline] is performed by Property and its filial systems of debt and credit. Debt, grinding debt, whose iron face the widow, the orphan and the sons of genius fear and hate;—debt which consumes so much time, which so cripples and disheartens a great spirit with cares that seem so base, is a preceptor whose lessons cannot be forgone, and is needed most by those who suffer from it most. Moreover, property, which has been well compared to snow,—"if it fall today, it will be blown into drifts tomorrow,"—is the surface action of internal machinery, like the index on the face of a clock. Whilst now it is the gymnastics of the understanding, it is hiving, in the foresight of the spirit, experience in profounder laws. (26–27)

17 Emerson, "Experience," ibid., 492.

18 Emerson, "Self-Reliance," 272.

19 Emerson, "Experience," 492.

20 Ahab's last is structured by imploding, collapsing dualities, these having been the very timbers of the Captain's distorted, unviable cosmos.

> Oh, lonely death on lonely life! Oh, now I feel my topmost greatness lies in my topmost grief. Ho, ho! from all your furthest bounds, pour ye now in, ye bold billows of my whole foregone life, and top this one piled comber of my death! Towards thee I roll, thou all-destroying but unconquering whale; to the last I grapple with thee; from hell's heart I stab at thee; for hate's sake I spit my last breath at thee. Sink all coffins and all hearses to one common pool! and since neither can be mine, let me then tow to pieces, while still chasing thee, though tied to thee, thou damned whale! *Thus,* I give up the spear!

Melville, *Moby Dick,* 1406.

21 Here is Julien's speech to the jury:

> . . . My crime is atrocious, and it was *premeditated.* I have therefore, Gentlemen of the Jury, deserved death. But even were I less guilty, I see before me men who, without pausing to consider what pity my youth may deserve, will wish to punish in my person and forever discourage that body of young men who, born in an inferior station, and in some degree oppressed by poverty, have the good fortune to secure for themselves a sound education, and the audacity to mingle with what the pride of rich men calls society.
>
> That is my crime, Gentlemen, and it will be punished with all the more severity in that, in point of fact, I am not being tried by my peers. In the jury-box I see not a single peasant who has grown rich, but simply and solely men of the middle-class enraged against me. . . .

Stendhal, *The Red and the Black* (London: Penguin, 1953), 484.

22 And here is Hester's vision and her recognition that she is forever barred from participating in its realization:

> She assured [women who came to her seeking comfort in unhappy marriages] of her firm belief, that, at some brighter period, when the world should have grown ripe for

it, in Heaven's own time, a new truth would be revealed, in order to establish the whole relation between man and woman on a surer ground of mutual happiness. Earlier in life, Hester had vainly imagined that she herself might be the destined prophetess, but had long since recognized the impossibility that any mission of divine and mysterious truth should be confided to a woman stained with sin, bowed down with shame, or even burdened with a lifelong sorrow. The angel and apostle of the coming revelation must be a woman, indeed, but lofty, pure, and beautiful; and wise, moreover, not through dusky grief, but the ethereal medium of joy; and showing how sacred love should make us happy, by the truest test of a life successful to such an end!

Nathaniel Hawthorne, *The Scarlet Letter,* in *Nathaniel Hawthorne, Collected Novels,* ed. Millicent Bell (New York: Library of America, 1983), 344–45. That last sentence is a veritable "catch-22" which ensures that whatever other world Hawthorne may envisage in the future, one certainly cannot get there from here.

23 Emerson, "Experience," 492.

24 Chase, *American Novel,* 25.

25 Emerson, "American Scholar," 492.

26 Henry James, introduction to *Madame Bovary,* by Gustave Flaubert (London, 1904), xviii–xix.

27 Emile Faguet, *Flaubert* (Paris, 1899), 106–7, my translation.

28 Henry James, *The Portrait of a Lady,* in *Henry James, Novels 1881–1886,* ed. William T. Stafford (New York: Library of America, 1985), 379.

29 Honoré de Balzac, *Old Goriot* (London: Penguin), 286.

30 William Faulkner, *Absalom, Absalom!* In *William Faulkner, Novels 1936–1940,* ed. Joseph Blotner and Noel Park (New York: Library of America, 1990), 311.

CHAPTER FOUR

1 "Benito Cereno," *Herman Melville* (New York: Library of America, 1984), 755.

2 Slaves do appear in white novels before emancipation, notably in plantation fiction but also in cameo roles in Northern stories such as Cooper's. There is also Friday in *Robinson Crusoe.* But all these slaves are in the story as objects, not subjects; and when they are expressive it is rather in the mode of dogs or horses than of people. In the construction of fictional characters societal oppression becomes ontological suppression.

3 Not only of fiction. When Frederick Douglass wrote his *Narrative of the Life of Frederick Douglass* in 1845 the publishers found it necessary to append to the author's name "Written by Himself."

4 Harriet Beecher Stowe, *Uncle Tom's Cabin* (New York: Library of America, 1982). Page references are cited parenthetically in the text.

5 Melville self-mockingly claimed to have intended to write in *Pierre* a sentimental novel that would finally sell after the financial disappointment of *Moby-Dick.* From its parodic opening *Pierre,* however, takes on sentimentalism itself as passionately as any social or moral evil. As Melville constructs him, the archetypally individualistic Pierre cannot contemplate Stowe's mediations without fatally compromising the essence of his character.

6 *American Slavery, American Freedom: The Ordeal of Colonial Virginia* (New York: W. W. Norton, 1975).

7 More should be made of the clear indication that George's master is not a true gentleman but possibly an upstart, a recent climber, perhaps of the class of the "coarse" slave trader Haley about whom one of the first and most damaging things we learn is that he is "a low man who is trying to elbow his way upward in the world" (11). A discussion of Stowe's class attitudes would be a little digressive here but in passing we might note that her pref-

erence for "gentlemen" and her contemptuous suspicion for climbers reflects her commitment to gentry rule. It is very much to her point that the threat to such rule here comes through the institution of slavery.

8 The role of the growing working class as an independent antislavery constituency is equally important. Post-Revolution immigration, overwhelmingly working class, is probably the single most important factor in the transformation of the American polity between the Revolution and the Civil War. Although Stowe does not address this development directly, the class bigotry of her treatment of Haley and her insistence on identifying "gentlemen" as her constituency surely reflect its unsettling effects.

9 Three of the most influential works in the development of this account of women's writing are: Janice Radway, *Reading the Romance: Women, Patriarchy, and Popular Literature* (Chapel Hill: University of North Carolina Press, 1984); Jane Tompkins, *Sensational Designs: The Cultural Work of American Fiction, 1790–1860* (New York: Oxford University Press, 1985); and Cathy Davidson, *Revolution and the Word: The Rise of the Novel in America* (New York: Oxford University Press, 1986).

CHAPTER FIVE

1 All references are to the Library of America edition of *Huckleberry Finn*, in *Mark Twain: Mississippi Writings*, ed. Guy Cardwell (New York, 1982), 615–912. Page references are cited parenthetically in the text.

2 Cited in Justin Kaplan, *Mr. Clemens and Mark Twain: A Biography* (New York: Simon and Schuster, 1966), 268.

3 Bernard DeVoto, *Mark Twain's America* (New York: Houghton Mifflin, 1932), 308, 310–20.

4 Leo Marx, "Mr. Eliot, Mr. Trilling, and *Huckleberry Finn*," *American Scholar* 22 (autumn 1953): 423–40.

5 Ernest Hemingway, *Green Hills of Africa* (New York: Scribner, 1935), 22, 21.

6 Cited in DeVoto, *Twain's America,* 308.

7 Adam Gopnik, "The Wise Innocent," *New Yorker,* November 8, 1993, 119.

8 "The American Scholar," in *Emerson: Essays and Lectures,* ed. Joel Porte (New York: Library of America, 1983), 69.

9 The date of *Huckleberry Finn's* publication, 1885, is in fact a likely one for a populist work. Although the People's Party was not established until later (running its first presidential candidate in 1892), anti-Northern industrialist agitation in the agrarian South and Southwest had already given rise to Farmers' Alliances and other populist movements in the 1880s.

10 Nineteenth-century readers need not have been very well educated to know Shakespeare, who was the most popular playwright on the circuit. On the breadth of Shakespeare's nineteenth-century audience see Lawrence Levine, "William Shakespeare in America," Chapter 1 in *Highbrow/Lowbrow: The Emergence of Cultural Hierarchy in America* (New York: Harvard University Press, 1988), 11–81.

11 Jonathan Arac, "Nationalism, Hypercanonization, and *Huckleberry Finn*," *boundary 2* 19, no. 1 (1992): 14–33.

12 See in this respect Neil Schmitz, "Twain, *Huckleberry Finn,* and the Reconstruction," *American Studies* 12 (1971): 59–67.

13 The writing of *Huckleberry Finn* was prolonged and difficult. Albert Bigelow Paine, who was Twain's first literary executor, and Bernard DeVoto, who was the second, both described exceptional problems in the composition of the author's masterpiece, but the definitive account is probably Walter Blair's "When Was *Huckleberry Finn* Written?" (*American Literature* 30 [1958]: 1–25). Of particular relevance to this essay is Blair's proof that Twain had not initially planned to have the entire story unfold on the river but decided to do so about halfway through the writing.

14 In an essay on Benjamin Franklin's *Autobiography*, I have traced Franklin's formulation of a civic morality explicitly in response to the organic duplicity of the modern self and its opaque interiority (see above, chapter 1). Civil morality in *Huckleberry Finn* is a mockery, a burlesque like those the duke and the dauphin make of Shakespeare.

15 Forrest G. Robinson, *In Bad Faith: The Dynamics of Deception in Mark Twain's America* (Cambridge, Mass.: Harvard University Press, 1986), 17.

16 All citations to this episode are from chapters 21 and 22, pages 757–72.

17 This is essentially the perspective of Twain's last and uncompleted work, *The Mysterious Stranger.*

18 Shelley Fisher Fishkin, *Was Huck Black? Mark Twain and African-American Voices* (New York: Oxford University Press, 1993).

CHAPTER SIX

1 I use "sex" instead of "gender" in the title not to reject the argument that sexual identity is a social construction, but to sidestep it in order to evoke the material condition itself; the way sex is interpreted into gender being precisely the subject of this essay. I am aware that one view holds that no material condition as such exists, or none we can apprehend, so that the language of gender is all we know of sex and all we need to know. To this, my response is implicit in what follows, that gender, like any ideological construction, describes the interactions of several realities, at least one of which is not the creature of language but material—the world out there. Gender is all we know of sex, but not all we need to know. This essay also depicts the inadequacy of ideological knowledge.

2 Samuel Langhorne Clemens, *Pudd'nhead Wilson and Those Extraordinary Twins*, ed. Signey E. Berger (New York: W. W. Norton, 1980), 114. Subsequent page references are cited parenthetically in the text.

3 The first description of the two children distinguished only by the "soft muslin and . . . coral necklace" of one and the "coarse tow-linen shirt" of the other (9) recalls the similarly contrasting costumes of the Prince and the Pauper. In that story, however, the little pauper fulfills all sentimental expectations, and far from usurping the throne, returns it more secure to its rightful owner. Are there implications in the virtue of this poor boy, versus the vice of the black boy, for different authorial attitudes toward class and race?

4 Here I would mention specifically that portion of the literature that has reevaluated the sentimental tradition as a female, sometimes feminist, critique of the male ideology of the market. See especially Jane Tompkins, *Sensational Designs: The Cultural Work of American Fiction, 1790–1860* (New York: Oxford University Press, 1985) and Elizabeth Ammons, "Stowe's Dream of the Mother-Savior: *Uncle Tom's Cabin* and American Women Writers before the 1920s," in *New Essays on Uncle Tom's Cabin,* ed. Eric J. Sundquist (Cambridge: Cambridge University Press, 1986).

5 I have discussed this phenomenon more fully in an essay, "Archimedes and the Paradox of Feminist Criticism," *Signs* 6 (winter 1981): 575–601. Reprinted in this book as chapter 7.

CHAPTER SEVEN

1 Kate Millett, *Sexual Politics* (Garden City, N.Y.: Doubleday, 1970).

2 Jean-Paul Sartre, *What Is Literature?* (New York: Harper Colophon, 1965), 40; emphasis in original.

3 Pierre Macherey, *Pour une théorie de la production littéraire* (Paris: Librairie François Maspero, 1966), 66–68.

4 Patricia Meyer Spacks, *The Female Imagination* (New York: Avon Books, 1976), 5, 6.

5 Ellen Moers, *Literary Women: The Great Writers* (Garden City, N.Y.: Doubleday, 1976), xvi.

6 Elaine Showalter, *A Literature of Their Own: British Women Novelists from Brontë to Lessing* (Princeton, N.J.: Princeton University Press, 1977), 319, 11–12.

7 Sandra Gilbert and Susan Gubar, *The Madwoman in the Attic: The Woman Writer and the Nineteenth-Century Literary Imagination* (New Haven, Conn.: Yale University Press, 1979). The chapter referred to at some length in this discussion is chapter 7, "Horror's Twin: Mary Shelley's Monstrous Eve."

8 I want to cite two works that do deal with the traditions of male writing. Judith Fetterley in *The Resisting Reader: A Feminist Approach to American Fiction* (Bloomington: Indiana University Press, 1978) writes that "the first act of the feminist critic must be to become a resisting rather than an assenting reader and, by this refusal to assent, to begin the process of exorcizing the male mind that has been implanted in us" (xxii). Lee Edwards in *Psyche as Hero: Female Heroism and Fictional Form* (Middletown, Conn.: Wesleyan University Press, 1984), expresses the somewhat different but related purpose of reclaiming language and mythology for women. My objections to both these approaches will be clear from the essay. Let me add here only that I also find them nonetheless extremely suggestive and often persuasive.

9 Henry Nash Smith, "The Scribbling Women and the Cosmic Success Story," *Critical Inquiry* 1, no. 1 (September 1974): 49–70.

10 Smith, "Scribbling Women," 51.

11 Ann Douglas, *The Feminization of American Culture* (New York: Avon Books, 1978).

12 Quentin Anderson, *The Imperial Self* (New York: Alfred A. Knopf, 1971).

13 Leslie Fiedler, *Love and Death in the American Novel* (New York: Delta Books, 1966).

14 Nina Baym, *Woman's Fiction: A Guide to Novels by and about Women, 1820–1870* (Ithaca, N.Y.: Cornell University Press, 1978). Page references are cited parenthetically in the text.

15 Smith, "Scribbling Women," 49.

16 Fiedler, *Love and Death,* 259–60.

17 I am aware that this analysis assumes a modern psychology of art, that "creation" has not always been the artist's mission, or tacit acceptance of the established ethos considered fatal. But we are here speaking of the nineteenth century, not of all time; and writers who did not challenge their society's values would also not have questioned its fundamental construction of artistic identity as individualistic and as authentically creative.

18 For an illuminating discussion of this phenomenon—of women novelists being unable to imagine female characters as strong as themselves—see Carolyn Heilbrun, "Women Writers and Female Characters: The Failure of Imagination," in *Reinventing Womanhood* (New York: W. W. Norton, 1979), 71–92.

CHAPTER EIGHT

1 I am grateful to Rick Livingston for an illuminating discussion of the dynamic between the concepts of "difference" and of the "other."

2 Christopher Columbus, *Four Voyages to the New World,* trans. and ed. R. H. Major (Gloucester, Mass.: Peter Smith Publisher, 1978), 1–2.

3 Arkady Plotnitsky has brought to my attention in connection with this Marlow's account of the horrifying Africans in *Heart of Darkness.* The landscape, Marlow recalls shuddering, "was unearthly, and the men were—No, they were not inhuman. Well, you know, that was the worst of it—this suspicion of their not being inhuman." *Youth, Heart of Darkness, the End of the Tether* (New York: Oxford University Press, 1984), 96–97.

4 Citations from both "Of Cannibals" and "Of Coaches" are from *The Complete Works of Montaigne: Essays, Travel Journal, Letters,* trans. Donald Frame (Stanford: Stanford University Press, 1957), 150–59, 685–99, esp. 152. Subsequent page references are cited parenthetically in the text.

5 It should be noted that there is no unimpeachable evidence for the existence of cannibals

in the New World. For a particularly illuminating analysis of the evidence, see David Beers Quinn, "The New Geographical Literature," in *First Images of America: The Impact of the New World on the Old,* ed. Fredi Chiapelli (Berkeley: University of California Press, 1976), 635–57. A more recent discussion of this ongoing controversy is in Peter Hulme, *Caribbean Encounters: Europe and the Native Caribbean, 1492–1797* (London: Methuen, 1986).

6 Marcel Gutwirth, "Des coches, ou la structuration d'une absence," *L'Esprit créateur* 15, nos. 1–2 (spring–summer 1975), 8–20. Since Montaigne's time, anthropologists have determined that the Incas did make wheels but only on toys. Of course this only deepens the distinction between Europeans and Americans being projected here. I am indebted to Rolph Trouillot for this correction.

7 Tzvetan Todorov, *The Conquest of America: The Question of the Other,* trans. Richard Howard (New York: Harper Torchbooks, 1987), 3. Originally published as *La conquête de l'Amérique* (Paris: Editions du Seuil, 1982).

8 Tzvetan Todorov, "'Race,' Writing and Culture," in *'Race,' Writing and Difference,* ed. Henry Louis Gates, Jr. (Chicago: University of Chicago Press, 1986), 370–80. Todorov's essay responds to one published earlier in the Special Issue of *Critical Inquiry* which was the first version of this book: Abdul R. JanMohamed, "The Economy of Manichean Allegory: The Function of Racial Difference in Colonialist Literature," *'Race,' Writing and Difference,* Special Issue of *Critical Inquiry,* ed. Henry Louis Gates, Jr., 12, no. 1 (autumn 1985), 59–87. The passage from which Todorov cites is on page 65. To clarify Jan Mohamed's part in this argument, I should say that Todorov seems to me to misrepresent it a little. JanMohamed also seeks a way out of the predicament of absolute alterity and, as I read him, only stresses the difficulties it entails on the way to proposing a way of overcoming them.

9 An interesting version of this argument is made in Rey Chow's "'It's You, and not Me': Domination and 'Othering' in Theorizing the 'Third World,'" in *Coming to Terms: Feminism, Theory, Politics,* ed. Elizabeth Weed (New York: Routledge, 1989), 152–61. Rey Chow uses a short story by the twentieth-century Chinese writer Lu Xun to criticize current Western projections of an absolutely other Third World. Lu Xun's story, according to her, "foretells much that is happening in the contemporary 'Western' theoretical scene." This foretelling, of course, demonstrates a shared universe of concerns. An equally telling discussion occurs in V. Y. Mudimbe's *Invention of Africa: Gnosis, Philosophy, and the Order of Knowledge* (Bloomington: Indiana University Press, 1988) in a section of chapter 3, "The Power of Speech," entitled "The Panacea of Otherness: J. P. Sartre as an African Philosopher." Mudimbe here analyses the effect of the theory of "Negritude" set forth in Sartre's essay *"Black Orpheus"* which attempts precisely to identify a different culture without rendering it in any way inferior. On the contrary, Sartre is prepared to find in the values and energies of Negritude the next world-important culture to take over in the twilight of European culture. Without attempting to rehearse an exceptionally complex and dense argument, I want to invoke it here as a particularly penetrating treatment of the contradictions of the concept of difference and particularly of its fatal tendency to move toward an obliterating otherness.

10 Michael Dorris, "Indians on the Shelf," in *The American and the Problem of History,* ed. Calvin Martin (New York: Oxford University Press, 1987), 98–105. Interestingly, Calvin Martin himself argues the opposite in his introduction. Attempts to write Indian history in the conventional Western terms so distort its fundamental structures of meaning, Martin claims, as to render the results either meaningless or, worse, new instances of ethnic and racial suppression. A recent theoretical study of Indian literature urges on the contrary that the same models of interpretation be applied to it as to any literature and that not to do so is to continue excluding this literature from United States culture: Arnold Krupat, *The Voice in the Margin: Native American Literature and the Canon* (Berkeley: University of California Press, 1989).

11 A selection from these writings is available in a paperback collection edited by Miguel Leon-Portilla, *The Broken Spears: The Aztec Account of the Conquest of Mexico* (Boston: Beacon Press, 1966).

12 La Malinche is a figure of enormous interest who would repay more attention from historians. A woman and a slave, Mexican and woman, she was at once helpless and decisively powerful, victim of an oppressive gender and class system, yet also a significant agent in the defeat of her people.

13 These are Indian figures (Leon-Portilla, *Broken Spears,* 124). They also estimate that of the 300,000 on the Aztec side, 240,000 were killed by the end of the final siege.

14 Alfred Crosby, *The Columbian Exchange: Biological and Cultural Consequences of 1492* (Westport, Conn.: Greenwood Press, 1972). Within five years of the arrival of Europeans, nine out of ten Americans were dead of diseases ranging from the common cold to smallpox. A contemporary account of the North American part of the holocaust, which puzzled the whites almost as much as it terrified the Indians, is in Thomas Harriot's 1588 *Briefe and True Report of the New Found Land of Virginia.*

15 The full citation, from *1984,* is "who controls the past controls the future; who controls the present controls the past." This is the Party's slogan.

16 Todorov interprets the same phenomenon differently, suggesting that what the Aztecs preserve through the invention of the omens is a meaningful past, demonstrating the orderliness of their universe by having it forecast its own end. I am suggesting on the contrary that what is safeguarded in the omens is the future, that is, after the end of their universe, the possibility of an ongoing orderliness however horrific the order.

17 One of the most problematical aspects of the Todorov account is its failure to incorporate any effects from the historical process itself of the conquest. The Spanish learn to see others as others, but this is already implicit or anyway potential in Spanish culture; the Aztecs do not learn about otherness and that is also implicit in their culture. The events and experiences of the conquest itself dramatize and illustrate, but they do not really inform, let alone form.

18 By "common ground" here I intend something quite different from "bridge." Bridging two cultures emphasizes their distinctness while on the contrary I want to sketch their interactions. I am grateful to Arkady Plotnitsky for suggesting this distinction.

CHAPTER NINE

1 Samuel Eliot Morison, *Admiral of the Ocean Sea: A Life of Christopher Columbus* (Boston, 1942), 236; quoted in Peter Hulme, *Colonial Encounters: Europe and the Native Caribbean, 1492–1797* (London: Methuen, 1986), 158. Subsequent page references to *Colonial Encounters* are cited parenthetically in the text.

2 See Edmundo O'Gorman, *The Invention of America: An Inquiry into the Historical Nature of the New World and the Meaning of Its History* (Bloomington, Ind.: Indiana University Press, 1961).

3 Perry Miller, *Errand into the Wilderness* (Cambridge, Mass.: Harvard University Press, 1956), vii. See also Henry Nash Smith, *Virgin Land: The American West as Symbol and Myth* (Cambridge, Mass.: Harvard University Press, 1950) and R. W. B. Lewis, *The American Adam: Innocence, Tragedy, and Tradition in the Nineteenth Century* (Chicago: University of Chicago Press, 1955).

4 When I presented one version of this essay at a conference on the discovery of America held at Vanderbilt University in October 1992, by a fortunate coincidence Peter Hulme was present. The ensuing discussion was for me remarkably illuminating and entered deeply into the revised essay published here.

5 Ivan Illich gives a detailed account of this incident in "Vernacular Values," chapter 2 of his *Shadow Work* (Boston: M. Boyars, 1981). Illich sees the grammar, the work of Elio Anto-

nio de Nebrija who was a classical scholar (his first book in 1482 was a Latin grammar) turned to the study of vernacular languages, as an instrument of control, a "declaration of war" against the vernacular and for the universal. The grammar (published just fifteen days after Columbus sailed) is called *Gramática Castellana* and is intended to make it possible for the queen to replace the language of her subjects with her own. Nebrija proposes a union between the sword and the learned man, the *letrado* in the conquest of the empire: an army of *armas y letras*. For Illich, therefore, Columbus and Nebrija represent the same development. Jim Hicks called *Shadow Work* to my attention.

6   Carlo Ginzburg, "Checking the Evidence: The Judge and the Historian," *Critical Inquiry* 18 (autumn 1991): 83.

7   See William Arens, *The Man-Eating Myth: Anthropology and Anthropophagy* (New York: Oxford University Press, 1979).

8   Gananath Obeyesekere makes this point about another region, maintaining that "the British discourse on cannibalism produced, in very complicated ways, the Maori practice of cannibalism." Gananath Obeyesekere, "'British Cannibals': Contemplation of an Event in the Death and Resurrection of James Cook, Explorer," *Critical Inquiry* 18 (summer 1992): 653.

9   Ginzburg, "Checking the Evidence," 83.

10   See the brief but penetrating discussion of this problem in Patricia Seed, "On Caribbean Shores: Problems of Writing History of the First Contact," *Radical History Review* 53 (spring 1992): 5-11.

11   John Smith, *The Generall Historie of Virginia, New England, and the Summer Isles . . .* (1624) in Volume II of *The Complete Works of Captain John Smith (1580-1631) in Three Volumes,* edited by Philip L. Barbour, published for The Institute of Early American History and Culture in Williamsburg, Virginia, by The University of North Carolina Press (Chapel Hill, N.C., 1986), 184.

12   Smith, *Generall Historie,* 1:141-42.

13   Thomas Harriot's *A Briefe and True Report of the New Found Land of Virginia* (London, 1588-90) combines the two ascents. Harriot was a very important Renaissance scientist sent by Sir Walter Raleigh to the New World to report on its resources. His *True Report* seeks objectivity while also self-consciously serving the empire. The conjunctions and intersections, as well as the incoherences, of these two projects emerge here with great clarity.

14   See Bruno Latour, *Science in Action: How to Follow Scientists and Engineers through Society* (Cambridge, Mass., 1987). Three historians of science—Evelyn Fox Keller, Jessica Riskin, and Arnold Davidson—have objected that I cite Latour to make a case apparently the opposite of his. They have explained that Latour's denial that science is the progressive discovery of natural facts has in view a relativist refutation of the very existence of natural facts. My effort to exhume from the historical record the traces of multiple inconclusive moments would imply the contrary about history: that the facts exist and manifest themselves outside discursive explanations (such facts might constitute Ginzburg's "evidence.") I still persist in using Latour's terms, however, in the belief that my misreading is actually an adaptation. Latour studies the making of science while I am concerned with the making of history. To strip scientific stories of their telos requires replacing natural facts with historical facts—the facts, for instance, of the construction of the "discovery" of DNA. Latour is therefore no more relativistic about history than I am.

CHAPTER TEN

1   Myra Jehlen, "History before the Fact; or, Captain John Smith's Unfinished Symphony." *Critical Inquiry* 19 (1993): 677-92. Reprinted in this book as chapter 9.

2   I have benefited in this discussion from chapter 2 of Krishnakali Ray Lewis's dissertation,

"Ambivalence and Pastoral Strategy: Colonization in the Caribbean, Wilson Harris, and Zora Neale Hurston (Guyana)."

3   Included in John Oldmixon's *British Empire in America, 1708;* then in the March 13, 1711, *Spectator;* this version translated into German in 1713, French 1714, Swedish 1734, Danish 1742, Russian 1759. See Lawrence Marsden Price, *Inkle and Yarico Album* (Berkeley: University of California Press, 1937).

4   Richard Ligon, Gent., *A True and Exact History of the Island of Barbadoes* (London: printed for Humphrey Moseley at the Prince's Armes in St. Paul's Church-yard, 1657), 46–47. Subsequent page references are cited parenthetically in the text.

5   I have elsewhere suggested that the seventeenth-century Montaigne may not have been our Montaigne either: "Why Did the European Cross the Ocean?" in *Discovering Difference: Contemporary Essays in American Culture,* ed. Christopher K. Lohman (Bloomington, Ind.: Indiana University Press, 1993), 1–15; reprinted in *Cultures of United States Imperialism,* ed. Amy Kaplan and Donald Pease (Durham, N.C.: Duke University Press, 1994), 41–58; reprinted in this book as chapter 8.

6   David Brion Davis, *The Problem of Slavery in Western Culture* (Ithaca, N.Y.: Cornell University Press, 1996), 108.

CHAPTER ELEVEN

1   Virginia Woolf, *The Voyage Out* (New York: Harcourt, Brace, Jovanovich, 1948). Page references are cited parenthetically in the text.

2   Walter Raleigh, "The discoverie of the large, rich and beutiful empyre of Guiana." Imprinted by R. Robinson, 1596. (Facsimile ed., Cleveland: World Publication Company, 1966).

CHAPTER TWELVE

1   Coosje van Bruggen, *Frank O. Gehry: Guggenheim Museum Bilbao.* (New York: Guggenheim Museum Publications, 1998).

2   Arthur G. Smith, *Pittsburgh: Then and Now* (Pittsburgh: University of Pittsburgh Press, 1990).

Index